The Complexity of the Irregular Verbal and Nominal Forms & the Phonological Changes in Arabic

The Complexity of the Irregular Verbal and Nominal Forms & the Phonological Changes in Arabic

Joyce Åkesson

Pallas Athena Distribution

Lund

2009

The Complexity of the Irregular Verbal and Nominal Forms & the Phonological Changes in Arabic

2009 Pallas Athena Distribution,
Skarpskyttevägen 10 A, 226 42 Lund, Sweden.
E-mail: pallas.athena@netatonce.net

ISBN: 978-91-977641-2-4
PRINTED IN THE UNITED STATES OF AMERICA

TABLE OF CONTENTS

the elision of one of the identical segments 9
1.2.1.7. Some derived forms of the verb: the sequence of a vowelled segment preceding a vowelless identical segment: the substitution of one of the doubled segments by a *y* 10
1.3. Conclusion 11

CHAPTER TWO 13
2. The assimilation 13
2.1. The assimilation in the pronunciation and in the writing 14
2.2. The points of articulation and some of the characters of the segments that lead to the assimilation 14
2.2.1. The segments' common and neighboring points of articulation 15
2.2.2. Some of the segments' characters 16
2.3. The sequences of two identical segments: cases in which the assimilation is or is not carried out 17
2.3.1. The sequence of two identical segments of which the 1st is vowelless and the 2nd vowelled: the necessity of the assimilation 18
2.3.1.1. The assimilation that is carried out in one word 18
2.3.1.2. The assimilation that is carried out in two words following each other 19
2.3.2. The sequence of two identical segments which are both vowelled 19
2.3.2.1. The assimilation that is carried out in one word 20
2.3.2.2. Cases in which the assimilation is not carried out in one word 21
2.3.2.2.1. An anomalous case: *ḥayiya* 21
2.3.2.2.2. The coordinatives and some special measures 22
2.3.2.3. The assimilation that is carried out in two words following each other 23
2.3.3. The sequence of two identical segments of which the 1st is vowelled and the 2nd vowelless: the prohibition of the assimilation. The assimilation in some anomalous cases 23
2.4. The sequence of two different segments: cases in which the assimilation is or is not carried out 25
2.4.1. The sequence of two different segments of which the 1st is vowelless and the 2nd is vowelled: the assimilation 25

2.4.1.1. The assimilation that is carried out from the 1st vowelless segment to a 2nd different vowelled segment in one word 25

2.4.1.1.1. The assimilation of the vowelless *l-* of the article *al-* to the vowelled solar segment that begins a noun 26

2.4.1.1.2. The assimilation of the 3rd radical *d* in verbs that occur in the perfect, to the vowelled suffixed pronoun of the agent that begins with the *t* 26

2.4.1.1.3. The assimilation that is carried out between the vowelled infixed *t* of Form VIII of the perfect *ʾiftaʿala* and the 1st vowelless radical preceding it 27

2.4.1.1.3.1. Cases in which the 1st vowelless radical is assimilated to the infixed vowelled *t* of Form VIII of the perfect *ʾiftaʿala* 27

1- The assimilation of the 1st radical vowelless *ʾ* to the vowelled infixed t of Form VIII *ʾiftaʿala* 28

2- The assimilation of the 1st radical vowelless *t* to the vowelled infixed *t* of Form VIII *ʾiftaʿala* 28

3- The assimilation between the 1st radical vowelless *ṯ* and the vowelled infixed *t* of Form VIII *ʾiftaʿala* 29

4- The assimilation of the 1st radical vowelless *w* to the vowelled infixed t of Form VIII *ʾiftaʿala* 29

5- The assimilation of the 1st radical vowelless *y* to the vowelled infixed *t* of Form VIII *ʾiftaʿala* 29

2.4.1.1.3.2. Cases in which the infixed vowelled *t* of Form VIII of the perfect *ʾiftaʿala* is assimilated to the 1st vowelless radical preceding it 30

1- The assimilation of the vowelled infixed *t* of Form VIII *ʾiftaʿala* to the 1st radical vowelless *d* preceding it 31

2- The assimilation of the vowelled infixed *t* of Form VIII *ʾiftaʿala* to the 1st radical vowelless *ḏ* preceding it 31

3- The assimilation of the vowelled infixed *t* of Form VIII *ʾiftaʿala* to the 1st radical vowelless *z* preceding it 32

4- The assimilation of the vowelled infixed *t* of Form VIII *ʾiftaʿala* to the 1st radical vowelless *ṣ* preceding it 33

5- The assimilation of the vowelled infixed *t* of Form VIII *ʾiftaʿala* to the 1st radical vowelless *ḍ* preceding it 33

6- The assimilation of the vowelled infixed *t* of Form VIII *ʾiftaʿala* to the 1st radical vowelless *ṭ* preceding it 34

7- The assimilation of the vowelled infixed *t* of Form VIII *ʾiftaʿala* to the 1st radical vowelless *ẓ* preceding it 35

8- The assimilation of the vowelled infixed *t* of Form VIII *ʾiftaʿala* to the 1st radical vowelless *ṯ* pre ceding it 36

9- The assimilation of the vowelled infixed *t* of Form VIII *ʾiftaʿala* to the 1st radical vowelless *s* preceding it 36

10- The assimilation of the vowelled infixed *t* of Form VIII *ʾiftaʿal* to the 1st radical vowelless *š* preceding it 37

2.4.1.2. The assimilation that is carried out from the 1st vowelless segment to a 2nd different vowelled segment in two words following each other 37

2.4.2. The sequence of two different segments which are both vowelled: the assimilation 38

2.4.2.1. The assimilation that is carried out from the 1st vowelled segment to a 2nd vowelled segment in one word 38

2.4.2.1.1. The assimilation of the vowelled prefixed *t* of Form V *tafaʿʿala* or Form VI *taf(a)āʿala* to the 1st vowelled radical following it 39

1- The assimilation of the vowelled prefixed *t* of Form V *tafaʿʿala* or Form VI *taf(a)āʿala* to the 1st vowelled radical *t* following it 40

2- The assimilation of the vowelled prefixed *t* of Form V *tafaʿʿala* or Form VI *taf(a)āʿala* to the 1st vowelled radical *ṯ* following it 40

3- The assimilation of the vowelled prefixed *t* of Form V *tafaʿʿala* or Form VI *taf(a)āʿala* to the 1st vowelled radical *d* following it 40

4- The assimilation of the vowelled prefixed *t* of Form V *tafaʿʿala* or Form VI *taf(a)āʿala* to the 1st vowelled radical *ḏ* following it 41

5- The assimilation of the vowelled prefixed *t* of Form V *tafaʿʿala* or Form VI *taf(a)āʿala* to the 1st vowelled radical *z* following it 42

6- The assimilation of the vowelled prefixed *t* of Form V *tafaʿʿala* or Form VI *taf(a)āʿala* to the 1st vowelled radical *s* following it 42

7- The assimilation of the vowelled prefixed *t* of Form V *tafaʿʿala* or Form VI *taf(a)āʿala* to the 1st vowelled radical *š* following it 43

8- The assimilation of the vowelled prefixed *t* of Form V *tafa*[cc]*ala* or Form VI *taf(a)ā*[c]*ala* to the 1st vowelled radical *ṣ* following it 43

9- The assimilation of the vowelled prefixed *t* of Form V *tafa*[cc]*ala* or Form VI *taf(a)ā*[c]*ala* to the 1st vowelled radical *ḍ* following it 43

10- The assimilation of the vowelled prefixed *t* of Form V *tafa*[cc]*ala* or Form VI *taf(a)ā*[c]*ala* to the 1st vowelled radical *ṭ* following it 44

11- The assimilation of the vowelled prefixed *t* of Form V *tafa*[cc]*ala* or Form VI *taf(a)ā*[c]*ala* to the 1st vowelled radical *ẓ* following it 44

2.4.2.1.2. The assimilation of the infixed vowelled *t* of the imperfect of Form VIII *yafta*[c]*ilu* to the vowelled 2nd radical 45

1- The assimilation of the vowelled infixed *t* of Form VIII of the imperfect *yafta*[c]*ilu* to the 2nd vowelled radical *t* following it in the imperfect 45

2- The assimilation of the vowelled infixed *t* of Form VIII of the imperfect *yafta*[c]*ilu* to the 2nd vowelled radical *d* following it 45

3- The assimilation of the vowelled infixed *t* of Form VIII of the imperfect *yafta*[c]*ilu* to the vowelled 2nd radical *d̲* following it 46

4- The assimilation of the vowelled infixed *t* of Form VIII of the imperfect *yafta*[c]*ilu* to the vowelled 2nd radical *z* following it 46

5- The assimilation of the vowelled infixed *t* of Form VIII of the imperfect *yafta*[c]*ilu* to the vowelled 2nd radical *s* following it 47

6- The assimilation of the vowelled infixed *t* of Form VIII of the imperfect *yafta*[c]*ilu* to the vowelled 2nd radical *ṣ* following it 47

7- The assimilation of the vowelled infixed *t* of Form VIII of the imperfect *yafta*[c]*ilu* to the vowelled 2nd radical *ḍ* following it 47

8- The assimilation of the vowelled infixed *t* of Form VIII of the imperfect *yafta*[c]*ilu* to the vowelled 2nd radical *ṭ* following it 48

9- The assimilation of the vowelled infixed *t* of Form VIII of the imperfect *yafta*ᶜ*ilu* to the *ẓ* following it 48
2.4.2.2. The assimilation that is carried out from the 1st vowelled segment to a 2nd vowelled segment in two words following each other 48
2.5. Conclusion 49

CHAPTER THREE 51
3. The hamzated verb and some of its derivatives 51
3.1. The conjugations of the verb with 1st radical hamza 51
3.2. Examples of some derivatives of the verb with 1st radical hamza 52
3.2.1. Remarks concerning the phonological procedures in some of its forms 52
3.2.1.1. The imperative and the passive voice: the sequence of two hamzas of which the 1st is vowelled and the 2nd is vowelless: the change of the vowelless hamza into a glide 53
1- The imperative 53
2- The passive voice 54
3.3. The conjugations of the verb with 2nd radical hamza 54
3.4. Examples of some derivatives of the verb with 2nd radical hamza 55
3.4.1. Remarks concerning the phonological procedures in some of its forms 55
3.4.1.1. The imperfect: the sequence of a hamza vowelled by a fatḥa preceded by a sukūn: the transfer of the fatḥa to the vowelless segment and the elision of the hamza 55
3.5. The conjugations of the hamzated verbs with 3rd radical hamza 56
3.6. Examples of some derivatives of the hamzated verb with 3rd radical hamza 56
3.6.1. Remarks concerning the phonological procedures in some of its forms 57
3.7. The occurrence of the hamza in some of the other classes of irregular verbs 57
3.8. Conclusion 58

CHAPTER FOUR 59
4. The phonological changes due to the hamza 59

4.1. The hamza. Its retaining or alleviation 59
4.1.1. The hamza as the initial segment of a word 60
4.1.2. The hamza preceded by another segment in the middle of the word 60
4.1.2.1. The hamza is vowelless and the segment preceding it is vowelled: its retaining or the alleviation by the change of the hamza into a glide 62
1- The alleviation by the change of the vowelless hamza, the ʾ, into an *ā* 63
2- The alleviation by the change of the vowelless hamza, the ʾ, into an *ū* 63
3- The alleviation by the change of the vowelless hamza, the ʾ, into an *ī* 64
4.1.2.2. The hamza and the segment preceding it are vowelled 64
4.1.2.2.1. The hamza is vowelled by one of the three vowels and is preceded by a fatḥa: its retaining or its alleviation by its change into a *hamza bayna bayna* "an intermediary hamza" 64
1- The alleviation by the change of the hamza vowelled by a fatḥa, the *ʾa* into an *ā* 66
2- The alleviation by the change of the hamza vowelled by a ḍamma, the *ʾu,* into *wu* 66
3- The alleviation by the change of the hamza vowelled by a kasra the *ʾi,* into *yi* 67
4.1.2.2.2. The hamza is vowelled by a fatḥa and is preceded by a ḍamma or kasra: its alleviation by its change into a glide 67
1- The change of the hamza preceded by a ḍamma into *w* 67
2- The change of the hamza preceded by a kasra into *y* 67
4.1.2.3. The hamza is vowelled and the segment preceding it is vowelless 68
4.1.2.3.1. The hamza is vowelled by a fatḥa and is preceded by a sukūn: its elision together with the hamza's fatḥa shifted to the vowelless segment preceding it 69
4.1.2.3.1.1. The vowelless segment preceding the hamza is a strong segment 69

4.1.2.3.1.2. The vowelless segment preceding the hamza is a vowelless *w* or *y* 70
4.1.2.3.1.2.1. The elision of the hamza in one word and the transfer of its fatḥa to the segment preceding it 70
1- The segment preceding the hamza is a vowelless *w* 71
2- The segment preceding the hamza is a vowelless *y* 71
4.1.2.3.1.2.2. The elision of the hamza vowelled by a fatḥa in one word following a vowelless *w*, *y* or a strong segment in the word preceding it and the transfer of its fatḥa to this segment 72
1- The segment preceding the hamza in the word preceding it is a vowelless *w* 72
2- The segment preceding the hamza in the word preceding it is a vowelless *y* 73
3- The segment preceding the hamza in the word preceding it is a vowelless strong segment 73
4.1.2.3.2. The hamza is vowelled by a fatḥa and is preceded by a sukūn [i.e. a vowelless infixed glide of prolongation]: its assimilation to the glide 74
1- The segment preceding the hamza is an infixed vowelless *w* 75
2- The segment preceding the hamza is an infixed vowelless *y* 75
4.1.2.3.3. The hamza is vowelled by a kasra and is preceded by a sukūn [i.e a vowelless infixed glide of prolongation]: its assimilation to the glide 76
4.1.2.3.4. The hamza is vowelled by a kasra or ḍamma and is preceded by a sukūn [i.e .a vowelless infixed glide of prolongation]: its change into a *hamza bayna bayna* 76
4.1.2.4. The hamza is vowelless and the hamza preceding it is vowelled by a fatḥa: Its alleviation by its change into an *ā* 77
4.1.2.4.1. An anomalous example: *ʾayimmatun* 78
4.1.2.5. The hamza is vowelless and the hamza preceding it is vowelled by a kasra: its alleviation by its change into a *y* 79
4.1.2.6. The hamza is vowelless and the hamza preceding it is vowelled by a ḍamma: its change into a *w* or its elision 79

4.1.2.7. The hamza and the hamza preceding it are vowelled by a fatḥa 80
4.1.2.7.1. The hamza and the hamza preceding it are vowelled by a fatḥa in one word: their assimilation into a *madda* and the anomalous insertion of an *ā* in some cases 80
4.1.2.7.2. The hamza is vowelled by a fatḥa in one word and follows a hamza vowelled by a fatḥa in the word preceding it: the elision of one hamza or of both 81
4.1.3. The hamza as the final segment of a word 82
4.1.3.1. The vowelled hamza is preceded by a vowel 82
4.1.3.2. The vowelled hamza is preceded by a sukūn 82
4.1.3.2.1. Some anomalous cases that concern the alleviation of the hamza 83
4.2. Conclusion 83

CHAPTER FIVE 85
5. The verb with 1st radical *w* or *y* 85
5.1. The conjugations of the verb with 1st radical *w* 86
5.1.1. An anomalous case: *waǧada yaǧudu* 87
5.2. Examples of some derivatives of the verb with 1st radical *w* 88
5.2.1. Remarks concerning the phonological procedures in some of its forms 88
5.2.1.1. The perfect: the sequence in which the 1st radical *w* is the initial segment: the soundness of the glide 89
5.2.1.2. The verbal noun: the sequence in which the 1st radical *w* is the initial segment: the elision of the *w* and the compensation with the prefixed *tāʾ marbūṭā* 90
5.2.1.3. The imperfect: the sequence in which the 1st radical *w* is vowelless and followed by a kasra in the conjugation *yafʿilu:* the elision of the *w* 91
5.2.1.4. The imperfect: the sequence in which the 1st radical *w* is vowelless and followed by a fatḥa in the conjugation *yafʿalu:* the retaining or the change of the *w* into a *y* or an *ā*, or the elision of the *w* 92
5.2.1.5. The imperative: the sequence in which the 1st radical *w* is vowelless and preceded by the kasra of the connective hamza: the *w* is changed into a *y* and can be retained or is elided together with the hamza vowelled by a kasra 92

5.2.1.6. The active participle: the sequence in which the 1st radical *w* is vowelled by a fatḥa and followed by the infix vowelless *ā:* the retaining of the *w* or the anomalous transposition of segments 93

5.2.1.7. The noun of place and time: the sequence in which the 1st radical *w* is vowelless and preceded by a fatḥa: the soundness of the *w* 94

5.2.1.8. Form VIII of the perfect: the sequence in which the 1st vowelless radical *w* is preceded by a kasra and followed by the vowelled infixed *t:* the change of the *w* into a *y* and the assimilation of the *y* to the vowelled infixed *t* 94

5.3. The conjugations of the verb with 1st radical *y* 94

5.4. Examples of some derivatives of the verb with 1st radical *y* 95

5.4.1. Some remarks concerning the phonological procedures in some of its forms 95

5.4.1.1. The imperfect of the passive voice of Form I, the active voice of Form IV of the imperfect and the active participle of Form IV: the *y* is vowelless and preceded by a ḍamma: the change of the *y* into a *w* 96

5.4.1.2. Form VIII of the perfect: the sequence in which the 1st vowelless radical *y* is preceded by a kasra and followed by the vowelled infixed *t:* the assimilation of the *y* to the vowelled infixed *t* 97

5.5. Conclusion 97

CHAPTER SIX 99

6. The verb with 2nd radical *w* or *y* 99

6.1. The conjugations of the verb with 2nd radical *w* 101

6.2. Examples of some derivatives of the verb with 2nd radical *w* 101

6.3. The conjugations of the verb with 2nd radical *y* 101

6.4. Examples of some derivatives of the verb with 2nd radical *y* 101

6.5. Remarks concerning the phonological procedures in some of the forms of the verb with 2nd radical *w* or *y* 102

6.5.1. The 3rd persons of the perfect of the verb with 2nd radical *w* or *y:* the sequence of the vowelled 2nd weak radical preceded by a fatḥa: the change of the vowelled weak radical into

an *ā* 105
6.5.1.1. The verb with 2nd radical *w* 105
1- The conjugation *faᶜala* 105
2- The conjugation *faᶜula* 106
3- The conjugation fa*ᶜila* 106
6.5.1.2. The verb with 2nd radical *y* 106
1- The conjugation *faᶜala* 107
2- The conjugation *faᶜila* 107
6.5.2. The persons in the perfect of the verb with 2nd radical *w* or *y* in which the vowelled pronoun of the agent is suffixed: the sequence of the vowelless 2nd radical *ā* (that is substituted for the 2nd weak radical) preceded by a fatḥa and followed by the vowelless 3rd radical: the elision of the *ā* and the change of the 1st radical's fatḥa into another vowel 107-8
6.5.2.1. The verb with 2nd radical *w* 108
1- The conjugation *faᶜala* 108
2- The conjugation *faᶜila* 109
6.5.2.2. The verb with 2nd radical *y* 109
6.5.3. The imperfect of the verb with 2nd radical *w* or *y* of the conjugation *yafᶜalu:* the sequence of the 2nd weak radical vowelled by a fatḥa and preceded by a sukūn: the transfer of the fatḥa to the vowelless segment preceding it and the change of the vowelled weak radical into an *ā* in all forms with the remark that the *ā* is elided in the imperfect forms of the fem. pl. in which the vowelled *–n, the -na,* is suffixed to 110
6.5.3.1. The verb with 2nd radical *w* 110
6.5.3.2. The verb with 2nd radical *y* 111
6.5.4. The imperfect of the verb with 2nd radical *w* of the conjugation *yafᶜulu:* the sequence of the 2nd radical *w* vowelled by a ḍamma and preceded by a sukūn: the transfer of the ḍamma to the vowelless segment preceding it, the change of the *wu* into an *ū* with the remark that the *-ū* is elided in the forms of the fem. pl. in which the vowelled *–n, the -na,* is suffixed to 112
6.5.5. The imperfect of the verb with 2nd radical *y* of the conjugation *yafᶜilu:* the sequence of the 2nd radical *y* vowelled by a kasra and preceded by a sukūn: the transfer of the kasra to the vowelless segment preceding it and the change of the *yi* into an *ī* in all forms with the remark that the *ī* is elided in the imperfect forms of the fem. pl. in which the vowelled *–n, the -na,* is

suffixed to 113

6.5.6. The passive participle of the verb with 2nd radical *w* *maf*ᶜ*(u)wlun / maf*ᶜ*(u)ūlun:* the sequence of the 2nd radical *w* vowelled by a ḍamma preceded by a sukūn and followed by the infixed vowelless *ū:* the transfer of the ḍamma to the vowelless segment preceding it, the change of the *wu* into an *ū* and the elision of one of the wāws 114

6.5.7. The passive participle of the verb with 2nd radical *y* *maf*ᶜ*(u)wlun / maf*ᶜ*(u)ūlun:* the sequence of the 2nd radical *y* vowelled by a ḍamma, preceded by a sukūn and followed by the infixed vowelless *ū:* the transfer of the ḍamma to the vowelless segment preceding it, the change of the ḍamma into a kasra, the elision of the infixed *ū* or the 2nd radical *y*, and the change of the *y* into an *ī* or the *ū* into an *ī* respectively 115

6.5.8. The imperative of the verb with 2nd radical *w* or *y*: the sequence of the 2nd vowelled radical *w* or *y* that is preceded by a sukūn: the transfer of the vowel to the vowelless segment preceding it, the lengthening of the vowel into an *ū* or an *ī* respectively, and the elision of the *ū* or *ī* in both the 3rd person of the masc. sing. and the 3rd person of the fem. pl. and its retaining in the remaining persons 117

6.5.8.1. The verb with 2nd radical *w* 117

6.5.8.2. The verb with 2nd radical *y* 118

6.5.9. The active participle of the verb with 2nd radical *w* or *y:* the sequence of the 2nd radical *w* or *y* vowelled by a kasra and preceded by a vowelless *ā:* the change of the *wi* or *yi* into *ʾi* respectively 119

6.5.9.1. The verb with 2nd radical *w* 119

6.5.9.2. The verb with 2nd radical *y* 119

6.5.10. Anomalous cases of active participles of the verb with 2nd radical *w:* the sequence of the 2nd radical *w* vowelled by a kasra and preceded by a vowelless *ā:* the elision of the *w* or the transposition of segments together with the elision of the glide 120

1- The elision of the 2nd radical *w* 120

2- The transposition of segments together with the elision of the glide 121

6.5.11. The verbal noun of Form I of the verb with 2nd radical *w* or *y:* the sequence in which the 2nd radical *w* or *y* is vow-

elless and preceded by a fatḥa: the soundness of the *w* or *y* 122
6.5.12. The verbal nouns of Form IV *ʾifʿ(a)ālun* and Form X *ʾistifʿ(a)ālun* of the verb with 2nd radical *w:* the sequence in which the *w* is vowelled by a fatḥa and preceded by a sukūn: the transfer of the *w's* fatḥa to the segment preceding it, the change of the *w* into an *ā,* the elision of one of the alifs and the compensation with the *tāʾ marbūṭa* 122
6.5.13. The passive voice of the perfect of the verb with 2nd radical *w* or *y:* the sequence of the 2nd radical *w* or *y* vowelled by a kasra and preceded by a ḍamma: the transfer of the kasra to the 1st radical and hence the change of the 1st radical's ḍamma into a kasra, the change of the *w* into a *y* or the *y* into an *ī* respectively, or the elision of the 2nd radical *w's* or *y's* kasra and the lengthening of the ḍamma preceding it into an *ū* 123
6.5.13.1. The verb with 2nd radical *w* 124
6.5.13.2. The verb with 2nd radical *y* 125
6.5.14. The passive voice of the imperfect of the verb with 2nd radical *w* or *y:* the sequence of the 2nd radical *w* or *y* vowelled by a fatḥa and preceded by a sukūn: the transfer of the fatḥa to the 1st vowelless radical and the change of the *w* or the *y* into an *ā* 125-6
6.5.15. The noun of place of the verb with 2nd radical *w:* the sequence of the 2nd radical *w* vowelled by a fatḥa and preceded by a sukūn: the transfer of the fatḥa to the vowelless segment preceding it and the change of the *w* into an *ā* 126
6.6. A few remarks concerning some homonymous forms 127
6.7. Conclusion 128

CHAPTER SEVEN 131
7. The verb with 3rd radical *w* or *y* 131
7.1. The conjugations of the verb with 3rd radical *w* 132
7.2. Examples of some derivatives of the verb with 3rd radical *w* 132
7.3. The conjugations of the verb with 3rd radical *y* 132
7.4. Examples of some derivatives of the verb with 3rd radical *y* 133
7.5. Remarks concerning the phonological procedures in some of the forms of the verb with 3rd radical *w* or *y* 133

8.2. Examples of some derivatives of the verb with 1st and 3rd weak radical 152
8.2.1. Remarks concerning the phonological procedures in some of its forms 152
8.3. The conjugations of the verb with 1st and 3rd weak radical 152
8.4. Examples of some derivatives of the verb with 2nd and 3rd weak radical 153
8.4.1. Remarks concerning the phonological procedures in some of its forms 153
8.5. Conclusion 153

CHAPTER NINE 155
9. The soundness or the unsoundness of the glide 155
9.1. The soundness or the unsoundness of the glide: the sequences involved and the conditions 155
9.1.1. The glide is vowelless and preceded by a fatḥa: its soundness or its change into an *ā* 160
9.1.1.1. Some anomalous cases 161
9.1.2. The glide is vowelled by a fatḥa and preceded by a fatḥa: its change into an *ā* 161
9.1.2.1. The phonological change that is carried out in verbs 162
9.1.2.1.1. The soundness of the glide 162
1- The combination of two phonological changes due to the unsound glides should be avoided 163
2- The fatḥa preceding the glide is ruled by the sukūn of another form 163
9.1.2.2. The phonological change that is carried out in nouns and adjectives 164
9.1.2.2.1. The soundness of the glide 165
1- The noun or the adjective is not formed according to the verbal form *faᶜal* through the sufixation of the *tāʾ marbūṭa* or the *alif maqṣūra* 165
2- The glide is meant to give clues to the base form 166
3- The word refers in its meaning to intensive mobility 167
9.1.3. The glide is vowelled by a kasra and preceded by a fatḥa: its change into an *ā* 167

9.1.3.1. The soundness of the glide 168
1- The fatḥa preceding the glide is ruled by the sukūn of another form 168
2- The form should remain unchanged to prevent that the last glide becomes vowelled by a ḍamma in the imperfect 169
9.1.4. The glide is vowelled by a ḍamma and preceded by a fatḥa: the change of the *wu* or *yu* into an *ā* 169
9.1.4.1. The soundness of the glide 169
1- The glide should not be vowelled by a vowel that is not supplied by the basic form 170
9.1.5. The glide, the *y*, is vowelless and preceded by a ḍamma: its change into a *w* 170
9.1.6. The glide is vowelled by a kasra and preceded by a ḍamma: the transfer of the kasra to the preceding segment and hence the change of the preceding segment's ḍamma into a kasra, the change of the *w* into a *y* or the *y* into an *ī* respectively, or the elision of the glide's kasra and the lengthening of the ḍamma preceding it into an *ū* 171
9.1.7. The glide is vowelled by a ḍamma and preceded by a vowel: the glide's ḍamma is elided 172
9.1.8. The glide is vowelled by a fatḥa and preceded by a ḍamma: its soundness 173
9.1.9. The glide, the *w*, is vowelled by a fatḥa and preceded by a kasra: its change into a *y* 174
9.1.9.1. Some anomalous cases 175
9.1.10. The glide, the *y*, is vowelled by a ḍamma and preceded by a kasra: the transfer of the ḍamma before the *y* and hence the change of the preceding segment's kasra into a ḍamma, the elision of the *y* and the lengthening of the ḍamma into an *ū* according to a theory, or the elision of the *y's* ḍamma together with the elision of the *y* and the change of the preceding segment's kasra into a ḍamma according to another theory 176
9.1.11. The glide, the *y*, is vowelled by a kasra and preceded by a kasra: the elision of the vowel of the *y* together with the *y* 177
9.1.12. The glide is vowelled by a fatḥa and preceded by a sukūn: the transfer of the fatḥa to the segment preceding it and the change of the *w* into an *ā* 177
9.1.12.1. The soundness of the glide 178

1- The noun or the adjective is not formed according to the verbal form *faᶜal* 178
9.1.12.2. Some anomalous cases 179
9.1.13. The glide, the *y*, is vowelled by a kasra and preceded by a sukūn: the transfer of the kasra to the segment preceding it and the change of the *y* into an *ī* 182
9.1.13.1. Anomalous cases 182
9.1.14. The glide is vowelled by a kasra and preceded by a vowelless *ā:* the change of the *wi* or *yi* into *ʾi* 183
9.1.15. The glide, the *w*, is vowelled by a ḍamma and preceded by a sukūn: the transfer of the ḍamma to the segment preceding it and the change of the *w* into *ū* 184
9.1.15.1. The soundness of the glide 184
1- The glide should not be vowelled by a vowel that is not supplied by the basic form 184
9.1.16. The glide, the *y*, is vowelled by a ḍamma and preceded by a sukūn: the transfer of the ḍamma to the vowelless segment preceding it, the change of the ḍamma into a kasra and the change of the *y* into *ī* 185
9.1.16.1. The soundness of the glide 185
1- The glide should not be vowelled by a vowel that is not supplied by the basic form 186
9.1.17. The glide, the *w* or *y*, is vowelless and preceded by a kasra: its change into a *y* or *ī* respectively 187
9.1.18. The transposition of segments in some nouns 187
9.2. Conclusion 188

CHAPTER TEN 191
10. The substitution 191
10.1. The segments of substitution 191
10.1.1. The substitution of the hamza 192
10.1.1.1. The substitution of the hamza for the alif of feminization, the *ā (alif maqṣūra)* 192
10.1.1.2. The substitution of the hamza for the *w* 192
1- The hamza vowelled by a fatḥa 193
2- The hamza vowelled by a ḍamma 193
3- The hamza vowelled by a kasra 194
10.1.1.3. The substitution of the hamza for the *y* 195
1- The hamza vowelled by a fatḥa 195

2- The hamza vowelled by a kasra 195
10.1.1.4. The substitution of the hamza for the *h* 195
10.1.1.5. The substitution of the hamza for the *ā* 196
10.1.1.6. The substitution of the hamza for the ᶜ 196
10.1.2. The substitution of the *s* 197
10.1.2.1. The substitution of the *s* for the *t* 197
10.1.3. The substitution of the *t* 197
10.1.3.1. The substitution of the *t* for the *w* 198
10.1.3.2. The substitution of the *t* for the *y* 198
10.1.3.3. The substitution of the *t* for the *d* and the *s* 199
10.1.3.4. The substitution of the *t* for the *ṣ* 199
10.1.3.5. The substitution of the *t* for the *b* 200
10.1.4. The substitution of the *n* 200
10.1.4.1. The substitution of the *n* for the *w* 200
10.1.4.2. The substitution of the *n* for the *l* 201
10.1.5. The substitution of the *ǧ* 201
10.1.5.1. The substitution of the *ǧ* for the *y* 201
10.1.6. The substitution of the *d* 202
10.1.6.1. The substitution of the *d* for the *t* 202
10.1.7. The substitution of the *h* 202
10.1.7.1. The substitution of the *h* for the hamza 203
10.1.7.2. The substitution of the *h* for the *ā* 203
10.1.7.3. The substitution of the *h* for the *y* 204
10.1.7.4. The substitution of the *h* for the *t* 204
10.1.8. The substitution of the *y* 204
10.1.8.1. The substitution of the *ī* for the *ā* 205
10.1.8.2. The substitution of the *y* for the *w* 205
10.1.8.3. The substitution of the *y* for the hamza 206
10.1.8.4. The substitution of the *y* for one of the doubled segments in the doubled verb 206
10.1.8.5. The substitution of the *y* for the *n* 207
10.1.8.6. The substitution of the *ī* for the ᶜ 207
10.1.8.7. The substitution of the *y* for the *t* 208
10.1.8.8. The substitution of the *y* for the *b* 208
10.1.8.9. The substitution of the *y* for the *s* 209
10.1.8.10. The substitution of the *y* for the *ṯ* 209
10.1.9. The substitution of the *w* 210
10.1.9.1. The substitution of the *w* for the *ā* 210
10.1.9.2. The substitution of the *w* for the *y* 210

10.1.9.3. The substitution of the *w* for the hamza 211
10.1.10. The substitution of the *m* 211
10.1.10.1. The substitution of the *m* for the *w* 211
10.1.10.2. The substitution of the *m* for the *l* 212
10.1.10.3. The substitution of the *m* for the *n* 212
10.1.10.4. The substitution of the *m* for the *b* 213
10.1.11. The substitution of the *ṣ* 213
10.1.11.1. The substitution of the *ṣ* for the *s* 213
10.1.12. The substitution of the *ā* 214
10.1.12.1. The substitution of the *ā* for the *w* 214
10.1.12.2. The substitution of the *ā* for the *y* 214
10.1.12.3. The substitution of the *ā* for the hamza 214
10.1.13. The substitution of the *l* 215
10.1.13.1. The substitution of the *l* for the *n* 215
10.1.13.2. The substitution of the *l* for the *ḍ* 215
10.1.14. The substitution of the *z* 216
10.1.14.1. The substitution of the *z* for the *s* 216
10.1.14.2. The substitution of the *z* for the *ṣ* 216
10.1.15. The substitution of the *ṭ* 216
10.1.15.1. The substitution of the *ṭ* for the *t* 217
10.2. Conclusion 218

BIBLIOGRAPHY 221
I. Literature 221
I.1. Primary sources 221
II.2. Secondary sources 224

INDEX OF QUR'ANIC QUOTATIONS 227

INDEX OF VERSES 229

INDEX OF NAMES 231

PREFACE

After having written my comprehensive work *Arabic Morphology and Phonology based on the Marāḥ al-arwāḥ by Aḥmad b. ᶜAlī b. Masᶜūd,* I felt that a deepened study of the morphophonology of the irregular classes of the verbal and nominal forms and the phonological changes would be of interest for the reader.

For this purpose I have divided this book into two main topics. The first one is a presentation and analysis of the morphological classes of the irregular verbs and the second one is a study of the main phonological changes in the language.

These irregular verbs are the doubled, the hamzated, the verb with 1st radical *w* or *y,* the verb with 2nd radical *w* or *y,* the verb with 3rd radical *w* or *y,* and the verb that is doubly weak.

The common verbal forms are the perfect, the imperfect and the imperative, and the nominal forms are the infinitive noun, the active participle, the passive participle, the noun of time, the noun of place and the noun of instrument.

The existence of a doubled segment, a hamza or a weak segment in the word can result in different phonological changes which lead it from one base form to another derived form. These procedures are recognized as the addition of one segment or more to a word's structure, the substitution of a segment for another, the elision of a segment or more, the addition or the elision of a vowel, the assimilation of a segment to another, the transfer of a vowel from one segment to another and the transfer of a segment to the position of another. In the many cases that I study, I discuss the reasons forcing or hindering a specific change. My approach explains for instance in which manner a phonological change is carried out from one base form to another derived form without that a change in meaning is implied, e.g. the verb with 2nd radical *w* in the perfect *qawala* "to say" that becomes *q(a)āla* after that a change is carried out in its structure.

The phonological changes that I study in detail in the separate chapters are the assimilation, the changes due to the hamza, the changes due to the unsound segment and the substitution. As it is remarked, the changes due to the assimilation and substitution do not only occur in the irregular classes of verbs, but also in the classes of the regular verb.

For the purpose of studying these changes I have adopted a specific model that takes into consideration the succession of different segments occurring in one word and in some cases in two words following each other.

I refer a lot to my previous study *Arabic Morphology and Phonology.*

I do not neglect however to refer to other grammarians, ancient as well as modern, Arabs as well as Westerners. Among some of the ancient Arab grammarians that I take up, I can mention Sībawaihi with his *al-Kitāb,* Ibn Ǧinnī with his works *Muḫtaṣar al-taṣrīf al-mulūkī* (Ibn Ǧinnī, *de Flexione), al-Munṣif fī šarḥ taṣrīf al-Māzinī, al-Ḫaṣā'iṣ* and *Sirr ṣinā'at al-i'rāb,* Zamaḫšarī with his *al-Mufaṣṣal,* Ibn Ya'īš with his works *Šarḥ al-mulūkī fī l-taṣrīf* and *Šarḥ al-Mufaṣṣal* and Ibn 'Uṣfūr with his *al-Mumti' fī l-taṣrīf.* Among Westerners who have written works on grammar I can mention Howell with the *Grammar of the Classical Arabic Language,* Wright with the *A Grammar of the Arabic Language,* de Sacy with the *Gram-*

maire arabe, Vernier with the *Grammaire arabe,* Blachère et Gaudefroy-Demombynes with the *Grammaire de l'Arabe classiqe* and Fleisch with the *Traité de Philologie Arabe.* Among the many modern researchers who have developed the theoretical studies, I can mention Cantineau with the *Études de linguistique arabe,* Verseegh with *The Arabic language* and *The explanation of linguistic causes*, Bohas and Kouloughli with *The Arabic Linguistic Tradition,* Carter with the *Arab Linguistics,* Roman with the *Étude de la phonologie et de la morphologie de la koinè arabe* and Mokhlis with the *Théorie du taṣrīf.* Among the modern Arab researchers I can mention Hindāwī with the *Manāhiǧ al-ṣarfīyīn wa-maḏahibuhum fī l-qarnain al-ṯāliṯ wa-l-rābiᶜ mina l-hiǧra,* Bakkūš with al-*Taṣrif al-ᶜarabī,* ᶜAbd al-Raḥīm with his *Muqaddamat fī ᶜilm al-ṣarf* and ᶜAbd al-Tawwāb with his *al-Taṭawwur al-luġawī, maẓāhiruhu wa-ᶜilaluhu wa-qawānīnuhu.*

Hence, the material contains numerous examples, topics and theories referring to works from the 8th century A.D. until our days. The topics of the work are made accessible by the table of contents that facilitates their use.

The set-up of the work is as follows: chapter 1 is a study of the doubled verb an0d some of its derivatives, chapter 2 is a study of the assimilation, chapter 3 is a presentation of the hamzated verb and some of its derivatives, chapter 4 is a study of the phonological changes due to the hamza, chapter 5 is a presentation of the verb with 1st *w* or *y* radical and some of its derivatives, chapter 6 is a presentation of the verb with 2nd *w* or *y* radical and some of its derivatives, chapter 7 is a presentation of the verb with 3rd *w* or *y* radical and some of its derivatives, chapter 8 is a presentation of the verbs which are doubly weak, chapter 9 is a study of the soundness or the unsoundness of the weak segment and chapter 10 is a study of the substitution.

My thanks are due to the late Gösta Vitestam, Professor emeritus of the Semitic languages at the University of Lund, who has directed my research into the study of Arabic morphology and phonology. His encouragement and positive criticism have greatly influenced this work.

I extend my gratitude to the reviewers who have reviewed my two previous books, *"Aḥmad b. ^{c}Alī b. Mas^{c}ūd on Arabic Morphology, part 1: The Strong Verb" and "Arabic Morphology and Phonology".* Their insights and comments have been very inspiring.

Last but not least, my friends and family deserve my deepest gratitude.

To my late father, Mounir Hakim, my mother, Irene Egeland, my parents-in-law, Carl and Ellen Åkesson, my brother, Senior System Manager James Hakim, my nieces, Amanda and Mia, my husband, Dr. Anders Åkesson, and our son, MA Filip Åkesson, I owe all that one can owe for their love and support during the production of this book.

Lund, March 2009

CHAPTER ONE

1. The doubled verb and some of its derivatives

In this chapter I shall take up the doubled verb and some of its derivatives. I shall discuss as well the phonological procedures due to the doubled segment in its structure.

The doubled verb, *al-muḍāᶜaf,* is the verb in which the 2nd and 3rd radicals are identical segments. It is also termed as *al-ʾaṣamm* "the solid verb" (cf. Åkesson, *Ibn Masᶜūd* 194: fol. 17b), because of its *šadda* as both the 2nd and 3rd radical are assimilated together.

1.1. The conjugations of the doubled verb

The doubled verb falls into four conjugations, of which the fourth occurs very rarely:

1- *faᶜala yafᶜulu,* e.g. *sarara yasruru* "to gladden" that becomes after the assimilation *sarra yasurru.*

2- *faᶜala yafᶜilu,* e.g. *farara yafriru* "to escape" that becomes after the assimilation *farra yafirru.*

3- *faᶜila yafᶜalu,* e.g. *ᶜaḍiḍa yaᶜḍaḍu* "to bite" that becomes after the assimilation *ᶜaḍḍa yaᶜaḍḍu.*

4- *faᶜula yafᶜulu.* Only a few verbs seem to be formed according to this conjugation. Some examples are *ḥabuba yaḥbubu* that becomes after the assimilation *ḥabba yaḥubbu* "to love", *labuba yalbubu* that becomes *labba yalubbu.* Other examples are *sarura* "to become evil", *ramuma* "to repair" and *ḫafufa* "to be light". According to Ibn Ǧinnī, *Munṣif I,* 240, the example *labubta fa-ʾanta labībun* "you became possessed by understanding, so you are a person of understanding" has been said by Yūnus, and *šarurta fī l-šarri* "I became evil, or acted with evil" has been said by Quṭrub.

1.2. Examples of some derivatives of the doubled verb

An example of a doubled verb in the perfect is *madda* "to stretch" underlyingly *madada.* It becomes *yamuddu* in the imperfect of the indicative active. Its imperative is *mudd,* its active participle is *māddun,* its *maṣdar* is *maddun,* its perfect passive is *mudda,* its imperfect is *yumaddu,* its passive participle is *mamdūdun,* the nouns of time and place are *mamaddun* and the noun of instrument is *mimaddun.*

1.2.1. Remarks concerning the phonological procedures in some of its forms:

I intend here to select many of the representative forms by underlining on the one hand the sequences that lead to the assimilation or to any other phonological procedure, and on the other hand, those that prohibit any possible change. Each of the presented sequences is formed of two identical segments that can either be vowelled or vowelless. It goes without saying that two vowelless segments cannot be combined together. The presentation of these sequences will enable me to discuss the rules determining these procedures.

As it shall be remarked, the assimilation is not carried out in all the forms of the doubled verb and some of its derivatives. There exist some forms in which the assimilation of the two identical segments is prohibited. A few examples are the forms of the perfect, imperfect and imperative in which the vowelled pronoun of the agent is suffixed, e.g. the perfect *madad-tu* "I stretched", the imperfect *tamdud-na* "you stretch /fem. pl." and the imperative *ʾumdud-na* "stretch!" (cf. 1.2.1.3.).

Other forms are affected by the following changes:

1) the assimilation of the identical segments that is carried out in the perfect, e.g. *sarra* from *sarara* "he gladdened", in the imperfect *yasurru* from *yasruru* "he gladdens" (cf. 1.2.1.2.) and in some cases of anomalous imperatives, e.g. *mudda, muddi* and *muddu* from *ʾumdud* "stretch! /2nd person of the masc. sing." (cf. 1.2.1.5.).

2) the elision of one of the identical segments in some cases of anomalous perfects, e.g. *ẓal-ta* from *ẓalil-ta* "you continued" (cf. 1.2.1.4.).

3) the substitution of one of the segments by a *y* in some cases of derived forms of the doubled verb, e.g. *taẓannay-tu* from *taẓannan-tu* "I formed an opinion" (cf. 1.2.1.7.).

The forms and the sequences that I shall discuss are the following:

1.2.1.1. The verbal noun: the sequence of two identical segments of which the 1st is vowelless and the 2nd is vowelled: the assimilation.

1.2.1.2. The perfect and the imperfect: the sequence of two vowelled identical segments: the assimilation.

1.2.1.3. The forms of the perfect, imperfect and imperative in which the vowelled pronoun of the agent is suffixed: the sequence of a vowelled segment preceding a vowelless identical segment: the prohibition of the assimilation.

1.2.1.4. Some cases of anomalous perfects: the sequence of a vowelled segment preceding a vowelless identical segment: the elision of one of the identical segments.

1.2.1.5. Some cases of anomalous imperatives: the sequence of a vowelled segment preceding a vowelless identical segment: the assimilation.

1.2.1.6. Some cases of anomalous imperatives: the sequence of a vowelled segment preceding a vowelless identical segment: the elision of one of the identical segments.

1.2.1.7. Some derived forms of the verb: the sequence of a vowelled segment preceding a vowelless identical segment: the substitution of one of the doubled segments by a *y*.

1.2.1.1. The verbal noun: the sequence of two identical segments of which the 1st is vowelless and the 2nd is vowelled: the assimilation:

The phonological procedure that can be carried out in a word in which the sequence invoved is that of a vowelless segment preceding a vowelled identical segment is the assimilation of the first segment to the second (for discussions see par. 2.3.1.). An example of such a case is the verbal noun *maddun* "an extension" (مَدْدٌ)، which is formed according to the pattern *fa*ᶜ*lun,* with two dāls written of which the 1st *d* is vowelless and the 2nd is vowelled (cf. par. 2.3.1.1.). After the assimilation of the dāls it becomes *maddun* with the doubled *d* referred to in Arabic by the *d* carrying the *šadda:* (مَدٌّ) .

1.2.1.2. The perfect and the imperfect: the sequence of two vowelled identical segments: the assimilation:

The common procedure that can affect the stucture of the doubled verb in which the sequence invoved is that of two vowelled identical segments is the assimilation of both the identical vowelled segments (for discussions see par. 2.3.2.).

In Form I of the 3rd person of the perfect of the doubled verb in which the assimilation is carried out, the vowel of the 2nd radical is dropped and the 2nd radical is assimilated to the 3rd. Thus:

sarara → *sarra* "he gladdened"
farara → *farra* "he escaped"
ᶜaḍiḍa → *ᶜaḍḍa* "he bit"
ḥabuba → *ḥabba* "he loved"

As what concerns its imperfect, the phonological procedure that is observed is that the vowel of the 2nd radical is not dropped but switched to the 1st vowelless radical and the 2nd radical is assimilated to the 3rd:

yasruru → *yasurru* "he gladdens"
yafriru → *yafirru* "he escapes"
yaᶜḍadu → *yaᶜaḍḍu* "he bites"
yaḥbubu → *yaḥubbu* "he loves"

The following variations occur concerning the verbs *radda, farra* and *ᶜaḍḍa* (for them see Howell, IV, fasc. II, 1699). Asad and some other people say *rudda, firra* and *ᶜaḍḍa* by vowelling the 1st radical with a ḍamma, kasra or fatḥa respectively and by assimilating the 2nd radical to the 3rd vowelled by a fatḥa. Kaᶜb and Numair say *ruddi, firri* and *ᶜaḍḍi* by vowelling the 1st radical with a ḍamma, kasra or fatḥa respectively and by assimilating the 2nd radical to the 3rd radical vowelled with the kasra. Other variants pertaining to their dialect are *ruddu, firri* and *ᶜaḍḍa* with the alliteration of the vowel of the 1st radical and with the 2nd radical assimilated to the 3rd that is given the same vowel as the 1st radical's vowel.

1.2.1.3. The forms of the perfect, imperfect and imperative in which the vowelled pronoun of the agent is suffixed: the sequence of a vowelled segment preceding a vowelless identical segment: the prohibition of the assimilation:

As a general rule, the sequence of a vowelled segment preceding a vowelless segment prevents in most cases the assimilation (cf. par. 2.3.3.).

In the forms of the doubled verb occurring in the perfect, imperfect and imperative in which the vowelled agent pronouns are suffixed, the 3rd radical becomes vowelless to prevent the disliked succession of four vowelled segments. Hence the sequence is that of a vowelled segment preceding a vowelless segment.

In the case of the perfect, the vowelled agent pronouns are the *-tu* "/1st person of the sing.", the *-ta* "2nd person of the masc. sing.", the *-ti* "2nd person of the fem sing., the *-n(a)ā* "1st person of the pl.", the *-tum* "2nd person of the masc. pl.", the -*tunna* "2nd person of the fem. pl." and the *-na* "3rd person of the fem. pl.". Hence the forms implied for instance by the example *madada* "to stretch" are: *madad-tu, madad-ta, madad-ti,* *madad-n(a)ā, madad-tum, madad-tunna* and *madad-na* which all occur with the elision of the fatḥa from the 2nd *d* of *madada.*

The vowelled agent suffix pronoun in the cases of the imperfect and of the imperative is the *-na.* It marks the 2nd and 3rd person of the fem. pl. in the case of the imperfect, namely *tamdud-na* "you stretch /fem. pl." and *yamdud-na* "they stretch /fem. pl." respectively, and the 2nd person of the fem. pl. in the case of the imperative, namely *ʾumdud-na* "stretch!". In all these cases the assimilation of the two identical segments, namely the 2nd radical vowelled *d,* the *du,* to the 3rd radical vowelless *d* is forbidden because of the vowellessness of this 2nd *d* that has lost its vowel in order to prevent the succession of the vowels when the suffixed *-na* of the fem. pl. is suffixed to the word, and because this vowellessness marks as well the imperative.

1.2.1.4. Some cases of anomalous perfects: the sequence of a vowelled segment preceding a vowelless identical segment: the elision of one of the identical segments:

The sequence of a vowelled segment preceding a vowelless segment allows in some anomalous cases the elision of one of the identical segments (cf. par. 2.3.3.).

In some anomalous cases of verbs occurring in the perfect in which one of the vowelled pronouns of the agent is suffixed, the elision of one of the identical segments can be carried out. An example is *ẓalil-ta* "you continued all day /masc. sing." and *ẓalil-ti* "you continued all day /fem. sing.", with the 3rd radical *l* made vowelless on account of the suffixation of the vowelled agent pronoun in order to prevent the succession of four vowels. This sequence of a vowelled segment, namely the vowelled 2nd radical *l,* preceding a vowelless identical segment, namely the vowelless 3rd radical *l,* forbids the assimilation (for this sequence see par. 2.3.3.). The elision of one of the lāms is carried out by some, which implies that *ẓalil-ta* and *ẓalil-ti* become *ẓal-ta* or *ẓal-ti* respectively (cf. Ibn Mālik, *La Alfīya* 222, Ibn ᶜAqīl, II, 584, Åkesson, *Ibn Masᶜūd* 196: fol. 18b, Wright, II, 69, Howell, IV, fasc. II, 1836 sqq., de Sacy, I, 228). The alleviated form *ẓalta* occurs in the sur. 20: 97 *(l-laḏī ẓalta ᶜalayhi ᶜākifan)* "Of whom thou hast become a devoted worshipper", and *ẓaltum* in the sur. 56: 65 *(fa-ẓaltum tafakkahūna)* "And ye would be left in wonderment" (cf. Howell, IV, fasc. II, 1836).

1.2.1.5. Some cases of anomalous imperatives: the sequence of a vowelled segment preceding a vowelless identical segment: the assimilation:

In some cases of doubled verbs occurring in the imperative, the assimilation of the identical segments is carried out in spite of the vowelless state of the 2nd segment following a vowelless segment, which by principle should prevent the assimilation (cf. par. 2.3.3.).

An example is the imperative of the 2nd person of the masc. sing. *ʾumdud* "stretch!" with the 1st *d* vowelled by a ḍamma and the 2nd *d* vowelless, which becomes *mudda, muddi* and *muddu* (cf. Åkesson, *Ibn Masᶜūd* 196: fol. 18b, Wright, II, 70). Those who dissolute are the Ḥiğāzīs whereas those who assimilate are the people of Tamīm (cf. Wright, II, 70 in the notes).

By contrast to the variant of the imperative of the 2nd person of the masc. sing. *muddu* in which the ḍamma is given to the *d* on the analogy of the ḍamma of the 1st radical *m* (cf. Åkesson, *Ibn Masᶜūd* 196: fol. 18b), it is impossible to use the variant *firru* "flee!" for the imperative of the 2nd person of the masc. sing. of *farra* "to flee", with the ḍamma vowelling the *r* instead of the usual form *ʾifrir,* as the ḍamma is disliked after the kasra of the 1st radical (cf. ibid). However *firra* and *firri* are possible variants to be used instead of *ʾifrir,* with the fatḥa and the kasra vowelling the r respectively (cf. de Sacy, I, 229, Wright, II, 70), as *mudda* and *muddi* mentioned above.

Both *ʿaḍḍa* and *ʿaḍḍi* are used as well as variants with the assimilation of the ḍāds instead of *ʾiʿḍaḍ* bite! /masc. sing. (cf. Wright, II, 70).

1.2.1.6. Some cases of anomalous imperatives: the sequence of a vowelled segment preceding a vowelless identical segment: the elision of one of the identical segments:

In some cases of doubled verbs occurring in the imperative of the 2nd person of the fem pl. in which the vowelled person of the agent, namely the *-na,* is suffixed to, the elision of one the identical segments can be carried out (compare the cases of anomalous perfects in par. 1.2.1.4.).

An example is *ʾiqrir-na* "stay quietly! /2nd person of the fem. pl.", from the root *q r r* with 2nd and 3rd radical r (cf. Ibn Manẓūr, V, 3578-3579), in which the 2nd *r* is vowelless on the basis that the sukūn marks the imperative and that the vowelled agent pronoun is suffixed to it. The sequence of the identical segments in *ʾiqrir-na* is that of a vowelled segment, namely the 2nd radical *r,* preceding a vowelless segment, namely the 3rd radical *r,* which by principle should prevent the assimilation (for discussions concerning this sequence see 2.3.3.). The elision of the 1st *r* of the sequence is however a possibility after that its vowel is shifted to the *q,* and then the hamza of the imperative is also elided as it is not more needed now that the 1st radical *q* is vowelled. The resulting alleviated form is *qir-na* (cf. Ibn ʿAqīl, II, 584-585, Åkesson, *Ibn Masʿūd* 196: fol. 18b, Penrice, *Dic-*

tionary 116). The variant *qarna* exists as well which pertains to another dialectal variant, and its base form is then the variant *ʾiqrar-na.* It can be mentioned that *wa-qarna* occurs instead of *wa-qirna* in the sur. 33: 33 *(wa-qarna fī buyūtikunna)* and that it is the reading of Nāfiᶜ and ᶜĀṣim (cf. Ibn ᶜAqīl, II, 585).

1.2.1.7. Some derived forms of the verb: the sequence of a vowelled segment preceding a vowelless identical segment: the substitution of one of the doubled segments by a y:

The phonological procedure that is observed in some cases of the derived forms of the doubled verbs is that their 3rd radical, which is the second of two identical segments, is substituted by the *y* (for this substitution see par. 10.1.8.4.). Sībawaihi, II, 447 mentions the following verbs in which this substitution has been carried out (cf. Roman, *Étude I,* 361):

- Form V *tasarrartu* "I had a concubine" that becomes after the change of the 3rd radical *r* into a *y tasarraytu.*

- Form V *taẓannantu* "I formed an opinion" that becomes after the change of the 3rd radical *n* into a *y taẓannaytu.*

- Form V *taqaṣṣaṣtu* "I remembered [his words]" that becomes after the change of 3rd radical *ṣ* into a *y taqaṣṣaytu.*

- Form IV *ʾamlaltu* "I dictated" that becomes after the change of 3rd radical l into a *y ʾamlaytu.*

- Another example that can be added is Form V *taqaḍḍiya* used instead of *taqaḍḍaḍa* "to fly down swiftly" (cf. Zamaḫšarī, 173, Åkesson, *Ibn Masᶜūd* 194: fol. 17b), in which the 3rd radical *ḍ* is changed into the *y,* and the *ḍ* is vowelled with a kasra instead of a fatḥa. The verb is found in the example *taqaḍḍiya l-bāzī* "the hawk flew down swiftly" of the verse said by ᶜAǧǧāǧ cited by Ibn Ǧinnī, *Sirr II,* 759, Muʾaddib, *Taṣrīf* 438, Ibn Yaᶜīš, X, 24, Åkesson, *Ibn Masᶜūd* 204: (170):

> *"ʾIḏā l-kirāmu btadarū l-bāᶜa badar*
> *taqaḍḍiya l-bāzī ʾiḏā l-bāzī kasar".*
> "When the generous hasten to the noble deed,
> he hastens with the swoop of the falcon, when the falcon contracts his wings".

1.3. Conclusion

I have presented the doubled verb and some of its derivatives in this chapter. The phonological procedures due to the identical segments in some of its forms have been briefly discussed. It has been remarked that the assimilation is carried out if the sequence is that of two identical segments of which the 1st is vowelless and the 2nd is vowelled, e.g. *maddun* "an extension" (مَدْدٌ) that becomes after the assimilation *maddun* (مَدٌّ) with one *d* given the *šadda* (for discussions see par. 1.2.1.1.), or a sequence of two identical segments of which both segments are vowelled, e.g. *sarara* that becomes after the assimilation *sarra* "to gladden" (for discussions see par. 1.2.1.2.).

The assimilation is mostly forbidden if the sequence is that of a vowelled segment preceding a vowelless segment, e.g. *madad-tu* "I stretched" (for discussions see par. 1.2.1.3.), but it is in some anomalous cases carried out as in the imperative *ʾumdud* "stretch!" that becomes *mudda, muddi* and *muddu* (for discussions see par. 1.2.1.5.).

The elision of one of the identical segments is another possibility in some anomalous cases, as the perfect *ẓalil-ta* "you continued all day /masc. sing." that becomes after the elision *ẓal-ta* (for discussions see par. 1.2.1.4.) or the imperative *ʾiqrir-na* "stay quietly! /2nd person of the fem. pl." that becomes after the elision *qir-na* (for discussions see par. 1.2.1.6.).

The substitution of one of the identical segments by a *y* is another alternative that can be carried out in some anomalous cases of the derived forms of the doubled verb, as Form V *ta-sarrartu* "I had a concubine" that becomes after the change of the 3rd radical *r* into a *y* *tasarraytu* (for discussions see par. 1.2.1.7.).

What remains is to extend a general discussion and analysis of the assimilation in the next chapter.

CHAPTER TWO

2. The assimilation

In connection with the doubled verb in which two identical segments are assimilated, I shall generally discuss the assimilation in this section.

The assimilation is termed *ʾidġām* or *ʾiddiġām*. It involves a sequence of two identical segments (for discussions see par. 2.3., par. 1.2.1.), or of two different segments originating from one common point of articulation or from two close points of articulation (for discussions see par. 2.4). It can be carried out in one word or in two words following each other. Furthermore it differs in the pronunciation and in the writing (cf. 2.1.).

The reason why the assimilation is carried out is the dislike of repeating twice the same segment or of pronouncing two segments that are close to each other in the point of articulation. On the basis that the assimilation can be carried out between segments that are different, I shall briefly discuss the segments' points of articulation and characters (cf. 2.2.). This presentation explains as well some of the procedures of the substitution that I discuss in chapter 10.

Hence I shall attempt to present the theories concerning the assimilation or the lack of assimilation in a few sequences formed of two identical or of different segments.

2.1. The assimilation in the pronunciation and in the writing

It can be remarked that there is a difference in the pronunciation and in the written representation of a word in which an assimilation is carried out.

In examples in which two identical segments are assimilated, e.g. *madda,* two dāls are uttered in the pronunciation, namely *mad-da,* of which the first *d* is vowelless and the second one vowelled: مَدْدَ. In the writing however, one *d* is written with a šadda over it: مَدَّ.

In examples of nouns beginning with one of the "solar segments" to which the *l-* of the definite article *al-* is assimilated to (for discussions see par. 2.4.1.1.1.), the nouns are pronounced with the doubling of the solar segment and written with both the *l-* of the article and the solar segment given the *šadda.* An example is *"ar-Raḥmān"* pronounced with a double *r* indicating the assimilation of the *l-* to the *r,* and written *al-Raḥmān* الرَّحْمن "the Merciful" with the *l* and with the *r* that carries the *šadda.*

2.2. The points of articulation and some of the characters of the segments that lead to the assimilation

An assimilation between two different segments requires that these segments originate either from a common point of articulation or from close points of articulation. There should as well exist an akinity in character between both these segments or that a segment exhibits a strength of character in relation to the other, which would explain why the assimilation is carried out to it.

2.2.1. The segments' common and neighbouring points of articulation:

Among the first grammarians who gave a detailed description of the segments' points of articulation and characters, Sībawaihi, II, 452-455 can be mentioned. The following segments have common or neighbouring points of articulation (cf. also Versteegh, *Language* 20).

- The *ʾ*, *h,* and *ā* originate from "the farthest part of the throat" and the *ġ* and *ḫ* from "the nearest part of the throat". They are characterized as laryngals.
- The *ʿ* and *ḥ* originate from "the middle of the throat". They are characterized as pharyngals.
- The *q* originates from "the farthest part of the tongue, and the part of the upper palate above it". The *k* is "lower than the *q* from the next parts of the tongue and palate towards the upper palate". They are characterized as post-palatals.
- The *ǧ, š* and *y* originate from "the middle of the tongue, and from the middle part of the upper palate". They are characterized as pre-palatals.
- The *ṭ, d* and the *t* originate from "the tip of the tongue and the roots of the two upper central incissors". The *ḍ* originates from "the first part of the side of the tongue, and the molars below (on the left or right side)". They are characterized as alveolars.
- The *l* originates from "between the nearest part of the side of the tongue, to the end of its tip, and the part of the upper palate next to it, a little above the premolar, canine, lateral incisor, and central incisor".

- The *ṣ, z* and *s* originate from "the part that is between the tip of the tongue and the tops of the two upper central incissors". The *n* is from the tip of the tongue and the parts over the incissors". They are characterized as dentals.

- The *ẓ, ḏ* and *ṯ* originate from "the tip of the tongue and the edges of the two upper central incisors". They are characterized as interdentals.

- The *f* originates from "the inside of the lower lip and the edges of the two upper central incisors". The *b, m* and *w* originate from "what is between the lips". These segments are characterized as labials.

2.2.2. Some of the segments' characters:

Among the most specifying characters of the segments are those of *al-mahmūsa* "surd, low, soft, whispered, voiceless" and of *al-maǧhūra* "vocal, loud, clear, sonorous, voiced".

The surd segments are comprised in the sentence *satašḥaṯuka Ḫaṣfah* (cf. for them Zamaḫšarī, 189, Åkesson, *Ibn Masᶜūd* 198: fol. 19a, Howell, IV, fasc. II, 1725). They are: the *s, t, š, ḥ, ṯ, k, ḫ, ṣ, f* and *h*. Sībawaihi, II, 453 presents them in this order: the *h, ḥ, ḫ, k, š, s, t, ṣ, ṯ* and *f*. They are weak in the stress laid upon them so that they do not impede the breath that therefore runs on with them.

The voiced segments are comprised in the sentence *ẓillu Qawwin rabaḍun ᵓiḏ ġazā ǧundun muṭīᶜun* "the shade of Qaww was a shelter, when an obediant host made a raid" (cf. Howell, IV, fasc. II, 1726). They prevent the breath from running on with them. Sībawaihi, II, 453 presents them in this order: the *ᵓ, ā, ᶜ, ġ, q, ǧ, y, ḍ, l, n, r, ṭ, d, z, ẓ, ḏ, b, m* and *w*.

There are other secondary characters that the segments of these main groups can present (for a detailed presentation of the characters see. Sībawaihi, II, 454-455) as:

- *al-mustaᶜliya* "the elevated", which are comprised in the combination *ṣaṭ ḍaẓ ḫaġaq* (cf. Zamaḫšarī, 190, Åkesson, *Ibn Masᶜūd* 198: fol. 19b), namely the *ṣ, ṭ, ḍ, ẓ, ḫ, ġ* and *q*. The first four segments, namely the *ṣ, ṭ, ḍ* and *ẓ* are recognized as *al-muṭbaqa* "the covered" (cf. Sībawaihi, II, 455, Åkesson, *Ibn Masᶜūd* 198: fol. 19b). Their point of articulation is covered by the upper palate. The three remaining segments, namely the *ḫ, ġ* and *q* do not present any covering.

- *al-munḫafiḍa* "the depressed segments" which are contrary to the elevated (cf. Zamaḫšarī, 190, Howell, IV, fasc. II, 1729-1731).

- *al-ṣafīr* "sibilant" which are the three segments: the *ṣ, z* and *s*, which make a whistling.

2.3. The sequences of two identical segments: cases in which the assimilation is or is not carried out

The sequences of two identical segments can occur in one word or in two words following each other. In the case of the assimilation which is carried out between two segments belonging to two different words, it is the ultimate segment of the first word that can be assimilated to the initial segment of the second word (for such cases see Sībawaihi, II, 455 sqq., Zamaḫšarī, 191 sqq., Roman, *Étude I,* 390-427, Wright, I, 15-16). This assimilation is not as usual as the assimilation that is carried out in one word, and can be seen as belonging to the rarities. I can mention the following sequences:

2.3.1. the sequence of two identical segments of which the 1st is vowelless and the 2nd vowelled: the necessity of the assimilation.

2.3.2. the sequence of two identical segments which are both vowelled.

2.3.3. the sequence of two identical segments of which the 1st is vowelled and the 2nd vowelless: the prohibition of the assimilation. The assimilation in some anomalous cases.

Not all the sequences can result in the assimilation of the 1st segment to the 2nd. It shall be noticed that the most important condition of the assimilation is the vowelling of the 2nd segment.

2.3.1. The sequence of two identical segments of which the 1st is vowelless and the 2nd vowelled: the necessity of the assimilation:

The vowelless state of the 1st segment preceding a vowelled identical segment answers to the condition that makes the assimilation necessary.

This sequence can be found in one word or in two words following each other.

2.3.1.1. The assimilation that is carried out in one word:

An example of such a case is *maddun* (مدّ) "an extension" that is formed according to the pattern *faᶜlun,* in which the necessary assimilation of the 1st *d* to the 2nd *d* is carried out (cf. 1.2.1.1.).

Another example is Form VIII *ᵓittağara* "to trade" (cf. Åkesson, *Ibn Masᶜūd* 196: fol. 19a, par. 2.4.1.1.3.1.:2) from *tağara* with 1st *t* radical. In the base form *ᵓittağara,* the 1st vowelless *t* radical is followed by the vowelled *t* infix, the *ta,* of Form VIII *ᵓiftaᶜala,* which necessitates the assimilation of the *t* to the *t*. Hence *ᵓittağara* is written with one *t* carrying the *šadda* in Arabic (إتّجر) as an indication of the assimilation (for discussions concerning the assimilation of the 1st vowelless radical to the infixed vowelled *t* of Form VIII of the perfect *ᵓiftaᶜala* see par. 2.4.1.1.3.1.).

2.3.1.2. The assimilation that is carried out in two words following each other:

The assimilation can be carried out from a 1st vowelless segment, which is the last segment of a word, to a 2nd identical vowelled segment that is the initial segment of the word following it.

An example of such a case is *(ᵓiḫšaw w(a)āqidan)* (إخشَوْ واقدا) "Fear [2nd person of the masc. pl. of the imperative] one who sets fire!" (cf. Sībawaihi, II, 457) in which the 1st *w* is vowelless and the 2nd *w* is vowelled by a fatḥa. The reason of the vowellessness of the 1st *w* is that the verb *ᵓiḫšaw* is an imperative in the 2nd person of the masc. pl. with the suffixed pronoun of the masc. pl., the *ū,* vowelless and preceded by a fatḥa which results in *aw*. The example becomes after the assimilation of the vowelless *w* to the vowelled *wa, ᵓiḫšaw w(a)āqidan* (إخشَو وّاقدا) with the 2nd *w* carrying the *šadda* as an indication of the assimilation.

2.3.2. The sequence of two identical segments which are both vowelled

The sequence of two identical vowelled segments leads mostly to the assimilation (cf. par. 1.2.1.2.), except in some anomalous cases as the case of *ḥayiya* "to live" (cf. par. 2.3.2.2.1.), in the coordinatives and in somes measures that can be mixed up with other measures (cf. par. 2.3.2.2.2.).

The assimilation can be carried out in one word or in two words, and in the latter case the assimilation is a possibility that pertains to the rarities.

2.3.2.1. The assimilation that is carried out in one word:

The sequence occurs in the common following cases:

1- In examples of doubled verbs in the perfect, e.g. *sarara* resulting after the assimilation in *sarra* (for discussions see par. 1.2.1.2.).

2- In examples of verbs of Form V *tafaʿʿala* or Form VI *taf(a)āʿala* in which the vowelled prefixed *t* is assimilated to the 1st vowelled radical t following it (for discussions see par. 2.4.2.1.1.). An example is Form V *tatarrasa* "shielded himself" that becomes after the assimilation *ʾittarasa* (cf. Howell, IV, fasc. II, 1829). The vowelled *t* prefix, i.e. the *ta,* is assimilated to the vowelled 1st radical *t,* i.e. the *ta,* resulting in *ttarasa* and the prosthetic hamza, the *ʾi,* is then prefixed to prevent beginning the word with a vowelless segment.

3- In examples of verbs of Form VIII in the imperfect *yaftaʿilu* in which the vowelled infixed *t* is assimilated to the 2nd vowelled radical *t* following it (for discussions see par. 2.4.2.1.2.). An example is *yaqtatilu* "to contend among themselves" that becomes after the assimilation *yaqattilu* (cf. Åkesson, *Ibn Masʿūd* 200: fol. 20b). The vowelled *t* prefix, i.e. the *ta,* is assimilated to the vowelled 2nd radical, i.e. *ti,* after that its fatḥa vowel is shifted to the 1st radical *q.* It can be noted that both variants *yaqattilu* and *yaqittilu* occur (cf. Zamaḫšarī, 195, Howell, IV, fasc. II, 1807).

2.3.2.2. Cases in which the assimilation is not carried out in one word:

The assimilation is mostly not carried out in the case of *ḥayiya* "to live" (cf. par. 2.3.2.2.1.), in the co-ordinatives and in some special measures (cf. 2.3.2.2.2.).

2.3.2.2.1. An anomalous case: ḥayiya

The assimilation is not carried out in some dialectal variants in the doubled verb with two weak radicals *ḥayiya* "to live" (for discussions concerning it see Sībawaihi, II, 430-431, Zamaḫšarī, 187, Ibn ᶜAqīl, II, 588, Åkesson, *Ibn Masᶜūd* 194: fol. 18a, Howell, IV, fasc. I, 1624 sqq., fasc. II, 1693 sqq., Wright, II, 94-95, Vernier, I, 342-343, de Sacy, I, 259-260). In spite of the fact that two vowelled identical segments are combined in it, namely the *yi* and the *ya,* they are not in most cases assimilated together resulting in *ḥayya.* The assimilation is carried out however in some dialectal variants. The reason why some prefer not to assimilate the yāᵓs in the perfect resulting in *ḥayya,* is that they feel obliged by analogy to assimilate them in the imperfect causing the ḍamma to vowel the *y* which is deemed as a heavy combination, i.e. *yaḥayyu* would have to be said instead of *yaḥy(a)ā* with final *ᵓalif maqṣūra.* Those who assimilate in the perfect by saying *ḥayya* consider both yāᵓs as two identical vowelled segments in one word. They avoid however to assimilate in the imperfect because of the implied heavy combination. This means that *yaḥy(a)ā* with final *alif maqṣūra* occurs by all instead of *yaḥayyu.* Furthermore, the 3rd radical *y* has been dropped by some in the perfect of the 3rd person of the masc. pl., who use *ḥay(u)ū* instead of *ḥayiyū* (cf. Sībawaihi, II, 431, Ibn Manẓūr, II, 1080). This elision of the *y* implies that it is considered as unnecessary to the word's structure (cf. Åkesson, *Ibn*

Mas^c^ūd 194: fol. 18a). In the light that the 2nd segment among two identical segments is not necessary for the structure of the word, it can be understood why the assimilation is not always carried out in the perfect *ḥayiya,* as the condition of the assimilation is that the 2nd segment among the identical segments should be existent in the structure and not submitted to an elision.

2.3.2.2.2. The coordinatives and some special measures:

The assimilation is forbidden in *al-ᵓilḥāqīyāt* "the coordinatives", in spite of the vowelling of two identical segments in them. These patterns refer to those words that are rendered quasi-coordinate to other words of which the radicals are greater in number than theirs (cf. Lane, II 3008). An example is *qardadun* "elevated ground" (cf. Sībawaihi, II, 448, Åkesson, *Ibn Mas^c^ūd* 194: 17b) from the root *qarida* "it became contracted together", in which the 2nd *d* is added to the form, and no assimilation is to be carried out from the first vowelled *d,* the *da,* to the other vowelled *d,* the *dun,* on account that the word is quasi-coordinate to the measure *fa^c^lalun* (cf. Lane, II, 2513).

The assimilation is as well forbidden in some words that are formed according to special measures (cf. Sībawaihi, II, 445-446, Åkesson, *Ibn Mas^c^ūd* 194: fol. 18a) as *fa^c^ilun, fu^c^ulun, fu^c^alun* and *fa^c^alun,* so that they are not mixed up with other words in which the assimilation is carried out. Some examples are:

- *ṣakikun* "the colliding of the knees in running" formed according to *fa^c^ilun* to avoid mixing it up with *ṣakkun* "a written acknowledgement of a debt".

- *sururun* "bedsteads" formed according to *fu^c^ulun* to avoid mixing it up with *surrun* "the navel- string of a child".

- *ǧudadun* "the stripes that are on the back of the ass" formed according to *fuᶜalun* to avoid mixing it up with *ǧuddun* "a part of the river near the land".

- *ṭalalun* "the remains of a dwelling or house" formed according to *faᶜalun* to avoid mixing it up with *ṭallun* "weak rain".

2.3.2.3. The assimilation that is carried out in two words following each other:

The assimilation can be carried out from a 1st vowelled segment, which is the lst segment of a word, to a 2nd identical vowelled segment that is the initial segment of the word following it. An example of such a case is the assimilation of the bāʾ's in the sur. 2: 19 *(la-ḏahaba bi-samᶜihim)* that becomes *la-ḏahab bi-samᶜihim* (لَذَهَب بِّسَمْعِهِم) "He would take away their faculty of hearing", read so by Abū ᶜAmr (cf. Zamaḫšarī, 195, Ibn Yaᶜīš, X, 147) with the fatḥa of the 1st *b,* the ba, elided and the šadda given to the 2nd *b* as an indication of the assimilation. An analysis of *la-ḏahaba bi-samᶜihim* before that the assimilation of the bāʾs is carried out in it, shows that the first *b* which is the 3rd radical of *ḏahaba,* is vowelled by a fatḥa that is the marker of the undeclinable perfect and the 2nd *b* which is the 1st segment of the word following it, is vowelled by the kasra as it is the preposition *bi.*

2.3.3. The sequence of two identical segments of which the 1st is vowelled and the 2nd vowelless: the prohibition of the assimilation. The assimilation in some anomalous cases:

The sequence of two identical segments of which the 1st is vowelled and the 2nd is vowelless forbids the assimilation in most of the cases (for discussions see 1.2.1.3.), because the condition of the assimilation is that the 2nd segment should be vowelled. However, it can be remarked that the assimilation is carried out in some anomalous cases, as e.g. the imperative of the 2nd person of the masc. sing. *ʾumdud* "stretch!" with the vowelled *du* followed by a vowelless *d,* that becomes after the assimilation *mudda, muddi* and *muddu* (for discussions see 1.2.1.5.).

The elision of one of the identical segments is however a possibility in some anomalous cases, e.g. the perfect of the 2nd person of the masc. sing. *ẓalil-ta* "you continued all day" that becomes after the elision of one of the lāms *ẓal-ta* (for discussions see 1.2.1.4.) and the imperative of the 2nd person of the pl. *ʾiqrir-na* "stay quietly!" that becomes after the elision of one of the rāʾs *qir-na* (for discussions see par. 1.2.1.6.).

The substitution of one of the identical segments by a *y* is another alternative in some anomalous cases, e.g. Form V *tasarartu* "I had a concubine" that becomes after the change of the 3rd radical *r* into a *y tasarraytu* (for discussions see par. 1.2.1.7.). Thus there are four possibilities to be considered concerning the sequence of a vowelled segment followed by a vowelless identical segment. One of them is that the assimilation is forbidden, the second is that the assimilation is possible, the third is that of one of the segments is elided, and the fourth is that one of the segments is substituted by a *y.*

It can be noted that the sequence of a vowelled segment preceding a vowelless segment can only occur in one word, and not in two words following each other, on account that the 1st segment in the second word can only be vowelled and not vowelless, as it is impossible to begin the word with a vowelless segment in Arabic.

2.4. The sequence of two different segments: cases in which the assimilation is or is not carried out

The sequence of two different segments can result in the assimilation of one to the other on the condition that they originate from the same point of articulation or from two close points of articulation. I can take up the following sequences in which the vowelling or the absence of a vowel of one of the segments is considered:

2.4.1. the sequence of two different segments of which the 1st is vowelless and the 2nd is vowelled: the assimilation.

2.4.2. the sequence of two different segments which are both vowelled.

2.4.1. The sequence of two different segments of which the 1st is vowelless and the 2nd is vowelled: the assimilation:

The vowelless state of the 1st segment preceding a vowelled segment that is close to it in the point of articulation or that is akin to it in character or that is different and having a stronger character than it, can result in the assimilation.

This sequence can be found in one word or in two words following each other, the latter pertaining to the rarities.

2.4.1.1. The assimilation that is carried out from the 1st vowelless segment to a 2nd different vowelled segment in one word:

I propose for this study the assimilation of the vowelless *l-* of the definite article *al-* to the vowelled solar segment of the word that it is prefixed to, the assimilation of the 3rd radical *d* of a verb in the perfect to the pronoun of the agent beginning with the *t* that is suffixed to it, and the vowelled infixed *t* of Form VIII *ʾiftaʿala* to the 1st vowelless radical preceding it.

2.4.1.1.1. The assimilation of the vowelless l- of the article al- to the vowelled solar segment that begins a noun:

It is carried out in some examples of definite nouns to which the article *al-* is prefixed to, that begin with one of the "solar segments", namely the *t, ṯ, d, ḏ, r, z, s, š, ṣ, ḍ, ṭ, ẓ, l* and *n* (cf. Wright, I, 15, Bakkūš, *Taṣrīf* 66). It can be remarked concerning them that the vowelless *l-* is assimilated to this vowelled segment. An example is الرَّحْمٰن *al-Raḥmān* "the Merciful" in which the *r* carries the *šadda* in Arabic as an indication of the assimilation of the *l-* to it (cf. par. 2.1.). The reason why the *l-* is assimilated to those segments is that they all originate from between the teeth to the lower part of the palate, and thus are all close to the point of articulation of the *l* (cf. Bakkūš, *Taṣrīf* 66).

2.4.1.1.2. The assimilation of the 3rd radical d in verbs that occur in the perfect, to the vowelled suffixed pronoun of the agent that begins with the t:

In the cases of verbs whose 3rd radical is a *d* that occur in the perfect in the persons in which the vowelled pronoun of the agent beginning with the *t* is suffixed to, namely the *-tu* "1st person of the sing.", *-ta* "2nd person of the masc. sing.", *-ti* "2nd person of the fem. sing.", *-tum* "2nd person of the masc. pl.", *-tunna* "2nd person of the fem. pl." and *-tumā* "2nd person of the dual", an assimilation is carried out from the vowelless *d* to the vowelled *t* following it (cf. Vernier, I, 57).

Some examples are *madad-tu* "I stretched", *madad-ta* "you stretched /masc. sing." and *madad-ti* "you stretched /fem. sing.", in which the *d* is assimilated to the *t* which is indicated in Arabic by the *šadda* over the *t*. The reason of this assimilation is the proximity of the *d* to the *t* in the point of articulation as they both are alveolars (for the segments see par. 2.2.1.).

2.4.1.1.3. The assimilation that is carried out between the vowelled infixed t of Form VIII of the perfect ʾiftaʿala and the 1st vowelless radical preceding it:

The infixed *t* of Form VIII of the perfect *ʾiftaʿala* is either assimilated to or is assimilated by one of the vowelless fourteen segments preceding it that is the 1st radical (for a general study of this assimilation see Wright, II, 66-67, Howell, IV, fasc. II, 1803 sqq.). These segments are: 1- the *ʾ*, 2- *t*, 3- *ṯ*, 4- *d*, 5- *ḏ*, 6- *z*, 7- *s*, 8- *š*, 9- *ṣ*, 10- *ḍ*, 11- *ṭ*, 12- *ẓ*, 13- *w* and 14- *y* (cf. Åkesson, *Ibn Masʿūd* 196-198: fol. 19a).

It is possible to distinguish between cases in which the 1st vowelless radical is assimilated to the infixed vowelled *t* of Form VIII of the perfect *ʾiftaʿala* (cf. 2.4.1.1.3.1.) and cases in which the infixed vowelled *t* of Form VIII of the perfect *ʾiftaʿala* is assimilated to the 1st vowelless radical (cf. 2.4.1.1.3.2.)

2.4.1.1.3.1. Cases in which the 1st vowelless radical is assimilated to the infixed vowelled t of Form VIII of the perfect ʾiftaʿala:

The 1st vowelless radical is assimilated to the vowelled infixed *t* if it is a: 1- *ʾ*, 2- *t*, 3- possibly *ṯ*, 4- *w* and 5- *y*.

I can illustrate the phonological procedure that is carried out in the perfect of Form VIII as follows: *ʾiftaʿala* with the vowelless 1st radical *f* followed by the vowelled infix *t* becomes *ʾittaʿala* after that the 1st radical *f* is assimilated to the vowelled *t*.

1- The assimilation of the 1st radical vowelless ʾ to the vowelled infixed t of Form VIII ʾiftaʿala:

An example is Form VIII *ʾiʾtaḫaḏa* which becomes after the assimilation *ʾittaḫaḏa* "to take" (cf. Åkesson, *Ibn Masʿūd* 196: fol. 19a, Howell, IV, fasc. II, 1848 sqq., de Sacy, I, 236, Wright, II, 76-77, Lane, I, 29, Fleisch, *Traité I,* 150). The base form *ʾiʾtaḫaḏa* is from *ʾaḫaḏa* "to take", a verb with 1st hamza radical. The process leading to the assimilation is not a direct process and involves as well the substitutions of segments, namely the *y* for the ʾ and the *t* for the *y*. For this reason this assimilation is considered as anomalous. The changes can be illustrated with the following: *ʾiʾtaḫaḏa* with the vowelless ʾ preceded by a kasra becomes *ʾiytaḫaḏa* with the ʾ changed into a *y* on account of the influence of the kasra preceding it. As the vowelless *y* precedes the vowelled *t,* the *y* is changed into the *t* and then the *t* is assimilated to the *t* so that it becomes *ʾittaḫaḏa* (إِتَّخَذَ). This change of the *y,* which is not the underlying radical from the form *ʾiytaḫaḏa,* into the *t* resulting in *ʾittaḫaḏa,* is considered as anomalous because the *y* is already substituted for the ʾ that is the radical of the form *ʾiʾtaḫaḏa.* For this reason some grammarians preferred to believe that *ʾittaḫaḏa* is formed from the variant *taḫiḏa* and not from *ʾaḫaḏa,* and their theory was integrated in the language (cf. Ibn Manẓūr, I, 37, Zağğāğī, *Mağālis* 333, Wright, II, 76-77, Lane, I, 29, Fleisch, *Traité I,* 150).

2- The assimilation of the 1st radical vowelless t to the vowelled infixed t of Form VIII ʾiftaʿala:

An example is Form VIII *ʾittağara* "to trade" that becomes after the assimilation *ʾittağara* with one *t* carrying the šadda in Arabic as an indication of the assimilation (cf. par. 2.3.1.1.).

3- The assimilation between the 1st radical vowelless ṯ and the vowelled infixed t of Form VIII ʾiftaʿala:

The vowelless 1st radical *ṯ* can be assimilated to the vowelled infixed *t* as well as the vowelled infixed *t* can be assimilated to the vowelless 1st radical *ṯ*. An example is Form VIII *ʾiṯtaʾara* "to get one's revenge" (cf. Åkesson, *Ibn Masʿūd* 196: fol. 19a) with the vowelless *ṯ* preceding the vowelled *t* that can become after the assimilation of the *t* to the *ṯ* *ʾiṯṯaʾara* or after the assimilation of the *ṯ* to the *t* *ʾittaʾara.*

4- The assimilation of the 1st radical vowelless w to the vowelled infixed t of Form VIII ʾiftaʿala:

An example is Form VIII *ʾiwtaʿada* "to accept a promise" (from *waʿada* "to promise") with the vowelless *w* preceding the vowelled *t* that becomes after the assimilation of the *w* to the *t* *ʾittaʿada* (cf. de Sacy, I, 240, Wright, II, 80-81, Lane, II, 2902, Åkesson, *Ibn Masʿūd* 200: fol. 20a-20b and this study par. 5.2.1.8.)

The *w* is changed into a *y* on account of the kasra preceding it before that the assimilation to the infixed *t* is carried out. Hence *ʾiwtaʿada* becomes at first *ʾiytaʿada* "(cf. Wright, II, 80), and then *ʾittaʿada.*

5- The assimilation of the 1st radical vowelless y to the vowelled infixed t of Form VIII ʾiftaʿala:

An example is Form VIII *ʾiytasara* "to play at hazard" (cf. Zamaḫšarī, 175, 178, Åkesson, *Ibn Masʿūd* 200: fol. 20b, de Sacy, I 240, Wright, II, 80-81 and this study par. 5.4.1.2.) from *yasara* "to be easy", with the vowelless *y* preceding the vowelled *t,* that becomes after the assimilation *ʾittasara* with the *y* assimilated to the *t* resulting in the doubled *t.* The variant

ʾittasara with this assimilation is preferred to the base form *ʾiytasara* because the vowelling of the ʾ with a kasra preceding the *y* in *ʾiytasara* is deemed as a heavy combination.

2.4.1.1.3.2. Cases in which the infixed vowelled t of Form VIII of the perfect ʾiftaʿala is assimilated to the 1st vowelless radical preceding it:

The surd and soft infixed *t* is assimilated to the 1st radical if this radical originates from the same point of articulation or from a close point of articulation to it, and that it is stronger than it in character. Thus the surd *t* is assimilated to the 1st radical if it is a voiced segment (for the voiced and surd segments see par. 2.2.2.) because the voiced segment is considered as stronger than the surd segment in the sound (cf. Bakkūš, *Taṣrīf* 40, 66), or if it is a covered segment (cf. ibid, 66; and for the covered segments see par. 2.2.2.) or if it is a sibilant segment (for the sibilant segments see 2.2.2.) on account of the strength of character of the covered segment and of the sibilant segment in relation to the soft segment. Among the fourteen segments mentioned above (see 2.4.1.1.3.), the 1st radical's segment to which the alveolar surd and soft *t* is assimilated to can be: 1- the alveolar and voiced *d,* 2- the interdental and voiced *ḏ,* 3- the dental, voiced and sibilant *z,* 4- the dental, surd and sibilant *ṣ,* 5- the alveolar and voiced *ḍ,* 6- the alveolar and voiced *ṭ,* 7- the interdental and surd *ṯ,* 8- the dental, surd and sibilant *s* and 9- the prepalatal and surd *š.*

The phonological procedure that is carried out in the perfect of Form VIII is illustrated as follows: *ʾiftaʿala* with the vowelless 1st radical *f* followed by the vowelled infix *t* becomes *ʾiffaʿala* after that the vowelled *t* is assimilated to the 1st radical *f*.

1- The assimilation of the vowelled infixed t of Form VIII ʾiftaᶜala to the 1st radical vowelless d preceding it:

An example is Form VIII *ʾidt(a)āna* "to buy upon credit" (cf. Zamaḫšarī, 176, Ibn ᶜAqīl, II, 582, Åkesson, *Ibn Masᶜūd* 198: fol. 19a, Lane, I, 942-943) with the vowelless *d* preceding the vowelled *t* that becomes after the assimilation *ʾidd(a)āna* with the *t* assimilated to the *d* resulting in the doubled *d*.

The reason of the substitution of the *d* for the *t* before that the assimilation is carried out in it resulting in the doubled *d,* is the common point of articulation of both these segments as they both are alveolars (for the segments see par. 2.2.1.). As for the reason why it is specifically the *t* that is assimilated to the *d* and not vice versa, it is so that the character of the voiced dental segment is considered as stronger than the surd segment.

ʾidt(a)āna	→	*ʾidd(a)āna*
d + *t*	→	*dd*
voiced + surd	→	voiced + voiced

2- The assimilation of the vowelled infixed t of Form VIII ʾiftaᶜala to the 1st radical vowelless ḏ preceding it:

An example is Form VIII *ʾiḏtakara* "to remember" with the vowelless *ḏ* preceding the vowelled *t* that becomes after the assimilation *ʾiḏḏakara* with the *t* assimilated to the *ḏ* resulting in the doubled *ḏ*. The reason why the *t* is assimilated to the *ḏ* and not vice versa is that the surd *t* is weaker in character than the voiced *ḏ* (cf. Bakkūš, *Taṣrīf* 66).

ʾiḏtakara	→	*ʾiḏḏakara*
ḏ + *t*	→	*ḏḏ*
voiced + surd	→	voiced + voiced

Other variants are *ʾiḏdakara* with the doubling of the *d* and *ʾiddakara* with the *d* following the *ḏ* (cf. Zamaḫšarī, 195, Ibn ᶜAqīl, II, 582, Åkesson, *Ibn Masᶜūd* 198: fol. 19a, de Sacy, I, 222, Vernier, I, 344-345, Wright, II, 66, ᶜAbd al-Tawwāb, *Taṭawwur* 29).

The process concerning the 1st variant *ʾiḏdakara* is that the *t* of the base form *ʾiḏtakara* is changed into the *d.* The reason of this substitution is the closeness of the points of articulation of the *d* and the *t* on account that they both are alveolars (for the segments see par. 2.2.1.). In the second variant *ʾiddakara,* the *ḏ* of *ʾiḏdakara* is changed into a *d* and both the *dāls* are than assimilated together. The reason why the substitution of the *d* for the *ḏ* is possible is the proximity of the alveolar *d* to the interdental *ḏ* and the similarity of both their characters as they are both voiced segments.

3- The assimilation of the vowelled infixed t of Form VIII ʾiftaᶜala to the 1st radical vowelless z preceding it:

An example is Form VIII *ʾizt(a)āna* "to be ornamented" (cf. Zamaḫšarī, 176, 196, Åkesson, *Ibn Masᶜūd* 198: fol. 19b, Wright, II, 66, Lane, I, 1279) with the vowelless *z* preceding the vowelled *t* that becomes after the assimilation *ʾizz(a)āna* with the *t* assimilated to the *z* resulting in the doubled *z.* The reason why the *t* is assimilated to the *z* is that there is a proximity between the alveolar *t* and the dental *z* (for the segments see par. 2.2.1.). As for why it is specifically the *t* that is assimilated to the *z* and not vice versa, it is that the surd and soft *t* is weaker in character than the voiced and sibilant *z* (for the segments' characters see par. 2.2.2.). Thus:

ʾizt(a)āna	→	*ʾizz(a)āna*
z + *t*	→	*zz*
voiced + surd	→	voiced + voiced
sibilant + soft	→	sibilant + sibilant

4- The assimilation of the vowelled infixed t of Form VIII ʾiftaᶜala to the 1st radical vowelless ṣ preceding it:

An example is Form VIII *ʾiṣtabara* "to acquire patience" (cf. Zamaḫšarī, 176, Åkesson, *Ibn Masᶜūd* 198: fol. 19b-20a, Wright, II, 67, Vernier, I, 345, this study par. 10.1.15.1.) with the vowelless *ṣ* preceding the vowelled *t* that becomes after the assimilation *ʾiṣṣabara* with the *t* assimilated to the *ṣ* resulting in the doubled *ṣ*. The reason why the *t* is assimilated to the *ṣ* is that there is a proximity between the alveolar *t* and the dental *ṣ* (for the segments see par. 2.2.1.). As for why it is the *t* that is assimilated to the *ṣ* and not vice versa, it is because the soft *t* is weaker in character than the sibilant *ṣ*. Thus:

ʾiṣtabara	→	*ʾiṣṣabara*
ṣ + *t*	→	*ṣṣ*
sibilant + soft	→	sibilant + sibilant

Another variant concerning this verb is the substitution of the emphatic *ṭ* for the *t* on account of the influence of the emphatic *ṣ*, namely *ʾiṣṭabara* for *ʾiṣtabara.*

5- The assimilation of the vowelled infixed t of Form VIII ʾiftaᶜala to the 1st radical vowelless ḍ preceding it:

An example is Form VIII *ʾiḍtaraba* "to acquire patience" (cf. Zamaḫšarī, 195, Åkesson, Ibn Masᶜūd 198-200: fol. 20a, de Sacy, I, 222, Wright, II, 67, Vernier, I, 345, par. 10.1.15.1.)

with the vowelless *ḍ* preceding the vowelled *t* that becomes after the assimilation *ʾiḍḍaraba* "to be in a state of agitation" with the *t* asimilated to the *ḍ* resulting in the doubled *ḍ*. The reason why the *t* is assimilated to the *ḍ* is the proximity of their points of articulation as they both are alveolars (for the segments see par. 2.2.1.). As for why it is specifically the *t* that is assimilated to the *ḍ* and not vice versa, it is because the soft *t* is weaker in character than the covered *ḍ*. Thus:

ʾiḍtaraba	→	*ʾiḍḍaraba*
ḍ + *t*	→	*ḍḍ*
covered + soft	→	covered + covered

Another possibility concerning this verb is the substitution of the *ṭ* for the *t* on account of the influence of the preceding 1st radical emphatic *ḍ*, namely *ʾiḍṭaraba* instead of *ʾiḍtaraba* (cf. par. 10.1.15.1.)

6- The assimilation of the vowelled infixed t of Form VIII ʾiftaᶜala to the 1st radical vowelless ṭ preceding it:

An example is Form VIII *ʾiṭṭalaba* "to seek" (cf. Zamaḫšarī, 195, Ibn Yaᶜīš, X, 46, Åkesson, *Ibn Masᶜūd* 200: fol. 20a, Wright, II, 67, par. 10.1.15.1.) with the vowelless *ṭ* preceding the vowelled *t* that becomes after the assimilation *ʾiṭṭalaba* with the *t* assimilated to the *ṭ* resulting in the doubled *ṭ*. The reason why the *t* is assimilated to the *ṭ* is their common point of articulation as they are both alveolars (for the segments see par. 2.2.1.). As for why it is specifically the *t* that is assimilated to the *ṭ* and not vice versa, it is because the soft *t* is weaker in character than the covered *ṭ*. Thus:

ʾiṭtalaba	→	*ʾiṭṭalaba*
ṭ + t	→	*ṭṭ*
covered + soft	→	covered + covered

7- The assimilation of the vowelled infixed t of Form VIII ʾiftaʿala to the 1st radical vowelless ẓ preceding it:

An example is Form VIII *ʾiẓtalama* "to take upon oneself the bearing of the wrong" with the vowelless *ẓ* preceding the vowelled *t* that becomes after the assimilation *ʾiẓẓalama* (cf. Åkesson, *Ibn Masʿūd* 200: fol. 20a, par. 10.1.15.1.). The reason why the *t* is assimilated to the *ẓ* is the proximity of the point of articulation of the alveolar *t* to the interdental *ẓ* (for the segments see par. 2.2.1). As for why it is the *t* that is specifically assimilated to the *ẓ* and not vice versa, it is that the soft *t* is weaker in character than the covered *ẓ*.

ʾiẓtalama	→	*ʾiẓẓalama*
ẓ + t	→	*ẓẓ*
covered + soft	→	covered + covered

Two other variants exist namely *ʾiẓṭalama* and *ʾiṭṭalama* (cf. Sībawaihi, II, 472, Ibn Ǧinnī, *Sirr I,* 224, *de Flexione* 29, Zamaḫšarī, 195, Ibn Yaʿīš, X, 47, Åkesson, *Ibn Masʿūd* 200: fol. 20a, Wright, II, 67, Lane, II, 1921, Vernier, I, 345, Howell, IV, fasc. II, 1813).

As what regards the variant *ʾiẓṭalama,* the *t* of its base form *ʾiẓtalama* is changed into the *ṭ* on account of the proximity of the points of articulation of the *t* and *ṭ,* as they both are alveolars (for the segments see 2.2.1.). As for why the *t* is assimilated to the *ṭ,* it is because the soft *t* is weaker in character than the covered *ṭ*.

Concerning the variant *ʾiṭṭalama,* the ẓāʾs from the variant *ʾiẓẓalama* are changed into the ṭāʾs. This substitution of the *ṭ* for the *ẓ* and vice versa is possibly carried out because of both these segments' common character in being among the emphatic segments. It can be mentioned that both Form I of the passive *yuẓlamu* and Form VIII of the active voice *yaẓṭalimu* occur in this verse said by Zuhair b. Abī Sulmā al-Muzanī praising Harim b. Sinān, cited by Sībawaihi, II, 472, Ibn Ǧinnī, *Sirr I,* 219, Muʾaddib, *Taṣrīf* 170 Zamaḫšarī, 195, Ibn Yaʿīš, X, 47, Howell, IV, fasc. II, 1813, Åkesson, *Ibn Masʿūd* 229: (197):

> *"Huwa l-ğawādu l-laḏī yuʿṭīka nāʿilahu*
> *ʿafwan wa-yuẓlamu ʾaḥyānan fa-yaẓṭalimu".*
> "He is the magnanimous, who gives you his largesse spontaneously;
> and is wronged at times, and than puts up with that wrong".

All the three variants *fa-yaẓẓalimu, fa-yaṭṭalimu* or *fa-yaẓṭalimu* as being the last word of the rime have been cited in different works (cf. Fischer/Braūnlich, *Šawāhid* 227).

8- The assimilation of the vowelled infixed t of Form VIII ʾiftaʿala to the 1st radical vowelless ṯ preceding it:

An example is Form VIII *ʾiṯtaʾara* "to get one's revenge" that becomes after the assimilation *ʾiṯṯaʾara* (cf. 2.4.1.1.3.1.:3).

9- The assimilation of the vowelled infixed t of Form VIII ʾiftaʿala to the 1st radical vowelless s preceding it:

An example is Form VIII *ʾistamaʿa* "to listen" with the vowelless *s* preceding the vowelled *t* that becomes after the assimilation of the *t* to the *s* *ʾissamaʿa* (cf. Sībawaihi, II, 472, Zamaḫšarī, 196, Åkesson, *Ibn Masʿūd* 198: fol. 19b, de Sacy, I, 220, Wright, II, 66).

The reason why it is possible to substitute the *s* for the *t* is that they originate from close points of articulation, as the alveolar *t* is close to the dental *s* (for the segments see par. 2.2.1.) and they are both similar in character in being among the surd segments (for the segments' characters see par. 2.2.2.). However it is only the *t* than can be assimilated to the *s* and not vice versa because the *s* is a sibilant segment, and thus offers a stronger character than the *t*.

ʾistamaʿa	→	*ʾissamaʿa*
s + *t*	→	*ss*
sibilant + soft	→	sibilant + sibilant

10- The assimilation of the vowelled infixed t of Form VIII ʾiftaʿala to the 1st radical vowelless š preceding it:

An example is Form VIII *ʾištabaha* "to liken" with the vowelless *š* preceding the vowelled *t* that becomes *ʾiššabaha* after the assimilation of the *t* to the *š* (cf. Åkesson, *Ibn Masʿūd* 198: fol. 19b).

The reason why this substitution is possible is the proximity of the point of articulation of the alveolar *t* to the pre-palatal *š* (for the segments see par. 2.2.1.) and both these segments' common character in being among the surd segments (for the segments' characters see par. 2.2.2.).

2.4.1.2. The assimilation that is carried out from the 1st vowelless segment to a 2nd different vowelled segment in two words following each other:

The assimilation can be carried out from a 1st vowelless segment which is the last segment of a word to a 2nd vowelled segment that is the initial segment of the word following it (for some references to different works that treat this sort of assimilation see 2.3.), if both different segments originate from a common point of articulation of from close points of articulation.

An example is the reading of the sur. 4: 81 *bayyat ṭāʾifatun* in which the surd and soft *t* is assimilated to the voiced and covered *ṭ* resulting in *bayyat ṭṭāʾifatun* (بَيَّتَ طَّائِفَةٌ) "A section of them meditate all night" (cf. Cantineau, *Études* 35). The sentence is written in Arabic with the *t,* which is the last segment of the first word *bayyat* without any vowel or sukūn, and with the *ṭ* which is the initial segment of the second word given a *šadda* as an indication of the assimilation. As what regards the common point of articulation of the *t* and the *ṭ* that enables the substitution of the *ṭ* for the *t* leading to the assimilation, they are both alveolars (for the segments see 2.2.1.). As for their characters, the covered *ṭ* is stronger than the soft *t,* which explains why it is the *t* specifically that is assimilated to the *ṭ* and not vice versa.

2.4.2. The sequence of two different segments which are both vowelled: the assimilation:

The vowelled state of the 1st segment preceding another different vowelled one that originates from the same point of articulation as it, or from a close point of articulation to it, or that is akin to it in character, can result in the assimilation. This sequence can be found as well in one word or in two words following each other, the latter pertaining to the rarities.

2.4.2.1. The assimilation that is carried out from the 1st vowelled segment to a 2nd vowelled segment in one word:

The cases that I discuss are the assimilation of the vowelled prefixed *t* of Form V *tafaᶜᶜala* or Form VI *taf(a)āᶜala* to the 1st vowelled radical following it (cf. par. 2.4.2.1.1.) and of the vowelled infixed *t* of Form VIII of the imperfect *yafta^cilu* to the 2nd vowelled radical following it (cf. par. 2.4.2.1.2.).

2.4.2.1.1. The assimilation of the vowelled prefixed t of Form V tafa^{cc}*ala or Form VI taf(a)ā*^{c}*ala to the 1st vowelled radical following it:*

The prefixed *t* of Form V and VI is assimilated to the 1st radical of the verb (cf. Zamaḫšarī, 196, Åkesson, *Ibn Mas*^{c}*ūd* 202: fol. 21a, de Sacy, I, 220-221, Wright, II, 64-65, ^{c}Abd al-Tawwāb, *Taṭawwur* 29) following it if it is: 1- the *t* (for the assimilation of two identical segments see par. 2.3.2.1.), 2- the interdental and surd *ṯ*, 3- the alveolar and voiced *d*, 4- the interdental and voiced *ḏ*, 5- the dental, voiced and sibilant *z*, 6- the dental, surd and sibilant *s*, 7- the pre-palatal and surd *š*, 8- the dental, surd and sibilant *ṣ*, 9- the alveolar and voiced *ḍ*, 10- the alveolar and voiced *ṭ*, or 11- the interdental and voiced *ẓ*. The assimilation implies that the prefixed *t* loses its vowel and that the prosthetic hamza vowelled by a kasra, the *^{ɔ}i*, is prefixed to the word to avoid beginning it with a vowelless segment.

The phonological procedure that is carried out in the perfect of Form V can be illustrated as follows: *tafa*^{cc}*ala* with the vowelled *t* prefix preceding the vowelled 1st radical *f* becomes *ffa*^{cc}*ala* after that the *t's* fatḥa is elided and the *t* is assimilated to the 1st radical *f* vowelled by a fatḥa. As it is prohibited to begin the word with a vowelless 1st radical *f*, the *^{ɔ}i* is prefixed so that it becomes *^{ɔ}iffa*^{cc}*ala.*

The same procedure is carried as what concerns Form VI *taf(a)ā*^{c}*ala* that becomes *^{ɔ}iff(a)ā*^{c}*ala.*

It can be remarked that the prosthetic alif is not needed in the imperfect of Form V *ʾiffaʿʿala* that becomes *yaffaʿʿalu* and Form VI *ʾiff(a)āʿala* that becomes *yaff(a)āʿalu.*

1- The assimilation of the vowelled prefixed t of Form V tafaʿʿala or Form VI taf(a)āʿala to the 1st vowelled radical t following it:

This assimilation has been taken up within the sub-paragraph discussing the assimilation of two vowelled identical segments (cf. 2.3.2.1.). The example there is Form V *tatarrasa* "shielded himself" that becomes after the assimilation *ʾittarasa.*

2- The assimilation of the vowelled prefixed t of Form V tafaʿʿala or Form VI taf(a)āʿala to the 1st vowelled radical ṯ following it:

An example is Form VI *taṯ(a)āqala* "to be borne down heavily" that becomes after the assimilation *ʾiṯṯ(a)āqala* (cf. Åkesson, *Ibn Masʿūd* 202: fol. 21a, Howell, IV, fasc. II, 1829, Lane, I, 344, Penrice, *Dictionary* 25). The vowelled alveolar and surd *t* prefix vowelled by a fatḥa, the *ta,* is assimilated to the vowelled interdental and surd 1st radical *ṯ* vowelled by a fatḥa, the *ṯa,* resulting in *ṯṯāqala* and the prosthetic hamza vowelled by a kasra, the *ʾi,* is prefixed to prevent beginning the word with a vowelless segment. I can mention that the 2nd person of the masc. pl. *ʾiṯṯāqaltum* occurs in the sur. 9: 38 *(ʾiṯṯāqaltum ʾilā l-ʾarḍi fī sabīli l-lāhi)* "In the Cause of God ye cling heavily to the earth?".

3- The assimilation of the vowelled prefixed t of Form V tafaʿʿala or Form VI taf(a)āʿala to the 1st vowelled radical d following it:

An example is Form VI *tad(a)āraʾa* "to repel" that becomes after the assimilation *ʾidd(a)āraʾa* (cf. Howell, IV, fasc. II,

1829, Lane, I, 865, Penrice, *Dictionary* 47). The vowelled alveolar and surd *t* prefix vowelled by a fatḥa, the *ta,* is assimilated to the vowelled alveolar and voiced 1st radical *d* vowelled by a fatḥa, the *da,* resulting in *ʾidd(a)āraʾa* and the prosthetic hamza vowelled by a kasra, the *ʾi,* is prefixed to prevent beginning the word with a vowelless segment. I can mention that the 2nd person of the masc. pl. *fa-ddāraʾtum* occurs in the sur. 2: 72 *(fa-ddāraʾtum fīhā)* "And fell into a dispute among yourselves as to the crime:".

4- The assimilation of the vowelled prefixed t of Form V tafaᶜᶜala or Form V taf(a)āᶜala to the 1st vowelled radical ḏ following it:

An example is Form VI *taḏ(a)ākara* "to be reminded" that becomes after the assimilation *ʾiḏḏ(a)ākara* (cf. Howell, IV, fasc. II, 1829, Lane, I, 968, Penrice, *Dictionary* 52). The vowelled alveolar and surd *t* prefix, the *ta,* is assimilated to the vowelled interdental and voiced 1st radical *ḏa* resulting in *ḏḏ(a)ākara* and the prosthetic hamza vowelled by a kasra, the *ʾi,* is prefixed to prevent beginning the word with a vowelless segment. I can mention that Form V of the imperfect of the 3rd person of the masc. sing. *yaḏḏakkaru* occurs in both the sur. 80: 3-4 *(wa-mā yudrīka laᶜallahu yazzakkā ʾaw yaḏḏakkaru fa-tanfaᶜahu l-ḏikrā)* "But what could tell thee but that perchance he might grow (in spiritual understanding)? Or that he might receive admonition, and he teaching might profit him?", and the sur. 2: 269 *(wa-mā yaḏḏakkaru ʾillā ʾūlū l-ʾalbābi)* "But none will grasp the Message but men of understanding".

*5- The assimilation of the vowelled prefixed t of Form V tafa*ᶜᶜ*ala or Form VI taf(a)ā*ᶜ*ala to the 1st vowelled radical z̧ following it:*

An example is Form V *taz̧ayyana* "to decorate itself" that becomes after the assimilation *ʾiz̧z̧ayyana* (cf. Howell, IV, fasc. II, 1829, Lane, I, 1279, Wright, II, 64, Penrice, *Dictionary* 64). The alveolar and soft vowelled *t* prefix, the *ta,* is assimilated to the vowelled dental and sibilant 1st radical *z̧,* the *z̧a,* resulting in *z̧z̧ayyana* and the prosthetic hamza vowelled by a kasra, the *ʾi,* is prefixed to prevent beginning the word with a vowelless segment. It can be mentioned that the 3rd person of the fem. sing. *wa-z̧z̧ayyanat* occurs in the sur. 10: 24 *(ḥattā ʾiḏā ʾaḫaḏati l-ʾarḍu zuḫrufahā wa-z̧z̧ayyanat)* "Till the earth is clad with its golden ornaments and is decked out (in beauty)".

*6- The assimilation of the vowelled prefixed t of Form V tafa*ᶜᶜ*ala or Form VI taf(a)ā*ᶜ*ala to the 1st vowelled radical s following it:*

An example is Form V *tasammaᶜa* "to listen" that becomes after the assimilation *ʾissammaᶜa* originally (cf. Howell, IV, fasc. II, 1829, Lane, I, 1427, 1428, Wright, II, 65, Penrice, *Dictionary* 72). The vowelled alveolar and soft *t* prefix, the *ta,* is assimilated to the vowelled dental and sibilant 1st radical *s,* the *sa,* resulting in *ssammaᶜa* and the prosthetic hamza vowelled by a kasra, the *ʾi,* is prefixed to prevent beginning the word with a vowelless segment. It can be mentioned that the imperfect of the 3rd person of the masc. pl. *yassammaᶜūna* occurs in the sur. 37: 8 *(lā yassammaᶜūna ʾilā l-malāʾi l-ʾaᶜlā)* "(So) they should not strain their ears in the direction of the Exalted Assembly".

7- The assimilation of the vowelled prefixed t of Form V tafa^{cc}ala or Form VI taf(a)ā^{c}ala to the 1st vowelled radical š following it:

An example is Form VI *tašāğara* "to be embroiled" that becomes after the assimilation *ʾiššāğara* (cf. Howell, IV, fasc. II, 1829). The vowelled alveolar and surd *t* prefix, the *ta,* is assimilated to the vowelled pre-palatal and surd 1st radical *š,* the *ša*, resulting in *sšāğara* and the prosthetic hamza vowelled by a kasra, the *ʾi,* is prefixed to prevent beginning the word with a vowelless segment.

8- The assimilation of the vowelled prefixed t of Form V tafa^{cc}ala or Form VI taf(a)ā^{c}ala to the 1st vowelled radical ṣ following it:

An example is Form VI *taṣ(a)ābara* "to bear patiently" that becomes after the assimilation *ʾiṣṣ(a)ābara* (cf. Howell, IV, fasc. II, 1829, Lane, II, 1643). The vowelled alveolar and surd *t* prefix, the *ta,* is assimilated to the vowelled dental and covered 1st radical *ṣ,* the *ṣa,* resulting in *ṣṣ(a)ābara* and the prosthetic hamza vowelled by a kasra, the *ʾi,* is prefixed to prevent beginning the word with a vowelless segment.

9- The assimilation of the vowelled prefixed t of Form V tafa^{cc}ala or Form VI taf(a)ā^{c}ala to the 1st vowelled radical ḍ following it:

An example is Form VI *taḍ(a)āraba* "to fight" that becomes after the assimilation *ʾiḍḍ(a)āraba* (cf. Howell, IV, fasc. II, 1829). The vowelled alveolar and surd *t* prefix, the *ta,* is assimilated to the alveolar and covered vowelled 1st radical *ḍ,* the *ḍa,* resulting in *ḍḍ(a)āraba* and the prosthetic hamza vowelled by a kasra, the *ʾi,* is prefixed to prevent beginning the word with a vowelless segment.

10- The assimilation of the vowelled prefixed t of Form V tafaᶜᶜala or Form VI taf(a)āᶜala to the 1st vowelled radical ṭ following it:

An example is Form V *taṭahhara* "to purify one's-self" that becomes after the assimilation *ʾiṭṭahhara* (cf. Åkesson, *Ibn Masᶜūd* 202: fol. 21a, Howell, IV, fasc. II, 1829, Lane, II, 1887, Penrice, *Dictionary* 91). The vowelled alveolar and surd *t* prefix, the *ta,* is assimilated to the vowelled alveolar and covered 1st radical *ṭ,* the *ṭa,* resulting in *ṭṭahhara* and the prosthetic hamza vowelled by a kasra, the *ʾi,* is prefixed to prevent beginning the word with a vowelless segment.

Another example is Form V *taṭayyara* "to see an evil omen" that becomes after the assimilation *ʾiṭṭayyara* originally (cf. Howell, IV, fasc. II, 1829, Wright, II, 65). I can mention that the 1st person of the pl. *ʾiṭṭayyarnā* occurs in the sur. 27: 47 *(qālū ṭṭayyarnā bi-ka wa-bi-man maᶜaka)* "They said: [1] omen do we augur from thee and those that are with thee".

11- The assimilation of the vowelled prefixed t of Form V tafaᶜᶜala or Form VI taf(a)āᶜala to the 1st vowelled radical ẓ following it:

An example is Form VI *taẓ(a)ālama* "to wrong" that becomes after the assimilation *ʾiẓẓ(a)ālama* (cf. Howell, IV, fasc. II, 1829). The vowelled alveolar and surd *t* prefix, the *ta,* is assimilated to the vowelled interdental and covered 1st radical *ẓ,* the *ẓa,* resulting in *iẓẓ(a)ālama* and the prosthetic hamza, the *ʾi,* is prefixed to prevent beginning the word with a vowelless segment.

*2.4.2.1.2. The assimilation of the infixed vowelled t of the imperfect of Form VIII yafta*ᶜ*ilu to the vowelled 2nd radical:*

The alveolar and surd infixed *t* of Form VIII can be assimilated to one of the nine segments following it (cf. Åkesson, *Ibn Mas*ᶜ*ūd* 200: fol. 20b, Wright, II, 64-65) that are:

1- the *t* (for the assimilation of two identical segments see par. 2.3.2.1.), 2- the alveolar and voiced *d,* 3- the interdental and voiced *ḏ,* 4- the dental, voiced and sibilant *z,* 5- the dental, surd and sibilant *s,* 6- the dental, surd and sibilant *ṣ,* 7- the alveolar and voiced *ḍ,* 8- the alveolar and voiced *ṭ,* and 9- the interdental and voiced *ẓ*. The assimilation is carried out in the imperfect of such verbs and rarely in their perfect, except in some anomalous cases as the case of *ʾiḫtaṣama* resulting in *ḥaṣṣama* (cf. Penrice, *Dictionary* 42).

The phonological procedure that is carried out in the imperfect is the following: *yafta*ᶜ*ilu* with the vowelled *t* infix following the vowelless 1st radical *f* becomes *yafat*ᶜ*ilu* after that the *t's* fatḥa is shifted to the 1st radical *f*. As the *t* preceding the vowelled 2nd radical ᶜ is vowelless, it is assimilated to the ᶜ, so that it becomes *yafa*ᶜᶜ*ilu.*

*1- The assimilation of the vowelled infixed t of Form VIII of the imperfect yafta*ᶜ*ilu to the 2nd vowelled radical t following it in the imperfect:*

This assimilation has been taken up within the sub-paragraph discussing the assimilation of two vowelled identical segments (cf. 2.3.2.1.). The example is Form VIII *yaqtatilu* "to contend among themselves" that becomes after the assimilation *yaqattilu.*

*2- The assimilation of the vowelled infixed t of Form VIII of the imperfect yafta*ᶜ*ilu to the 2nd vowelled radical d following it:*

An example is *yabtadilu* "to change" which becomes after the assimilation *yabaddilu* (cf. Åkesson, *Ibn Mas*ᶜ*ūd* 200: fol.

20b). The fatḥa of the *ta* in *yabtadilu* is shifted to the 1st radical *b* resulting in *yabatdilu* and the alveolar and surd *t* is assimilated to the alveolar and voiced *d,* because of their common point of articulation and because of the stronger character of the voiced segment in relation to the surd segment (for the segments see 2.2.) resulting in *yabaddilu.*

Another example of Form VIII verb with 2nd radical *d* in the imperfect is *yahtadī* that becomes after the assimilation *yahiddī* "he finds guidance" with the *h* vowelled by a kasra instead of a fatḥa. It occurs in the sur. 10: 35 *(ʾaman lā yahiddī)* "Or he who finds not guidance (himself)". Abū ^{c}Amr and Nāfi^{c} read it with both vowelless segments, the *h* and the *d,* combined, namely *yahddī*, which is disapproved by the majority, and Abū Bakr read it with both the *y* and the *h* being vowelled by a kasra, namely *yihiddī* (cf. Howell, IV, fasc. II, 1807-1808).

3- The assimilation of the vowelled infixed t of Form VIII of the imperfect yafta^{c}*ilu to the vowelled 2nd radical d̲ following it:*

An example is *ya*^{c}*tad̲iru* "to excuse one's-self" which becomes after the assimilation *ya*^{c}*ad̲d̲iru* (cf. Åkesson, *Ibn Mas*^{c}*ūd* 200: fol. 20b). The fatḥa of the *ta* in *ya*^{c}*tad̲iru* is shifted to the 1st radical ^{c} resulting in *ya*^{c}*atd̲iru* and the alveolar and surd *t* is assimilated to the interdental and voiced *d̲* resulting in *ya*^{c}*ad̲d̲iru.*

4- The assimilation of the vowelled infixed t of Form VIII of the imperfect yafta^{c}*ilu to the vowelled 2nd radical z following it:*

An example is *yantazi*^{c}*u* "to snatch, tear away" which becomes after the assimilation *yanazzi*^{c}*u* (cf. ibid). The fatḥa of the *ta* in *yantazi*^{c}*u* is shifted to the 1st radical *n* resulting in *yanatziᶜu* and the surd *t* is assimilated to the dental, voiced and sibilant *z* resulting in *yanazziᶜu*.

5- The assimilation of the vowelled infixed t of Form VIII of the imperfect yaftaᶜilu to the vowelled 2nd radical s following it:

An example is *yabtasimu* "to smile" which becomes after the assimilation *yabassimu* (cf. ibid). The fatḥa of the *ta* in *yabtasimu* is shifted to the 1st radical *b* resulting in *yabatsimu* and the surd *t* is assimilated to the dental, surd and sibilant *s* resulting in *yabassimu*.

6- The assimilation of the vowelled infixed t of Form VIII of the imperfect yaftaᶜilu to the vowelled 2nd radical ṣ following it:

An example is *yaḫtaṣimu* "to argue" which becomes after the assimilation *yaḫassimu* (cf. ibid). The fatḥa of the *ta* in *yaḫtaṣimu* is shifted to the 1st radical *ḫ* resulting in *yaḫatṣimu* and the surd and soft *t* is assimilated to the surd, covered, sibilant *ṣ* resulting in *yaḫaṣṣimu*. The variant *yaḫiṣṣimu* occurs as well with the *ḫ* given a kasra instad of a fatḥa (cf. de Sacy, I, 223). The 3rd person of the masc. pl. *yaḫiṣṣimūna* occurs in the sur. 36: 49 *(wa-hum yaḫiṣṣimūna)* "While they are yet disputing among themselves!". Seven different readings are known to have been transmitted concerning the verb in this sur. (cf. Ibn Manẓūr, II, 1177 in the note), namely: 1- *yaḫṣimūna*. 2- *yaḫtaṣimūna*. 3- *yaḫiṣṣimūna*. 4- *yiḫiṣṣimūna*. 5- *yaḫaṣṣimūna*. 6- *yaḫaṣimūna*. 7- *yaḫaṣṣimūna* read with a vowel of support (for discussions see Fleisch, *Traité I*, 144).

7- The assimilation of the vowelled infixed t of Form VIII of the imperfect yaftaᶜilu to the vowelled 2nd radical ḍ following it:

An example is *yantaḍilu* "to struggle" which becomes after the assimilation *yanaḍḍilu* (cf. Åkesson, *Ibn Masᶜūd* 200: fol.

20b). The fatḥa of the *ta* in *yantaḍilu* is shifted to the 1st radical *n* resulting in *yanatḍilu* and the surd and soft *t* is assimilated to the alveolar, voiced and covered *ḍ* resulting in *yanaḍḍilu.*

8- The assimilation of the vowelled infixed t of Form VIII of the imperfect yaftaᶜilu to the vowelled 2nd radical ṭ following it:

An example is *yaltaṭimu* "to collide, clash" which becomes after the assimilation *yalaṭṭimu* (cf. ibid). The fatḥa of the *ta* in *yaltaṭimu* is shifted to the 1st radical *l* resulting in *yalatṭimu* and the surd and soft *t* is assimilated to the voiced and covered *ṭ* resulting in *yalaṭṭimu.*

9- The assimilation of the vowelled infixed t of Form VIII of the imperfect yaftaᶜilu to the ẓ following it:

An example is *yantaẓiru* "to expect" which becomes after the assimilation *yanaẓẓiru* (cf. ibid). The fatḥa of the *ta* in *yantaẓiru* is shifted to the 1st radical *n* resulting in *yanatẓiru* and the alveolar, surd and soft *t* is assimilated to the interdental, voiced and covered *ẓ* resulting in *yanaẓẓiru.*

2.4.2.2. The assimilation that is carried out from the 1st vowelled segment to a 2nd vowelled segment in two words following each other:

The assimilation can be carried out from a 1st vowelled segment which is the last segment of a word to a 2nd vowelled segment that is the initial segment of the word following it (for a general study see Sībawaihi, II, 455 sqq., Zamaḫšarī, 191 sqq., Cantineau, *Études* 35 sqq., Fleisch, *Traité I,* 83 sqq., Roman, *Étude I,* 390-427, Wright, I, 15-16), if both different segments originate from a common point of articulation of from close points of articulation.

An example is the reading of some of the sur. 48: 29 *ʾaḫraǧa šaṭʾahu* "Which sends forth its blade", which after the assimilation of the vowelled pre-palatal *ǧ* to the vowelled pre-palatal *š* is pronounced *ʾaḫraššaṭʾahu* (cf. Zamaḫšarī, 193, Åkesson, *Ibn Masʿūd* 194: fol. 17b).

The sentence is written in Arabic as *ʾaḫraǧ ššaṭʾahu* (أَخْرَج شّطْأَهُ) with the *ǧ*, which is the last segment of the first word, deprived of a vowel or of a sukūn, and with the *š*, which is the initial segment of the second word, given a *šadda* as an indication of the assimilation of the *ǧ* to it.

2.5. Conclusion

I have studied the various sequences involving two identical or different segments that necessitate, allow or forbid the assimilation in one word or in two words following each other in this chapter.

The assimilation of the two differents segments in one word concerns the assimilation of the vowelless *t* infix of the perfect verbs that are formed according to Form VIII *ʾiftaʿala* to the vowelless 1st radical preceding it (cf. par. 2.4.1.1.3.), the assimilation of the vowelled prefixed *t* of Form V *tafaʿʿala* or Form VI *taf(a)āʿala* to the vowelled 1st radical following it (cf. par. 2.4.2.1.1.) and the assimilation of the vowelled infixed *t* of Form VIII of the imperfect *yaftaʿilu* to the vowelled 2nd radical following it (cf. par. 2.4.2.1.2.).

It has been observed that the assimilation is carried out in these cases if the two segments originate from a common point of articulation or from two points of articulation that are close to each other.

In the next chapter I shall discuss the hamzated verb and some of its derivatives.

CHAPTER THREE

3. The hamzated verb and some of its derivatives

The hamzated verb, *al-mahmūz* is the verb with a hamza radical.

The hamzated verb falls into three classes that refer to the position of the hamza in their forms:

1- verbs with hamza as their 1st radical, e.g. *ʾaḫaḏa* "to take", *ʾakala* "to eat".

2- verbs with hamza as their 2nd radical, e.g. *saʾala* "to ask", *raʾā* "to see".

3- verbs with hamza as their 3rd radical, e.g. *qaraʾa* "to read", *ǧāʾa* "to come".

In this approach of the phonological treatment I shall concentrate on a few forms in which the two hamzas are combined or in which the hamza is vowelled by a fatḥa and preceded by a vowelless segment.

3.1. The conjugations of the verb with 1st radical hamza

The verb with 1st radical hamza falls into the following conjugations:

1- *faʿala yafʿulu,* e.g. *ʾaḫaḏa yaʾḫuḏu* "to take".

2- *faʿala yafʿilu,* e.g. *ʾadaba yaʾdibu* "to invite (to a party or banquet)".

3- *faʿala yafʿalu,* e.g. *ʾahaba yaʾhabu* "to prepare".

4- *faʿila yafʿalu,* e.g. *ʾariqa yaʾraqu* "to find no sleep".

5- *faʿila yafʿulu,* e.g. *ʾariǧa yaʾruǧu* "to be flagrant".

6- *faʿala yafʿulu,* e.g. *ʾasala yaʾsulu* "to sharpen".

3.2. Examples of some derivatives of the verb with 1st radical hamza

An example of a hamzated verb with 1st radical hamza in the perfect is *ʾaḫaḏa* "to take". It becomes *yaʾḫuḏu* in the imperfect of the indicative active. Its imperative is *ḫuḏ,* its active participle is *ʾāḫiḏun,* its *maṣdar* is *ʾaḫḏun,* its perfect passive is *ʾuḫiḏa,* its imperfect is *yuʾḫaḏu* and its passive participle is *maʾḫūḏun.*

3.2.1. Remarks concerning the phonological procedures in some of its forms:

The verb with 1st radical hamza can present some forms as the imperative and the passive voice (cf. 3.2.1.1.) in which there occurs a sequence of two hamzas of which the 1st is vowelled and the 2nd is vowelless (for general discussions concerning this sequence see par. 4.1.2.4., 4.1.2.5., 4.1.2.6.).

In the case of the imperative the 1st hamza is the disjunctive hamza of Form I and the 2nd hamza is the 1st radical, e.g. *ʾiʾsir* "capture", and in the case of the passive voice the 1st hamza is the connective hamza of Form IV and the 2nd hamza is the 1st radical of the verb, e.g. *ʾuʾṯira* "he, or it was preferred /(passive)". In both these cases the 2nd vowelless hamza is changed into a glide of the nature of the vowel preceding it (cf. 3.2.1.1.).

3.2.1.1. The imperative and the passive voice: the sequence of two hamzas of which the 1st is vowelled and the 2nd is vowelless: the change of the vowelless hamza into a glide:

The forms of verbs with 1st radical hamza that present a combination of two hamzas of which the 1st is vowelled and the 2nd vowelless are the imperative in *ʾifʿil* of verbs of the conjugation *faʿala yafʿilu* and in *ʾufʿul* of verbs of the conjugation *faʿala yafʿulu* and the passive voice of Form IV *ʾufʿila.*

1- The imperative:

The formation of the imperative in *ʾifʿil* of verbs with 1st radical hamza of the conjugation *faʿala yafʿilu* implies the combination of two hamzas: the vowelled connective hamza of the imperative, the *ʾi,* followed by the vowelless 1st radical hamza of the verb. As the 1st radical hamza of the verb is vowelless, it is subjected to the influence of the connective hamza's vowel, - which is the kasra -, preceding it, and can therefore be changed into a glide of the nature of this vowel, which is the y. An example is *ʾiʾsir* that becomes *ʾiysir* "capture! /2 masc. sing. (imperative)" then *ʾ(i)īsir* (cf. Åkesson, *Ibn Masʿūd* 242: fol. 22b and par. 4.1.2.5.).

The formation of the imperative in *ʾufʿul* of verbs with 1st radical hamza of the conjugation *faʿala yafʿulu* results mostly in the elision of both hamzas (cf. par. 4.1.2.6.). Examples are *ḫuḏ* "take!", *kul* "eat!" and *mur* "order!" (cf. Ibn Ǧinnī, *de Flexione* 33, Åkesson, *Ibn Masʿūd* 242: fol. 23a, Howell, II-III, 89-90, IV, fasc. I, 957-958, Wright, II, 76, Vernier, I, 103). The elision of the hamza is obligatory in *ḫuḏ* which is not to be said *ʾuʾḫuḏ* with the combination of both hamzas, or *ʾuwḫuḏ* with the change of the 2nd hamza into a *w* resulting in *ʾu(ū)ḫuḏ,* and in *kul* which is not to be said *ʾuʾkul, ʾuwkul* or *ʾ(u)ūkul.* The elision however is not necessary in *mur* which is allowed, as well as in *ʾuwmur* in which the 1st hamza is maintained and the 1st radical hamza is changed into a *w* resulting in *ʾ(u)ūmur*. Also *ʾamur* with the vowelling of the hamza with a fatḥa occurs as in the sur. 20: 132 *(wa-ʾamur ʾahlaka bi-l-ṣalwati)* "Enjoin prayer on thy people" and in the sur. 7: 199 *(wa-ʾamur bi-l-ʿurfi ḫuḏi l-ʿafwa)* "Hold to forgiveness; Command what is right".

2-The passive voice:

The formation of the passive voice in Form IV *ʾufʿila* of verbs with 1st radical hamza implies the combination of the connective hamza, the *ʾu,* and the 1st radical hamza of the verb. The 1st radical hamza, which is vowelless, is subjected to the influence of the ḍamma of the disjunctive hamza preceding it, and is changed into a glide of the nature of this vowel, which is the *w*.

An example is the passive voice of Form IV *ʾuʾṯira* "he, or it was preferred /(passive)", of which the 2nd hamza is changed into a *w,* (cf. Åkesson, *Ibn Masʿūd* 242: fol. 22b-23a and par. 4.1.2.6.), namely *ʾuwṯira* which then becomes *ʾ(u)ūṯira.*

3.3. The conjugations of the verb with 2nd radical hamza

The verb with 2nd radical hamza falls into the following conjugations:

1- *faʿala yafʿalu,* e.g. *saʾala yasʾalu* "to ask". The fatḥa is given to its 2nd radical hamza because the hamza is a guttural consonant in the same manner as it is given to the 2nd radical of the strong verb of which the 2nd or 3rd radical is a guttural consonant (cf. par. 3.1.).

2- *faʿila yafʿalu,* e.g. *yaʾisa yayʾasu* "to despair".

3- *faʿula yafʿulu,* e.g. *laʾuma yalʾumu* "to be wicked".

3.4. Examples of some derivatives of the verb with 2nd radical hamza

An example of a hamzated verb with 2nd radical hamza in the perfect is *saʾala* "to ask". It becomes *yasʾalu* in the imperfect of the indicative active. Its imperative is *ʾisʾal,* its active participle is *sāʾilun,* its *maṣdar* is *suʾālun,* its perfect passive is *suʾila,* its imperfect is *yusʾalu* and its passive participle is *masʾūlun.*

3.4.1. Remarks concerning the phonological procedures in some of its forms:

The verb with 2nd radical hamza can present some forms as the imperfect (cf. 3.4.1.1.) in which there occurs a sequence of two segments of which the 2nd is a hamza vowelled by a fatḥa and preceded by a vowelless segment (for discussions concerning this sequence see par. 4.1.2.3.1.). The phonological procedure is that the fatḥa of the hamza is shifted to the vowelless segment preceding it, and the hamza is elided.

3.4.1.1. The imperfect: the sequence of a hamza vowelled by a fatḥa preceded by a sukūn: the transfer of the fatḥa to the vowelless segment and the elision of the hamza:

The 2nd radical hamza is elided by some in the imperfect for the sake of alleviation. Some examples are *yasʾalu* "he asks" that becomes anomalously *yasalu* (cf. de Sacy, I, 236, Wright, II, 77, Vernier, I, 74), and *yarʾ(a)ā* "he sees" that becomes *yar(a)ā* (cf. Sībawaihi, II, 170) on account of the frequency of its usage (cf. Åkesson, *Ibn Masᶜūd* 244: fol. 23a-23b). It can be remarked that in both *yasʾalu* and *yarʾ(a)ā,* the ʾ is elided and the hamza's fatḥa is shifted to the vowelless segment preceding it. Concerning *yarʾā,* it can be mentioned that in poetry, in consideration to the metric exigency, the ʾ can be retained. This is remarked in *tarʾayāhu* that is used instead of *tarayāhu* in this verse said by Surāqa b. Mirdās al-Azdī al-Bāriqī cited by Ibn Ǧinnī *Sirr I,* 77, II, 826, *Ḫaṣāʾiṣ III,* 153, *de Flexione* 34, Muʾaddib, *Taṣrīf* 422, Ibn Yaᶜīš, *Mulūkī* 370, Ibn Manẓūr, III, 1538, Ibn ᶜUṣfūr, II, 621, Howell, IV, fasc. I, 941, Åkesson, *Ibn Masᶜūd* 266: (236):

> *" ʾUrī ᶜaynayya mā lam tarʾayāhu*
> *kilānā ᶜālimun bi-l-turhāti".*
> "I make my eyes see what they have not seen:
> each of us is knowing in falsehoods".

3.5. The conjugations of the hamzated verbs with 3rd radical hamza

The verb with 3rd radical hamza falls into the following conjugations:

1- *faᶜala yafᶜulu,* e.g. *sāʾa yasūʾu* "to become evil".

2- *faᶜala yafᶜilu,* e.g. *ǧāʾa yaǧīʾu* "to come", and *hanaʾa yahniʾu* "to be beneficial".

3- *faᶜala yafᶜalu,* e.g. *našaʾa yanšaʾu* "to emerge", and *sabaʾa yasbaʾu.*

4- *faᶜila yafᶜalu,* e.g. *ṣadiʾa yaṣdaʾu* "to become rusty".

5- *faᶜula yafᶜulu,* e.g. *ǧaruʾa yaǧruʾu* "to dare, venture" (ibid).

3.6. Examples of some derivatives of the hamzated verb with 3rd radical hamza

An example of a hamzated verb with 3rd radical hamza in the perfect is *qaraʾa* "to read". It becomes *yaqraʾu* in the imperfect of the indicative active. Its imperative is *ʾiqraʾ,* its active participle is *qāriʾun,* its *maṣdar* is *qirāʾatun,* its perfect passive is *quriʾa,* its imperfect is *yuqraʾu* and its passive participle is *maqrūʾun.*

3.6.1. Remarks concerning the phonological procedures in some of its forms:

The verb with 3rd radical hamza is treated as the strong verb. The only peculiarity that can be remarked is that the hamza can be dropped in the pronunciation if it it is vowelless and not followed by a suffix (cf. Bakkūš, *Taṣrīf* 118, ᶜAbd al-Raḥīm, *Ṣarf* 26-27). Hence *lam yaqraʾ* "he did not read" can be pronounced *lam yaqra.*

3.7. The occurrence of the hamza in some of the other classes of irregular verbs

The hamza can occur as a radical in other classes of verbs than the "purely" hamzated (cf. Åkesson, *Ibn Masᶜūd* 248: fol. 24b-25a). I mention the following cases:

1- as a 1st radical in the doubled verb, e.g. *ʾanna yaʾinnu* "to groan, moan".

2- as a 2nd radical in verbs with weak 1st radical, e.g. *waʾada* "to bury alive (a newborn girl)", and as a 3rd radical in a verb with weak 1st radical, e.g. *waǧaʾa* "to beat".

3- as a 1st or 3rd radical in verbs with weak 2nd radical, e.g. *ʾāna* "to come, to approach" and *ǧāʾa* "to come" respectively.

4- as a 1st or 2nd radical in verbs with weak 3rd radical, e.g. *ʾabā* [with final *alif maqṣūra]* "to refuse" and *raʾā* [with final *alif maqṣūra]* "to see" respectively.

5- as a 2nd radical in verbs with weak 1st and 3rd radical, e.g. *waʾā* [with final *alif maqṣūra]* "to promise".

6- as a 1st radical in verbs with 2nd and 3rd weak radical, e.g. *ʾawā* [with final *alif maqṣūra]* "to seek refuge".

3.8. Conclusion

I have studied the hamzated verb, some of its derivatives and some other classes of irregular verbs in which the hamza occurs. I have as well touched upon the phonological procedures due to the hamza in some forms. It has been observed that the sequence of two hamzas of which the 1st is vowelled and the 2nd vowelless in the imperative of the verb with 1st radical hamza, e.g. *ʾiʾsir* "capture! /2 masc. sing. (imperative)" and in Form IV of the passive voice, e.g. *ʾuʾṯira* "he, or it was preferred /(passive)", leads to the change of the hamza into a glide, namely *ʾiysir* with a *y* and *ʾ(u)ūṯir* with an *ū* respectively (cf. 3.2.1.1.:1, 2), and that a hamza vowelled by a fatḥa and preceded by a sukūn in the imperfect of the verb with 2nd radical hamza, e.g. *yasʾalu* "he asks" leads to the transfer of the fatḥa to the vowelless consonant and the elision of the hamza, namely *yasalu* (cf. 3.4.1.1.).

I shall now study the phonological changes due to the hamza in the next chapter.

CHAPTER FOUR

4. The phonological changes due to the hamza

Having discussed the class of the hamzated verb I shall study the retaining of the hamza or the phonological changes affecting it in this section.

4.1. The hamza. Its retaining or alleviation

The hamza, which is characterized as the glottal stop, can either be pronounced fully, and is thus transcribed as ʾ, or can be alleviated (cf. Rabin, 130-131). The reason of its alleviation is that it is a hard heavy consonant uttered from the farthest part of the throat.

My intention in this chapter is to study some specific rules that determine the representation of the hamza whether it is maintained and the changes that are carried out in the word whether it is alleviated. These rules, as it shall be remarked, depend to a great extent on the hamza's position in a word, on whether it is the inial (cf. 4.1.1.), the middle (cf. 4.1.2.) or the last segment (cf. 4.1.3.). I shall study the different cases in the following paragraphs.

4.1.1. The hamza as the initial segment of a word

The hamza that occurs as the initial segment of a word is written over the alif when it is vowelled by a fatḥa, e.g. *ʾabun* "father" (أَبٌ) or by a ḍamma, e.g. *ʾummun* "mother" (أُمٌّ), and under the alif when it vowelled by a kasra, e.g. *ʾismun* "name" (إِسْمٌ).

The alleviation of the hamza is regular when it concerns the connective hamza following a vowel in the word preceding it, as it becomes a *waṣla* (for discussions see Wright, I, 19-20). An example is the hamza vowelled by a fatḥa, *ʾa,* of the definite article *-ʾal* that becomes *-l* after the alleviation with the *waṣla,* e.g. *bintu l-rāʿī* (بِنْتُ ٱلرَّاعِي) said instead of *bintu ʾal-rāʿī* (بِنْتُ أَلرَّاعِي) "the shepherd's daughter".

The alleviation of the hamza can be considered as anomalous in other cases. Some anomalous examples are *ʾunāsun* that becomes after the elision of the hamza *nāsun* "people" (cf. Ibn Ǧinnī, *Ḫaṣāʾiṣ III,* 151, Ibn Manẓūr, I, 147, Howell, I, fasc. I, 174, Fleisch, *Traité I,* 151) and *al-ʾilāhu* that becomes after the elision of the hamza *al-lāhu* (cf. Åkesson, *Ibn Masʿūd* 242-243: fol. 23a, Ibn Manẓūr, I, 114).

4.1.2. The hamza preceded by another segment in the middle of the word

The hamza can be found in other positions than as the initial segment of a word in a sequence in which it is preceded by another segment. This segment can be a consonant which is another consonant than the hamza, another hamza or a glide, and it can be vowelled or vowelless. Furthermore as it shall be remarked in some cases, the sequence can occur in one word or in two words following each other. For a better understanding of the retaining of the hamza or the change affecting it, I shall propose for its sudy the following sequences by separating two categories from each other: one in which the segment preceding the hamza is a consonant or a glide, and the other one in which it is a hamza. Thus I shall discuss the following sequences beginning with the first category and ending up with the second:

4.1.2.1. The hamza is vowelless and the segment preceding it is vowelled: its retaining or the alleviation by the change of the hamza into a glide.

4.1.2.2. The hamza and the segment preceding it are vowelled.

4.1.2.2.1. The hamza is vowelled by one of the three vowels and is preceded by a fatḥa: its alleviation by its change into a *hamza bayna bayna* "an intermediary hamza".

4.1.2.2.2. The hamza is vowelled by a fatḥa and is preceded by a ḍamma or kasra: its alleviation by its change into a glide.

4.1.2.3. The hamza is vowelled and the segment preceding it is vowelless.

4.1.2.3.1. The hamza is vowelled by a fatḥa and is preceded by a sukūn: its elision together with the hamza's fatḥa shifted to the vowelless segment preceding it.

4.1.2.3.2. The hamza is vowelled by a fatḥa and is preceded by a sukūn [i.e. a vowelless infixed glide of prolongation]: its assimilation to the glide.

4.1.2.3.3. The hamza is vowelled by a kasra and is preceded by a sukūn [i.e. a vowelless infixed glide of prolongation]: its assimilation to the glide.

4.1.2.3.4. The hamza is vowelled by a kasra or ḍamma and is preceded by a sukūn [i.e. a vowelless infixed glide of prolongation]: its change into a *hamza bayna bayna.*

With regards to the fact that the segment preceding the hamza can be another hamza, I present the following sequences:

4.1.2.4. The hamza is vowelless and the hamza preceding it is vowelled by a fatḥa: its alleviation by its change into an *ā*.

4.1.2.5. The hamza is vowelless and the hamza preceding it is vowelled by a kasra: its alleviation by its change into a *y*.

4.1.2.6. The hamza is vowelless and the hamza preceding it is vowelled by a ḍamma: its change into a *w* or its elision.

4.1.2.7. The hamza and the hamza preceding it are vowelled by a fatḥa.

4.1.2.7.1. The hamza and the hamza preceding it are vowelled by a fatḥa in one word: their assimilation into a madda and the anomalous insertion of an *ā* in some cases.

4.1.2.7.2. The hamza is vowelled by a fatḥa in one word and follows a hamza vowelled by a fatḥa in the word preceding it: the elision of one hamza or of both.

It shall be remarked in this study that the alleviation of the hamza is carried out by changing it either into a glide or a *hamza bayna bayna* "an intermediary hamza" or by eliding it.

4.1.2.1. The hamza is vowelless and the segment preceding it is vowelled: its retaining or the alleviation by the change of the hamza into a glide:

The hamza can be found in a sequence in which it occurs vowelless and the segment preceding it can be vowelled by a fatḥa, a ḍamma or a kasra. In all these three cases the hamza can be maintained or alleviated. In the latter case, it is changed into a glide of the same nature of the vowel of the segment preceding it (cf. Åkesson, *Ibn Masʿūd* 240: fol. 21b, Roman, *Étude I,* 330).

It is remarked that when the hamza is maintained, it is the vowel of the segment preceding it that determines its shape. If the hamza is preceded by a ḍamma it is changed into a *w* with a hamza over it, e.g. *luʾmun* "blame" (لُؤْمٌ) written with a hamza over the *w* instead of *lu*ʾ*mun* written with the hamza over the alif and when it is preceded by the kasra it is changed into a *hamza* ʿ*alā kursī l-yā*ʾ, e.g. *bi*ʾ*run* "well, spring" written with the *hamza* ʿ*alā kursī l-yā*ʾ (بِئْر) instead of *bi*ʾ*run* written with the hamza under the alif (cf. Wright, II, 72).

In other cases when the hamza is alleviated, it is noted that the vowel of the segment preceding it determines the nature of the glide that the hamza is changed into. If this vowel is a fatḥa the hamza is changed into an *ā* (cf. 4.1.2.1.: 1., 4.1.2.4.), if it is a ḍamma it is changed into an *ū* (cf. 4.1.2.1.: 2., 4.1.2.6.) and if it is a kasra it is changed into an *ī* (cf. 4.1.2.1.: 3., 4.1.2.5.).

1- The alleviation by the change of the vowelless hamza, the ʾ*, into an ā:*

If the segment preceding the hamza is vowelled by a fatḥa the hamza is changed into an *ā* (cf. par. 10.1.12.3.). Thus:

*-a*ʾ → *-(a)ā*

An example is *ra*ʾ*sun* with the vowelless ʾ preceded by a fatḥa that becomes *r(a)āsun* "a head" after the change of the ʾ into *ā*.

2- The alleviation by the change of the vowelless hamza, the ʾ*, into an ū:*

If the segment preceding the hamza is vowelled by a ḍamma the hamza is changed into an *ū* (cf. par. 10.1.9.3.). Thus:

*-u*ʾ → *-(u)ū*

An example is *lu*ʾ*mun* with the vowelless ʾ preceded by a ḍamma that becomes *l(u)ūmun* "blame" after the change of the ʾ into *ū*.

3- The alleviation by the change of the vowelless hamza, the ʾ, into an ī:

If the segment preceding the hamza is vowelled by a kasra the hamza is changed into an ī. Thus:

-iʾ → *-(i)ī*

An example is *biʾrun* with the vowelless ʾ preceded by a kasra that becomes *b(i)īrun* "well, spring" after the change of the ʾ into ī.

4.1.2.2. The hamza and the segment preceding it are vowelled:

The vowelled state of both the hamza and the segment preceding it give rise to the following eventualities:

4.1.2.2.1. The hamza is vowelled by one of the three vowels and is preceded by a fatḥa: its retaining or its alleviation by its change into a *hamza bayna bayna* "an intermediary hamza".

4.1.2.2.2. The hamza is vowelled by a fatḥa and is preceded by a ḍamma or kasra: its alleviation by its change into a glide.

4.1.2.2.1. The hamza is vowelled by one of the three vowels and is preceded by a fatḥa: its retaining or its alleviation by its change into a hamza bayna bayna "an intermediary hamza":

The hamza that is vowelled by one of the three vowels and preceded by a fatḥa can be changed into a *hamza bayna bayna* "intermediary hamza" (for discussions concerning it see Sībawaihi, II, 168-169, Åkesson, *Ibn Masʿūd* 240: 21b, Roman, 324-326, Lane, I, 288).

When the hamza that is vowelled by a ḍamma or a kasra is maintained, it is represented by its being written over - in the case of the *ʾu,* or under, - in the case of the *ʾi,* the particular glide that its vowel is connected to (for discussions see de Sacy, I, 95,

Wright, II, 75). If the hamza is vowelled by a ḍamma that is underlyingly written over an alif, the *ᵓu,* it is changed into a hamza over the *w*. An example is *laᵓuma* "to be wicked" (لَؤُم) written with the hamza over the *w* instead of the base form *laᵓuma* (لأُم) written with a hamza over the alif vowelled by a ḍamma. If the hamza is vowelled by a kasra that is underlyingly written under the alif, the *ᵓi,* it is changed into a *hamza ᶜalā kursī l-yāᵓ*. An example is *saᵓima* "to be weary" (سَئِم) written with the *hamza ᶜalā kursī l-yāᵓ* instead of the base form *saᵓima* (سَإِم) written with a hamza under the alif.

A closer look at the alleviated hamza will make one remark that it is a sort of mixture between the hamza itself and the glide to which its vowel is connected to. If the hamza's vowel is a fatḥa, then the glide that it is connected to is the *ā,* e.g. *s(a)āla* from *saᵓala* "to ask" (cf. 4.1.2.2.1.: 1), if it is a ḍamma then the glide that it is connected to is a *w,* e.g. *lawuma* from *laᵓuma* "he was base" (cf. 4.1.2.2.1.: 2), and if it is a kasra then the glide that it is connected to is a *y,* e.g. *sayima* from *saᵓima* "he was weary" (cf. 4.1.2.2.1.: 3).

Concerning the alleviated hamza Ibn Ǧinnī, *Sirr I,* 48 writes:

> "As what concerns the alleviated hamza it is the one that is termed *hamza bayna bayna.* The meaning with Sībawaihi's saying of *bayna bayna* is that it is intermediary between the hamza and the segment to which its vowel is connected to. If it is vowelled by the fatḥa it is then between the hamza and the alif, if it is vowelled by the kasra it is then between the hamza and the *y,* and if it is vowelled by the ḍamma it is then between the hamza and the *w*... As what concerns the one vowelled by the fatḥa it is in your saying about *saᵓala* "he asked": *sāla,* as what concerns the one vowelled by the kasra it is in your saying about saᵓima "he was weary": *sayima,* and as what concerns the one vowelled by the ḍamma it is in your saying concerning *laᵓuma* "he was base": *lawuma*".

1- The alleviation by the change of the hamza vowelled by a fatḥa, the ʾa, into an ā:

If the hamza is vowelled by a fatḥa and is preceded by one it can be changed into an *ā*. Thus:

-aʾa → *-(a)ā*

An example is *saʾala* "to ask" with the hamza vowelled by a fatḥa, the *ʾa*, preceded by a fatḥa, that becomes *s(a)āla.*

An example concerning the hamza alleviated for the sake of metric exigency, is the verb with 3rd radical hamza *hanaʾaki* that is said *han(a)āki* (cf. Åkesson, *Ibn Masʿūd* 240: fol. 22a) in a verse composed by Farazdaq, which is cited by Sībawaihi, II, 175, Ibn Ǧinnī, *Ḫaṣāʾiṣ III,* 152, *Sirr II,* 666, Ibn al-Sarrāǧ, *Uṣūl III,* 469, Muʾaddib, *Taṣrīf* 530, Zamaḫšarī, 166, Ibn Yaʿīš, IX, 113, *Mulūkī* 229, Ibn ʿUṣfūr, I, 405, Howell, IV, fasc. I, 951, Åkesson, *Ibn Masʿūd* 255: (220). It runs as follows:

"Rāḥat bi-Maslamata l-biġālu ʿašīyata
fa-rʿā Fazāratu lā hanāki l-martaʿu"
"The mules have gone away with Maslama at evening.
Then graze your camels, Fazāra. May the pasture not be pleasant to you!".

2- The alleviation by the change of the hamza vowelled by a ḍamma, the ʾu, into wu:

If the hamza is vowelled by a ḍamma and is preceded by a fatḥa, it can be changed into a *w*. Thus:

-aʾu → *-awu*

An example is *laʾuma* "to be base" with the hamza vowelled by a ḍamma: *ʾu,* and preceded by a fatḥa, that becomes *lawuma* with the change of the *ʾu* into *wu.*

3- The alleviation by the change of the hamza vowelled by a kasra the ᵓi, into yi:

If the hamza is vowelled by a kasra and is preceded by a fatḥa, it can be changed into a y vowelled by a kasra.

-aᵓi → *-ayi*

An example is *saᵓima* "he was weary" with the hamza vowelled by a kasra: *ᵓi,* preceded by a fatḥa that becomes *sayima* with the change of the *ᵓi* into *yi.*

4.1.2.2.2. The hamza is vowelled by a fatḥa and is preceded by a ḍamma or kasra: its alleviation by its change into a glide:

If the hamza is vowelled by a fatḥa and is preceded by a ḍamma or a kasra, it is changed into a glide of the same nature of the vowel of the segment preceding it (cf. Åkesson, *Ibn Masᶜūd* 240: fol. 21b). If the vowel preceding it is a ḍamma, then the hamza is changed into an *w* (cf. 4.1.2.2.2.: 1) and if it is a kasra it is changed into a *y* (cf. 4.1.2.2.2.: 2).

1- The change of the hamza preceded by a ḍamma into w:

If the segment preceding the hamza is a ḍamma, the hamza can be changed into a *w*. Thus:

-uᵓa → *-uwa*

An example is *guᵓanun* "receptable for bottles or the like" with the hamza vowelled by a fatḥa preceded by a ḍamma that becomes *ǧuwanun* with the change of the *ᵓ* into a *w* (cf. Zamaḫšarī, 174, Ibn Ǧinnī, *Sirr II,* 573, Åkesson, *Ibn Masᶜūd* 240: 21b).

2- The change of the hamza preceded by a kasra into y:

If the segment preceding the hamza is a kasra, the hamza can be changed into a *y*. Thus:

-iʾa → *-iya*

An example is *miʾarun* "exciting dissension among the people" with the hamza vowelled by a fatḥa preceded by a kasra that becomes *miyarun* with the change of the ʾ into a *y* (cf. Sībawaihi, II, 169, Zamaḫšarī, 166, Åkesson, *Ibn Masʿūd* 240: fol. 21b).

It can be observed that the hamza that is vowelled by a fatḥa and preceded by a ḍamma or kasra, is changed in the same manner as the hamza that is vowelless and preceded by a vowel (for it see par. 4.1.2.1.), i.e. into a glide of the nature of the specific vowel preceding it.

4.1.2.3. The hamza is vowelled and the segment preceding it is vowelless:

The vowelled state of the hamza and the vowelless state of the segment preceding it give rise to the following eventualities:

4.1.2.3.1. The hamza is vowelled by a fatḥa and is preceded by a sukūn: its elision together with the hamza's fatḥa shifted to the vowelless segment preceding it.

4.1.2.3.2. The hamza is vowelled by a fatḥa and is preceded by a sukūn [i.e. a vowelless infixed glide of prolongation]: its assimilation to the glide.

4.1.2.3.3. The hamza is vowelled by a kasra and is preceded by a sukūn [i.e. a vowelless infixed glide of prolongation]: its assimilation to the glide.

4.1.2.3.4. The hamza is vowelled by a kasra or ḍamma and is preceded by a sukūn [i.e. a vowelless infixed glide of prolongation]: its change into a *hamza bayna bayna.*

4.1.2.3.1. The hamza is vowelled by a fatḥa and is preceded by a sukūn: its elision together with the hamza's fatḥa shifted to the vowelless segment preceding it:

If the hamza is vowelled by a fatḥa and is preceded by a vowelless segment, it can be elided and its fatḥa is shifted to the segment preceding it (cf. Åkesson, *Ibn Masᶜūd* 240-242: fols. 22a-22b and for this sequence see par. 3.4.1.1.).

The vowelless segment preceding the hamza can be:

1- a strong segment.

2- an original *w* or *y*.

3- an augmentative *w* or *y* attached to the pattern.

4.1.2.3.1.1. The vowelless segment preceding the hamza is a strong segment:

The strong vowelless segment preceding the hamza vowelled by a fatḥa can be the *l*- of the definite article, *al*-, or a radical. The change procedure is that the hamza's fatḥa is shifted to the vowelless strong segment and the hamza is elided.

An example in which the segment preceding the hamza is the vowelless *l*- of the definite article is *al-ʾaḥmaru* "red" with the *l*- of the definite article, *al*-, vowelless preceding the hamza vowelled by a fatḥa. This sequence leads to the elision of the hamza and the transfer of its fatḥa to the *l* preceding it, namely *ʾalaḥmaru*. Another variant exists as well, namely *laḥmaru* with the hamza of the article elided (cf. Sībawaihi, II, 170, Zamaḫšarī, 166-167, Åkesson, *Ibn Masᶜūd* 240: fol. 22a, Howell, IV, fasc. I, 942-943, 959-963, Lane, I, 74, Wright, II, 269).

Some examples in which the segment preceding the hamza is a radical is the imperfect with the 2nd radical hamza *yasʾalu* "he asks" that becomes anomalously *yasalu* (cf. par. 3.4.1.1.) and its *maṣdar masʾalatun* "a matter" that becomes *masalatun* (cf.

Zamaḫšarī, 166, Åkesson, *Ibn Masᶜūd* 240: fol. 22a). In both these examples the 1st radical *s* is vowelless and precedes the hamza vowelled by a fatḥa. As it has been observed, this sequence results in the elision of the hamza and the transfer of its fatḥa to the *s* preceding it.

Another example is *malʾakun* "angel" (from *ʾalaka* "to convey") with the 2nd radical *l* vowelless, preceding the hamza vowelled by a fatḥa. This sequence results in the elision of the hamza and the transfer of its fatḥa to the *l* preceding it, namely *malakun* (cf. Ibn Ǧinnī, *Munṣif II*, 102-104, Ibn Manẓūr, I, 110-111, Åkesson, *Ibn Masᶜūd* 240: fol. 22a, Wright, II, 77, Vernier, I, 101-102, Lane, I, 81-82).

4.1.2.3.1.2. The vowelless segment preceding the hamza is a vowelless w or y:

The vowelless *w* or *y* preceding the hamza vowelled by a fatḥa can be an infixed segment or a radical. This sequence results in the elision of the hamza and the transfer of its fatḥa to the segment preceding it. It can be remarked that this sequence can occur in one word or in two words following each other.

4.1.2.3.1.2.1. The elision of the hamza in one word and the transfer of its fatḥa to the segment preceding it:

The vowelless segment preceding the hamza vowelled by a fatḥa in the same word can be an infixed glide, namely a *w* or a *y*. The conditions of the hamza's elision and consequently of the transfer of its fatḥa to the segment preceding it, is that the infixed segment is not a segment of prolongation, i.e. a glide lengthening the sound of the vowel preceding it, as the *w* in *mafᶜuwlatun (/ mafᶜ(u)ūlatun)* that lengthens the ḍamma preceding it (for discussions see 4.1.2.3.2.: 1), or the *y* in *faᶜiylatun (/ faᶜ(i)īlatun)* that lengthens the kasra preceding it (for discussions see 4.1.2.3.2. :2) and that the infixed segment is not specific for the diminutive, as the *y* in *ʾufayʾilun,* because in these cases the hamza is assimilated to the glide preceding it (for discussions see 4.1.2.3.3.).

1- The segment preceding the hamza is a vowelless w:

If the segment preceding the hamza is a vowelless *w* the procedure is the following:

-wʾa → *-wa*

An example *is ǧawʾabatun "Ǧawʾaba* [name of a water]", which is from the root *ǧ ʾ b* (cf. Howell, IV, fasc. I, 938), in which the infixed *w* is there to make it identical to the pattern *fawᶜalatun.* As it is noticed, the *w* infix is vowelless and precedes the hamza vowelled by a fatḥa. This sequence results in the elision of the hamza and the transfer of its fatḥa to the *w* preceding it, namely *ǧawabatun* (cf. Åkesson, *Ibn Masᶜūd* 240: fol. 22a).

2- The segment preceding the hamza is a vowelless y:

If the segment preceding the hamza is a vowelless *y* the procedure is the following:

-yʾa → *-ya*

An example is *ǧayʾalun* "female hyena", which is from the root *ǧ ʾ l* (cf. Ibn Manẓūr, I, 529, Lane, I, 370), in which the infixed *y* is to make it identical to the pattern *fayᶜalun.* As it is remarked, the *y* infix is vowelless and precedes the hamza vowelled by a fatḥa. This sequence results in the elision of the hamza and the transfer of its fatḥa to the *y* preceding it, namely *ǧayalun* (cf. Åkesson, *Ibn Masᶜūd* 240: fol. 22a).

4.1.2.3.1.2.2. The elision of the hamza vowelled by a fatḥa in one word following a vowelless w, y or a strong segment in the word preceding it and the transfer of its fatḥa to this segment:

The elision of the hamza that is vowelled by a fatḥa is as well carried out if the vowelless *w, y* or the strong segment preceding it, is not in the same word as the hamza. In this case the vowelled hamza, which is the initial segment of the second word, is elided, and its vowel, the fatḥa, is shifted to the vowelless segment preceding it which is the ultimate segment of the word preceding it (for a study see Sībawaihi, II, 171-172, Zamaḫšarī, 166, Åkesson, *Ibn Masᶜūd* 240-242: fol. 22a, Howell, IV, fasc. I, 938 sqq., Vernier, I, 104).

1- The segment preceding the hamza in the word preceding it is a vowelless w:

If the vowelless weak ultimate segment in the word preceding the hamza vowelled by a fatḥa is a *w,* the procedure is the following:

-w + ᵓa → *-wa*

An example is *ᵓAbuw ᵓAyyūba* "the father of Job", with the *w* vowelless in *ᵓAbuw (ᵓAb(u)ū),* marking its nominative's ending as it is the 1st element of the construct state, which precedes the hamza vowelled by a fatḥa that is the initial segment of the second word. This sequence results in the elision of the hamza from *ᵓAyyūba* and the transfer of its fatḥa to the *w* preceding it, namely *ᵓAbuwa yyūba* (cf. Åkesson, *Ibn Masᶜūd* 240-242: fol. 22a, Howell, IV, fasc. I, 940).

Some other examples with the alleviation of the hamza, just to mention a few, are *d̲uw ᵓamrihim* "the author of their matter" which becomes *d̲uwa mrihim* (Ibn Yaᶜīš, IX, 109) and *qāḍuw*

ʾabīka "the judges of your father" which becomes *qāḍuwa bīka* (cf. Ibn Yaᶜīš, IX, 110, Howell, IV, fasc. I, 940).

2- The segment preceding the hamza in the word preceding it is a vowelless y:

If the vowelless weak ultimate segment in the word preceding the hamza vowelled by a fatḥa is a *y,* the procedure is the following:

-y + *ʾa* → *-ya*

An example is *ʾabtaġiy ʾamrahu* "I seek for his matter" with the *y* vowelless occuring as the 3rd radical of the first word *ʾabtaġiy,* - which is the imperfect of 1st person of the sing. of *baġiya* -, preceding the hamza vowelled by a fatḥa that is the first initial segment of the second word, *ʾamrahu.* This sequence results in the elision of the hamza from *ʾamrahu* and the transfer of its fatḥa to the *y* preceding it, namely *ʾabtaġiya mrahu* (cf. Åkesson, *Ibn Masᶜūd* 240-242: fol. 22a, Howell, IV, fasc. I, 940).

3- The segment preceding the hamza in the word preceding it is a vowelless strong segment:

If the vowelless ultimate segment in the word preceding the hamza vowelled by a fatḥa is a strong segment, the procedure is the following [C stands for consonant]:

-C + *ʾa* → *-Ca*

An example is *man ʾabūka* with the strong segment, the *n,* vowelless occurring as the ultimate segment of the first word, namely the interrogative particle *man,* preceding the hamza vowelled by a fatḥa that is the first initial segment of the second word, *ʾabūka.* This sequence results in the elision of the hamza from *ʾabūka* and the transfer of its fatḥa to the *n* preceding it, namely *mana būka* "who is your father?" (cf. Ibn Yaʿīš, IX, 110, Howell, IV, fasc. I, 940, Roman, *Étude I,* 332).

Another example is *qad ʾaflaḥa* of the sur. 23: 1 *(qad ʾaflaḥa l-muʾminūna)* "The Believers must (eventually) win through", in which the strong segment, the *d,* of the first word, namely the particle *qad,* is vowelless and precedes the hamza vowelled by a fatḥa that is the initial segment of the second word, namely the verb in the Form IV *ʾaflaḥa.* This sequence results in the alleviation of the hamza from *ʾaflaḥa* in the reading of some, by methods of eliding it and shifting its vowel to the segment preceding it, namely *qada flaḥa l-muʾminūna* (cf. Ibn Yaʿīš, IX, 110).

Other examples, just to mention a few, are *law ʾanna* that becomes *lawa nna* "if" and *qad ʾaṣbaḥa* that becomes *qada ṣbaḥa* "he has become" (cf. Nöldeke, *Grammatik* 5).

4.1.2.3.2. The hamza is vowelled by a fatḥa and is preceded by a sukūn [i.e. a vowelless infixed glide of prolongation]: its assimilation to the glide:

The vowelless segment preceding the hamza vowelled by a fatḥa can be an infixed glide of prolongation. This sequence results in the alleviation of the hamza by its change into the same segment as the segment preceding it, namely a glide, and then the assimilation of the glides. It is worth to have in mind that if the infixed segment is not an infixed glide of prolongation, and the hamza's vowel is a fatḥa, the hamza is elided and its fatḥa is shifted to the segment preceding it (for discussions see par. 4.1.2.3.1.).

Some examples considering two vowelless segments of prolongation in some patterns are the *w* in *mafʿ(u)wlatun (/ mafʿ(u)ūlatun)* lengthening the ḍamma preceding it and the *y* in *faᶜ(i)ylatun (/ faᶜ(i)īlatun)* lengthening the kasra preceding it. I shall discuss the cases below.

1- The segment preceding the hamza is an infixed vowelless w:

If the infixed segment is a vowelless *w* as the *w* in *mafᶜ(u)wlatun (/ mafᶜ(u)ūlatun)* lengthening the ḍamma preceding it, the procedure leading to the assimilation is the following:

-uwʾa → *-uwwa*

An example is *maqruwʾatun (> maqr(u)ūʾatun)* "a writing read" which is formed according to the pattern *mafᶜuwlatun* with the infixed prolonged *w* lengthening the sound of the ḍamma preceding it. The hamza vowelled by a fatḥa is alleviated by its change into the same segment as the segment preceding it, which is a *w,* and then an assimilation of the wāws is carried out resulting in *maqruwwatun* (for discussions see Sībawaihi, II, 171, 175, Åkesson, *Ibn Masᶜūd* 242: fols. 22a-22b, Howell, IV, fasc. I, 936-937, de Sacy, I, 370, Vernier, I, 102, 350).

2- The segment preceding the hamza is an infixed vowelless y:

If the infixed segment is a vowelless *y* as the *y* in *faᶜiylatun (/ faᶜ(i)īlatun)* lengthening the kasra preceding it, the procedure leading to the assimilation is the following:

-iyʾa → *-iyya*

An example is *ḫaṭiyʾatun (> ḫaṭ(i)īʾatun)* "an error, sin", which is formed according to the pattern *faᶜiylatun* with the infixed *y* lengthening the sound of the kasra preceding it. The hamza vowelled by a fatḥa is alleviated by its change into the same segment as the segment preceding it, namely a *y,* and then an assimilation of the yāʾs is carried out resulting in *ḫaṭ(i)yyatun* (for discussions see Sībawaihi, II, 171, 175, Åkesson, *Ibn Mas^cūd* 242: fol. 22a-22b, Howell, IV, fasc. I, 936-937, de Sacy, I, 370, Vernier, I, 102, 350).

4.1.2.3.3. The hamza is vowelled by a kasra and is preceded by a sukūn [i.e. a vowelless infixed glide of prolongation]: its assimilation to the glide:

A pattern in which the hamza vowelled by a kasra is preceded by an infixed vowelless *y* is *ʾufayʿilun,* in which the *y* is specific for the diminutive. The procedure leading to the assimilation is the following:

-ayʾi → *-ayyi*

An example is *ʾufayʾisun* "a kind of little hoe, a little axe", which is formed according to the pattern *ʾufayʾilun* with the vowelless infixed *y* specific for the diminutive. The hamza vowelled by a kasra is alleviated by its change into the same segment as the segment preceding it, namely a *y,* and then an assimilation of the yāʾs is carried out resulting in *ʾufayyisun* (for discussions see Sībawaihi, II, 171, 175, Åkesson, *Ibn Masʿūd* 242: fol. 22a-22b, Howell, IV, fasc. I, 936-937, de Sacy, I, 370, Vernier, I, 102, 350).

4.1.2.3.4. The hamza is vowelled by a kasra or ḍamma and is preceded by a sukūn [i.e. a vowelless infixed glide of prolongation]: its change into a hamza bayna bayna:

As examples of two patterns in which the hamza vowelled by a kasra is preceded by an infixed vowelless *ā* of prolongation, I can take up the active participle *f(a)āʿilun* and the broken pl. of the nouns *maf(a)āʿilun* in which the alif lengthens the sound of the fatḥa preceding it. This sequence results in the alleviation of the hamza by its change into a *hamza bayna bayna* (for discussions see Sībawaihi, II, 171, Roman, *Étude I,* 333). The procedure leading to the assimilation is the following:

- *(a)āʾi* → *-(a)āyi*

Some examples that are formed according to the active participle *f(a)āᶜilun* are *s(a)āʾilun* "a questioner" with the 2nd radical hamza vowelled by a kasra, from *saʾala* "to ask", which results after the change of the hamza into a *hamza bayna bayna* in *s(a)āyilun,* and *q(a)āʾilun* "a teller" from *q(a)āwilun* with the 2nd radical *w* changed into a hamza vowelled by a kasra, from *qawala* "to tell", which results after the change in *q(a)āyilun* (cf. Åkesson, *Ibn Masᶜūd* 242: fol. 22b).

An example that is formed according to the broken pl. of the nouns *maf(a)āᶜilun* is *mas(a)āʾilun* "questions" (cf. Sībawaihi, II, 171, Roman, *Étude I*, 333) which results in *mas(a)āyilun.*

If the hamza is vowelled by a ḍamma an preceded by an *ā* of prolongation, the procedure leading to the assimilation is the following:

-āʾu → *-āwu*

An example in which the hamza vowelled by a ḍamma is preceded by an *ā* of prolongation is *ǧazā(a)ʾun* "a recompense" that is formed according to the pattern *faᶜ(a)ālun* in which the alif lengthens the sound of the fatḥa preceding it. It occurs in the sentence presented by Sībawaihi, II, 171 *ǧazāʾu ʾummihi* "his mother's recompense" (جَزاءُ أمّه) This hamza is changed into a *hamza bayna bayna* resúlting in *ǧazāwu mmihi* (جَزاوُامّه) (cf. ibid, Roman, *Étude I,* 333).

4.1.2.4. The hamza is vowelless and the hamza preceding it is vowelled by a fatḥa: Its alleviation by its change into an ā:

The hamza that is vowelless and preceded by a hamza vowelled by a fatḥa at the initial of the word is changed into an *ā,* and hence the hamza is assimilated to the *ā* resulting in a madda.

The procedure is the following:

-ʾaʾ → *-ʾ(a)ā*

Some examples that can be mentioned are those formed according to the pattern *ʾafᶜalu,* e.g. *ʾaʾḫaḏu* "the one who holds mostly against" that becomes *ʾ(a)āḫaḏu* and *ʾaʾdamu* "tawny, dark-complexioned" that becomes *ʾ(a)ādamu* with the *madda* as their initial segment (cf. Sībawaihi, II, 174, Ibn Ǧinnī, *Sirr II,* 579, 665, Åkesson, *Ibn Masᶜūd* 242: fol. 22b).

4.1.2.4.1. An anomalous example: ʾayimmatun

An anomalous example in which both hamzas are maintained is the base form of the plural of *ʾimām,* namely *ʾaʾmimatun* in which this combination of the hamzas takes place at the initial of the word. The 2nd hamza is changed into *y* for the purpose of alleviation and the kasra of the *m* is shifted to it, namely *ʾayimmatun* (cf. Zamaḫšarī, 167, Ibn Manẓūr, I, 133, Howell, IV, fasc. I 971 sqq., Lane, I, 91, Vernier, I, 101), because the combination of two hamzas at the initial of the word is deemed as heavy. The Kufans however maintain both the hamzas anomalously as they recite the sur. 9: 12 as *(fa-qātilū ʾaʾimmata l-kufri)* "Fight ye the chiefs of Unfaith", with *ʾaʾimmata* read instead of *ʾayimmata* (cf. Ibn Ḫālawaihi, *Qirāʾāt I,* 235, Åkesson, *Ibn Masᶜūd* 242: fol. 22b). This reading is disliked by Ibn Ǧinnī (cf. Ibn Ǧinnī, *Ḫaṣāʾiṣ III,* 143, *Sirr I,* 81).

It can be remarked that the combination of both hamzas at the interior of the word is more permitted. An example is *ḫaṭāʾiʾī* "my sins" used instead of *ḫaṭāyāya* in the sentence *ʾallahumma ġfir lī ḫaṭāʾiī* "O God forgive me my sins", which according to Zamaḫšarī, 167, Abū Zaid has heard from Abū l-Samḥ and his cousin Raddād.

4.1.2.5. The hamza is vowelless and the hamza preceding it is vowelled by a kasra: its alleviation by its change into a y:

The hamza that is vowelless and preceded by a hamza vowelled by a kasra is changed into a *y*.

The procedure is the following:

-ʾiʾ → *-ʾ(i)y*

An example in which such a combination occurs is the imperative of the 2nd person of the masc. sing. of a verb with 1st hamza radical *ʾasara* "to capture", namely *ʾiʾsir* "capture!" with the 2nd vowelless hamza preceded by a kasra which becomes *ʾ(i)ysir* with the *ʾ* changed into a *y*, and as the vowelless *y* in it is preceded by a kasra, it becomes *ʾ(i)īsir* with the *y* assimilated to the kasra resulting in the lengthened *ī* (cf. par. 3.2.1.1.: 1).

4.1.2.6. The hamza is vowelless and the hamza preceding it is vowelled by a ḍamma: its change into a w or its elision:

The hamza that is vowelless and preceded by a hamza vowelled by a ḍamma is in most cases changed into a *w*.

The procedure is the following:

-ʾuʾ → *-ʾ(u)w*

An example in which such a combination is carried out at the initial of the word is the passive voice of Form IV of *ʾaṯara* "to report" in the 3rd person of the masc. sing. formed according to *f(u)ūʿila,* namely *ʾuʾṯira* "it was reported" with the 2nd vowelless hamza preceded by a ḍamma. It becomes *ʾ(u)wṯira* with the hamza changed into a *w*, then as the vowelless *w* in it is preceded by a ḍamma, it becomes *ʾ(u)ūṯira* "he, or it was preferred /(passive)" with the *w* assimilated to the ḍamma resulting in the lengthened *ū* (cf. par. 3.2.1.1.: 2).

However it can be observed that in some cases of 1st radical hamzated verbs of the conjugation *faʿala yafʿulu* occurring in the imperative according to *ʾufʿul*, e.g. *ʾuʾḫuḏ* "take!" and *ʾuʾkul* "eat!" with the 2nd vowelless hamza preceded by the hamza of the imperative vowelled by a ḍamma, both hamzas are elided resulting respectively in *ḫuḏ* and *kul* (cf. par. 3.2.1.1.).

The procedure is then the following:

-ʾuʾ → -

4.1.2.7. The hamza and the hamza preceding it are vowelled by a fatḥa:

Two hamzas vowelled by a fatḥa combined together can occur in one word or in two words following each other.

The sequences that can be taken up are the following:

4.1.2.7.1. The hamza and the hamza preceding it are vowelled by a fatḥa in one word: their assimilation into a madda and the anomalous insertion of an *ā* in some cases.

4.1.2.7.2. The hamza is vowelled by a fatḥa in one word and follows a hamza vowelled by a fatḥa in the word preceding it: the elision of one hamza or of both.

4.1.2.7.1. The hamza and the hamza preceding it are vowelled by a fatḥa in one word: their assimilation into a madda and the anomalous insertion of an ā in some cases:

The possible assimilation of two hamzas vowelled by a fatḥa following each other at the beginning of the word concern some examples in which the interrogative particle, *ʾa*, is prefixed in a word which has the conjunctive hamza vowelled by fatḥa of the definite *ʾal-* attached to it, e.g. *ʾa-ʾal-Ḥasanu ʿindaka* "Is al-Ḥasan by you?" which becomes *ʾ(a)āl-Ḥasanu ʿindaka* (cf. Howell, IV, fasc. I, 1003).

Hence the procedure is the following:

-ʾa-ʾa → *-ʾ(a)ā*

The anomalous insertion of the *ā* in words in which the initial segment is the conjunctive hamza *ʾa,* to which the interrogative particle, *ʾa,* is prefixed to, can be remarked, e.g. *ʾa-ʾanti* "Are you /fem. sing.?" which becomes *ʾ(a)ā-ʾanti* (cf. Sībawaihi, II, 173, Åkesson, *Ibn Masʿūd* 242: fol. 23a).

Hence the procedure is the following:

-*ʾa-ʾa* → -*ʾ(a)ā-ʾa*

As an example, the anomalous *ʾ(a)ā-ʾanti* that occurs in this part of a verse said by D̲ū l-Rumma, cited by Sībawaihi, II, 173, Ibn Ǧinnī, *Sirr II,* 723, Muʾaddib, *Taṣrīf* 32, Zamaḫšarī, 14, 167, Ibn Yaʿīš, IX, 118-120, Howell, I, fasc. I, 119, IV, fasc. I, 982, Åkesson, *Ibn Masʿūd* 262: (233) can be mentioned:

> *"Fa-yā ẓabyata l-waʿsāʾi bayna ǧulāǧilin*
> *wa-bayna l-naqā ʾāʾanti ʾam ʾummu Sālimin"*
> "Then, O gazelle of the soft sandy ground between ˇGulāğil
> and the sand-hill, is this really you or Umm Sālim?".

4.1.2.7.2. The hamza is vowelled by a fatḥa in one word and follows a hamza vowelled by a fatḥa in the word preceding it: the elision of one hamza or of both:

Such a sequence occurs when the hamza vowelled by a fatḥa is the initial segment of a word and is preceded by a hamza vowelled by a fatḥa in the word preceding it (cf. Sībawaihi, II, 172, Zamaḫšarī, 167, Åkesson, *Ibn Masʿūd* 242: fol. 23a, Howell, IV, fasc. I, 983-986).

An example is the sur. 47: 18 *(fa-qad ǧāʾa ʾašrāṭuhā)* "But already Have come some tokens", in which *ǧāʾa ʾašrāṭuhā* presents a combination of two hamzas vowelled by a fatḥa. Al-Ḫalīl and some other Arabs alleviate the 2nd hamza and not the1st one, and recite it as *fa-qad ǧāʾa šrāṭuhā* فَقَدْ جاءَ ٱشراطُها whereas the Ḥiǧāzīs alleviate both the hamzas by eliding the 1st one and changing the 2nd one into a *waṣla,* namely *fa-qad ǧā šrāṭuhā* فَقَدْ جا أشراطُها (cf. Åkesson, *Ibn Mas^cūd* 242: fol. 23a).

4.1.3. The hamza as the final segment of a word

The hamza as the final segment of a word can either be vowelled and preceded by a vowel (cf. 4.1.3.1.) or vowelled and preceded by a sukūn (cf. 4.1.3.2.). In the first case, the vowel preceding it determines which is the glide that supports it, and in the 2nd case the hamza is written on the line unsupported, unless if it concerns some anomalous cases found in some dialectal variants.

4.1.3.1. The vowelled hamza is preceded by a vowel:

It is not the hamza's own vowel that is the factor determining whether it is supported by a glide, - namely if it is written over or under the alif or over the *ʾu,* - because its vowel marks the inflection and varies according to the word's position in the sentence. However it can be observed that it is the vowel preceding it that is the factor determining which is the glide that supports it (cf. Åkesson, *Ibn Mas^cūd* 248: fol. 25a).

Examples are *qaraʾa* "to read" with the hamza written over the alif (قَرَأَ) on account of the fatḥa of the *r* preceding it, *ṭaruʾa* "to descend, to break in" with the hamza written over the *w* (طَرُؤَ) on account of the ḍamma of the *r* preceding it, and *fatiʾa* "not to cease to be, to refrain" with the hamza written over the *kursī l-yāʾ* (فَتِئَ) on account of the kasra of the *t* preceding it.

4.1.3.2. The vowelled hamza is preceded by a sukūn:

The vowelled segment that is preceded by a sukūn is written as a pure hamza on the line without being supported by any glide (cf. Åkesson, *Ibn Mas^cūd* 248: fol. 25a-25b).

Some examples are *ḫab'un* "a hidden thing" (خَبْء) with the 1st radical given a fatḥa, *rid'un* "a buttress" (رِدْء) with the 1st radical given a kasra and *buṭ'un* "slowness" (بُطْء) with the 1st radical given a *ḍamma* (cf. Howell, IV, fasc. I, 807-812).

4.1.3.2.1. Some anomalous cases that concern the alleviation of the hamza:

The hamza in the examples *ḫab'un, rid'un* and *buṭ'un* is treated differently in the dialectal variants (for them see Howell, IV, fasc. I, 807-812). The Ḥiǧāzīs elide it on account of the pause, and say in the definite form *al-ḫab, al-rid* and *al-buṭ*. The Banū Tamīm give the 2nd radical a vowel that is similar to the vowel of the 1st radical and then change the hamza into a segment of the nature of the vowel preceding it by placing it over the glide, namely *al-ridi'* (الرِّدِئْ) and *al-buṭu'* (البُطُؤْ) in all the three cases of the nominative, accusative or genetive. Some Arabs elide and do not shift the vowel of the hamza, and then change the hamza into an unsound segment homogeneous with its vowel, i.e. *al-ridw* (الرِّدْوْ) and *al-buṭw* (البُطْوْ). Others shift the vowel of the hamza and change the 3rd radical into a glide, namely *al-ridiy* (الرِّدِي) and *al-buṭuw* (البُطُو).

4.2. Conclusion

I have studied the hamza's position as the initial, middle and the final segment in this chapter. I have discussed its retaining and the phonological changes due to its alleviation with regards to the different sequences in which it occurs. It has been remarked that the sequences in which it is vowelless and preceded by any of the three vowels, i.e. the fatḥa, e.g. *ra'sun,* "a head" (cf. 4.1.2.1.: 1), *'a'ḫaḏu* "the one who holds mostly against" (cf.

4.1.2.4.), the kasra, e.g. *biʾrun* "a well, spring" (cf. 4.1.2.1.: 3), *ʾiʾsir* "capture!" (cf. 4.1.2.5.), the ḍamma, e.g. *luʾmun* "blame", (cf. 4.1.2.1.: 2), *ʾuʾṯira* "it was reported" (cf. 4.1.2.6.) or vowelled by any of the three vowels and preceded by a fatḥa, e.g. *saʾala* "to ask", *laʾuma* "he was base", *saʾima* "he was weary" (cf. 4.1.2.2.1.), and vowelled by a fatḥa and followed by a hamza vowelled by a fatḥa in the second word, e.g. *ʾa-ʾal-Ḥasanu ʿindaka* "Is al-Ḥasan by you?" (cf. 4.1.2.7.) or vowelled by a fatḥa and preceded by a ḍamma, e.g. *ǧuʾanun* "receptable for bottles or the like" or vowelled by a fatḥa and preceded by a kasra, e.g. *miʾarun* "exciting dissension among the people" (cf. 4.1.2.2.2.), can result in its alleviation by its change into a glide, i.e. *r(a)āsun, ʾ(a)āẖaḏu, b(i)īrun, ʾ(i)ysir, l(u)ūmun, ʾ(u)wṯira, s(a)āla, lawuma, sayima, ʾ(a)āl-Ḥasanu ʿindaka, ǧuwanun* and *miyarun.* The sequence in which it is vowelled by a fatḥa and is preceded by a sukūn results in its elision and in the transfer of its fatḥa to the vowelless segment preceding it, e.g. *malʾakun* "angel" that becomes *malakun* (cf. 4.1.2.3.1.). This rule applies on the condition that this segment is not an infixed *w* or *y*, as the hamza in these cases is assimilated to the glide, e.g. *maqruwʾatun (> maqr(u)ūʾatun)* "a writing read" that becomes *maqruwwatun, ẖaṭiyʾatun (> ẖaṭ(i)īʾatun)* "an error, sin", that becomes *ẖaṭ(i)yyatun* (cf. 4.1.2.3.2.) and *ʾufayʾisun* "a kind of little hoe, a little axe" that becomes *ʾufayyisun* (cf. 4.1.2.3.3.).

In the next chapters I shall discuss the weak verbs and some of their derivatives.

CHAPTER FIVE

5. The verb with 1st radical *w* or *y*

The verb with 1st *w* or y radical is generally termed as *muᶜtal al-fāʾ*.

Another nomination is *miṯālun* "assimilated, similar", which is given to it because some of its patterns are similar to other patterns of verb classes.

This similarity is noticed in two cases:

1- Its pattern of the perfect that is formed of three radicals is similar to the pattern of the perfect of the strong verb, as its 1st weak radical is retained and sound as is the 1st strong radical of the strong verb. I illustrate this with the following examples:

a- verb with 1st radical w

waᶜada "to promise"		*ḍaraba* "to hit"
1st sound *w* radical	=	1st strong radical
wa+ᶜa+da		*ḍa+ra+ba*
1 + 2 + 3 radicals		1 + 2 + 3 radicals

b- verb with 1st radical y

yasara "to play at hasard"		*ḍaraba* "to hit"
1st sound *y* radical	=	1st strong radical

ya+sa+ra — *ḍa+ra+ba*

1 + 2 + 3 radicals — 1 + 2 + 3 radicals

2 - Its pattern of the imperative that is formed of two radicals is similar to the pattern of the imperative of the verb with 2nd *w* or *y* radical. I illustrate this with the following example:

ᶜid "promise!" (from *waᶜada)* — *zin* "decorate" (from *ẓayana)*

elision of 1st radical *w* = elision of 2nd radical *y*

ᶜi+d — *ẓi+n*

1 + 2 radicals — 1 + 2 radicals

The imperative of the verb with 1st radical *w: ᶜid* is underlyingly *ᵓiwᶜid* formed according to the measure *ᵓifᶜil* (from *waᶜada)* with the 1st radical *w* elided and the imperative of the verb with 2nd *y* radical *ẓin* is underlyingly *ᵓiẓyin* formed according to *ᵓifᶜil* (from *ẓayana)* with the 2nd *y* radical elided.

5.1. The conjugations of the verb with 1st radical *w*

The conjugations of the verb with 1st radical *w* can conveniently be grouped into the following ones:

1- *faᶜala yafᶜilu,* e.g. *waᶜada yawᶜidu* "to promise", of which the imperfect *yawᶜidu* becomes after the phonological change *yaᶜidu* with the 1st radical *w* elided.

2- *faᶜala yafᶜalu,* e.g. *wahaba yawhabu* "to give", of which the imperfect *yawhabu* becomes after the phonological change *yahabu* with the 1st radical *w* elided.

3- *faᶜila yafᶜalu,* e.g. *wağila yawğalu* "to be afraid", of which the 1st radical *w* is maintained in the imperfect *yawğalu.*

4- *faᶜila yafᶜilu,* e.g. *wamiqa yawmiqu* "to love", of which the imperfect *yawmiqu* becomes after the phonological change *yamiqu* with the 1st radical *w* elided.

5- *faᶜula yafᶜulu,* e.g. *wabula yawbulu* "to be unwholesome", of which the 1st radical *w* is maintained in the imperfect *yawbulu.*

5.1.1. An anomalous case: wağada yağudu

An anomalous case is the verb *wağada yağudu* "to find, to experience" in which the theme vowel is a ḍamma, and which would seem to be formed according to the conjugation *faᶜala yafᶜulu.* However a deeper level of analysis shows that its theme vowel is a kasra, as the underlying conjugation is *wağada yağidu* formed according to the conjugation *faᶜala yafᶜilu.* The imperfect *yağidu* is underlyingly *yawğidu* of which the 1st radical *w* is elided and the 2nd radical, the *ğ,* is given the kasra, namely *yağidu.* This procedure occurs by all the Arabs except by the Banu ᶜĀmir (cf. Ibn Manẓūr, VI, 4769, Åkesson, *Ibn Masᶜūd* 270: fol. 25b) who give the *ğ* the ḍamma, namely *yağudu.* I can mention the example of the imperfect of the 3rd person of the fem. pl. *yağudna* that occurs in their dialect in this verse said by Ğarīr, cited by Ibn ᶜUṣfūr, I, 177, Ibn Yaᶜīš, *Mulūkī* 49, Howell, II-III, 247-248, Åkesson, *Ibn Masᶜūd* 274: (243):

> *"Law šiʾti qad naqaᶜa l-fuʾāda bi-šarbatin*
> *tadaᶜu l-ṣawādiya lā yağudna ġalīlan".*
> "If you had wanted, your saliva would have quenched [the thirst] of the heart with a single draught
> leaving the thirsty [ribs of the breast in such a state that] they would not experience heat of thirst".

5.2. Examples of some derivatives of the verb with 1st radical *w*

An example of a verb with 1st radical *w* in the perfect is *waᶜada* "to promise". It becomes *yaᶜidu* in the imperfect of the indicative active. Its imperative is *ᶜid,* its active participle is *wāᶜidun,* its *maṣdar* is *waᶜdun* or *ᶜidatun,* its perfect passive is *wuᶜida,* its imperfect is *yūᶜadu* and its passive participle is *mawᶜūdun.*

5.2.1. Remarks concerning the phonological procedures in some of its forms:

The main changes are that it can have in some of its forms its 1st radical sound, in others elided and in others changed into another segment.

I shall focus on a few different forms and discuss some various sequences in them with the aim of determining the main rules.

5.2.1.1. The perfect: the sequence in which the 1st radical *w* is the initial segment: the soundness of the glide.

5.2.1.2. The verbal noun: the sequence in which the 1st radical *w* is the initial segment: the elision of the *w* and the compensation with the prefixed *tāᵓ marbūṭā.*

5.2.1.3. The imperfect: the sequence in which the 1st radical *w* is vowelless and followed by a kasra in the conjugation *yafᶜilu:* the elision of the *w.*

5.2.1.4. The imperfect: the sequence in which the 1st radical *w* is vowelless and followed by a fatḥa in the conjugation *yafᶜalu:* the retaining or the change of the *w* into a *y* or an *ā,* or the elision of the *w.*

5.2.1.5. The imperative: the sequence in which the 1st radical *w* is vowelless and preceded by the kasra of the connective hamza: the *w* is changed into a *y* and can be retained or is elided together with the hamza vowelled by a kasra.

5.2.1.6. The active participle: the sequence in which the 1st radical *w* is vowelled by a fatḥa and followed by the infix vowelless *ā:* the retaining of the *w* or the anomalous transposition of segments.

5.2.1.7. The noun of place and time: the sequence in which the 1st radical *w* is vowelless and preceded by a fatḥa: the soundness of the *w.*

5.2.1.8. Form VIII of the perfect: the sequence in which the 1st vowelless radical *w* is preceded by a kasra and followed by the vowelled infixed *t:* the change of the *w* into a *y* and the assimilation of the *y* to the vowelled infixed *t.*

5.2.1.1. The perfect: the sequence in which the 1st radical w is the initial segment: the soundness of the glide:

The 1st weak radical remains sound in the perfect, e.g. *waʿada* "he promised" on the basis that the glide can only be affected by a phonological change if it is preceded by another segment (for discussions see par. 9.1.), which is not the case here as the glide is the initial segment.

This rule implies that no phonological change can affect the initial segment. Hence, this means that the *w* in *waᶜada* cannot be made vowelless resulting in *wᶜada,* because of the impossibility of beginning the word with a vowelless segment. It could not either be changed into *ā* resulting in *āᶜada* as this would imply beginning the word with a vowelless segment which is forbidden, and it could not either be elided as the root would seem to be formed of two radicals, i.e. *ᶜada,* which is not allowed (cf. Åkesson, *Ibn Masᶜūd* 270: fol. 25b-26a).

5.2.1.2. The verbal noun: the sequence in which the 1st radical w is the initial segment: the elision of the w and the compensation with the prefixed tāᵓ marbūṭā:

It can be stated that the 1st weak radical can be elided in some cases of verbal nouns, e.g. *ᶜidatun* underlyingly *wiᶜdun* "a promise" (for some examples see Suyūṭī, *Muzhir II,* 158-159), in spite of the fact that it is the initial segment of the word. This opposes the rule that the glide should be preceded by another segment if a phonological change is to be carried out (cf. par. 5.2.1.1., 9.1). The breaking of this rule requests however that the *tāᵓ marbūṭa* is suffixed to it as a compensation for the elision of this initial glide (cf. Sībawaihi, II, 81, Wright, II, 118, Lane, II, 2952).

Not only the *tāᵓ marbūṭa* can occur as a compensation of a glide in the same word, but also another word, occurring as the 2nd element of an *ᵓiḍāfa* construction, can occur as a compensation for the elision of a *tāᵓ marbūṭa.* I can mention the case of the *tāᵓ marbūṭa* that is anomalously elided from the accusative *ᶜidata* which is said *ᶜida,* when it occurs as the first element of a construct state in this verse said by Abū Umayya al-Faḍl b. al-ᶜAbbās b. ᶜUtba b. Abī Lahab, that is cited by Ibn Ǧinnī, *Ḫaṣāᵓiṣ III,* 171, Muᵓaddib, *Taṣrīf* 285, Suyūṭī, *Ašbāh III,* 248, Ibn Manẓūr, VI, 4871, Howell, I, fasc. IV, 1527-1528, IV, fasc. I, 1423-1424, Åkesson, *Ibn Masᶜūd* 277: (248):

> *"ᵓInna l-ḫalīṭa ᵓaǧaddū l-bayna fa-nǧaradū*
> *wa-ᵓaḫlafūka ᶜida l-ᵓamri l-laḏī waᶜadū".*
> "Verily the familiar friends have renewed the separation, and made off, and have broken to you the promise of the matter which they promised".

There exist two different theories concerning the elision of the *tāᵓ marbūṭa* from *ᶜidatun* and its likes. One of them is

Sībawaihi's theory (cf. Sībawaihi, II, 260-261) who accepts the elision of the *tā*ᵓ *marbūṭa* even when the word to which it is suffixed is not the first element of a construct state, and the other one is al-Farrāᵓs, who can only accept this elision when the word is the first element of the construct state, as in the case of *ᶜida l-ᵓamri* of this verse, as he considers the second element of the construct, namely *l-ᵓamri,* as a compensation for the elided *tā*ᵓ *marbūṭa* (cf. Muᵓaddib, *Taṣrīf* 285, Åkesson, *Ibn Masᶜūd* 270-272: fol. 26a; and compare the case of *(wa-ᵓiqāmu l-ṣalāti)* in par. 6.5.12 in which *wa-ᵓiqāmu* is said instead of *wa-ᵓiqāmatu.*

5.2.1.3. The imperfect: the sequence in which the 1st radical w is vowelless and followed by a kasra in the conjugation yafᶜilu: the elision of the w:

In some examples of verbs occurring in the imperfect formed according to *yafᶜilu,* e.g. *yawᶜidu* "he promises", the *w* is elided as it precedes a kasra, which is deemed as a heavy combination resulting in *yaᶜidu* (cf. Zamaḫšarī, 178, de Sacy, I, 238, Vernier, I, 57).

The Kufans believed that the elision of the *w* is to distinguish the transitive verbs, e.g. *yaᶜidu-hu* underlyingly *yawᶜidu-hu* "he promises him/it", *yazinu-hu* underlyingly *yawzinu-hu* "he weights him/it", from the intransitive verbs in which the *w* is retained, e.g. *yawḥalu* "he/it falls into the mud", and *yawǧalu* "he fears". Their theory is however vicious as there exist verbs in the intransitive in which the *w* is elided, e.g. *yakifu* said with the elision of the *w* instead of *yawkifu* "it drips with rain-water" (for discussions see Ibn al-Anbārī, *Inṣāf* Q. 112, 326-327, Howell, IV, fasc. I, 1418).

5.2.1.4. The imperfect: the sequence in which the 1st radical w is vowelless and followed by a fatḥa in the conjugation yafᶜalu: the retaining or the change of the w into a y or an ā, or the elision of the w:

The *w* is usually maintained in the imperfect of the conjugation *faᶜila yafᶜalu,* e.g. *wağila yawğalu* "to be afraid". In some rare cases it is changed into a *y,* namely *wağila yawğalu* or *yayğalu, wağiᶜa yawğaᶜu* or *yayğaᶜu* "to have pain", and in some more rare cases into an *ā,* namely *y(a)āğalu* and *y(a)āgaᶜu* (cf. Wright, II, 79, Bakkūš, *Taṣrīf* 125).

The *w* is elided in the imperfect of the conjugation *faᶜala yafᶜalu,* e.g. *wahaba yahabu* "to give" underlyingly *wahaba yawhabu.*

As for the reason why the *w* is maintained in the conjugation *faᶜila yafᶜalu* and elided in *faᶜala yafᶜalu,* it seems to be to distinguish both these conjugations from each other (cf. Bakkūš, *Taṣrīf* 125, ᶜAbd al-Raḥīm, *Ṣarf* 28-29).

5.2.1.5. The imperative: the sequence in which the 1st radical w is vowelless and preceded by the kasra of the connective hamza: the w is changed into a y and can be retained or is elided together with the hamza vowelled by a kasra:

In the case of the imperative that is formed according to *ᵓifᶜal,* e.g. *ᵓiwğal,* the *w* is vowelless and preceded by the kasra of the connective hamza. The *w* is changed into a *y,* namely *ᵓiyğal* "be scared!" on account of the influence of the kasra (cf. Wright, II, 80).

In the case of *ᵓifᶜil,* e.g. *ᵓiwᶜid* "promise /masc sing.", the vowelless *w* is at first changed into a *y* on account of the kasra preceding it, namely *ᵓiyᶜid* (cf. Wright, II, 78, de Sacy, I, 238), then both the hamza vowelled by a kasra, namely the *ʾi,* and the *y* are elided resulting in *ᶜid.* This elision of the 1st radical *w* changed into *y* seems to be on the analogy of its elision in the imperfect (for it see par. 5.2.1.3.) *taᶜidu,* as the imperative can be considered to be derived from the imperfect.

5.2.1.6. The active participle: the sequence in which the 1st radical w is vowelled by a fatḥa and followed by the infix vowelless ā: the retaining of the w or the anomalous transposition of segments:

The active participle's form is *f(a)āᶜilun,* e.g. *w(a)āᶜidun* "promising", in which the *w* is sound.

In some anomalous cases the *qalb* "transfer of one segment to the position of another one" is carried out (for an example concerning the active participle of a verb with 2nd *w* radical, e.g. *š(a)āwikun* > *š(a)ākin* see par. 6.5.10.: 2).

An example is *w(a)āḥidun* "one (in higher ordinals)" resulting in *ḥ(a)ādin* (cf. Åkesson, *Ibn Masᶜūd* 292: fol. 30b). An analysis of the phonological changes that are carried out in it shows us that the 1st radical *w* is shifted after the 3rd radical *d* resulting in *āḥidwun.* As it is impossible to start the word with a vowelless *ā,* the 2nd radical *ḥ* is shifted before it and the kasra of the *ḥ* is shifted after the vowelless *d,* so that it became *ḥ(a)ādiwun.* The *w* in *ḥ(a)ādiwun* is changed into a *y* on account of the kasra preceding it, so it became *ḥ(a)ādiyun.* As it resembles the active participles of verbs with 3rd weak radical (for them see par. 7.5.12. and compare the case of the active participle of the verb with 2nd radical *š(a)ākin* par. 6.5.10.: 2), a phonological change was carried out in it so that it became *ḥādin.* So the pattern of *ḥādin* is not *fāᶜilun* but *ᶜālifun* (cf. Ibn Manẓūr, VI, 4779).

5.2.1.7. The noun of place and time: the sequence in which the 1st radical w is vowelless and preceded by a fatḥa: the soundness of the w:

The form of the noun of place and time of the verb with 1st radical *w* is *mafʿilun.* The 1st radical *w* is retained in it and the 2nd radical is invariably vowelled with a kasra. Examples are *mawʿidun* "time or place of a promise or appointment" from *waʿada yaʿidu* "to promise" of the conjugation *faʿala yafʿilu* and *mawǧilun* "a place that is dreaded" from *waǧila yawǧalu* "to be afraid" of the conjugation *faʿila yafʿalu.*

5.2.1.8. Form VIII of the perfect: the sequence in which the 1st vowelless radical w is preceded by a kasra and followed by the vowelled infixed t: the change of the w into a y and the assimilation of the y to the vowelled infixed t:

In the Form VIII of the perfect *ʾiftaʿala,* e.g. *ʾiwtaʿada* "to accept a promise", the *w* is changed into a *y* on account of the kasra of the connective hamza preceding it, namely *ʾiytaʿada,* and the *y* is assimilated to the infixed *t,* resulting in *ʾittaʿada* (for this assimilation see par. 2.4.1.1.3.1.: 4).

5.3. The conjugations of the verb with 1st radical *y*

The conjugations of the verb with 1st radical *y* can conveniently be grouped into the following ones:

1- *faʿala yafʿilu,* e.g. *yanaʿa yayniʿu* "to become ripe", of which the imperfect is inflected as the strong verb, namely *yayniʿu* or *yaynaʿu.*

2- *faʿala yafʿalu,* e.g. *yafaʿa yayfaʿu* "to be grown up", of which the imperfect is inflected as the strong verb, namely *yayfaʿu.*

3- *fa^{c}ila yaf^{c}alu,* e.g. *yaqiẓa yayqaẓu* "to be awake", of which the imperfect is inflected as the strong verb, namely *yayqaẓu.*

4- *fa^{c}ula yaf^{c}ulu,* e.g. *yaquẓa yayquẓu* "to be awake", of which the imperfect is inflected as the strong verb, namely *yayquẓu.*

5.4. Examples of some derivatives of the verb with 1st radical y

An example of a verb with 1st radical *y* in the perfect is *yasara* "to be easy". It becomes *yaysiru* in the imperfect of the indicative active. Its imperative is *ʾiysir* > *ʾīsir,* its active participle is *yāsirun,* its *maṣdar* is *yasrun,* its passive is *yusira,* its imperfect is *yūsaru* and its passive participle is *maysūrun.*

5.4.1. Some remarks concerning the phonological procedures in some of its forms:

It is possible to observe that the verb with 1st radical *y* has in most forms the *y* retained. However the *y* is changed into *w* when it occurs vowelless and preceded by a ḍamma (for this sequence see par. 9.1.5.; for the substitution see par. 10.1.9.2). The forms that present such a sequence are the imperfect of the passive voice of Form I *yuf^{c}alu,* the active voice of Form IV of the imperfect *yuf^{c}ilu* and the active participle of Form IV *muf^{c}ilun.* I shall consider the following forms in order to be able to determine the main rules concerning the various sequences in them:

5.4.1.1. The imperfect of the passive voice of Form I, the active voice of Form IV of the imperfect and the active participle of Form IV: the *y* is vowelless and preceded by a ḍamma: the change of the *y* into a *w.*

5.4.1.2. Form VIII of the perfect: the sequence in which the 1st vowelless radical *y* is preceded by a kasra and followed by the vowelled infixed *t:* the assimilation of the *y* to the vowelled infixed *t.*

5.4.1.1. The imperfect of the passive voice of Form I, the active voice of Form IV of the imperfect and the active participle of Form IV: the y is vowelless and preceded by a ḍamma: the change of the y into a w:

An example of an imperfect of the passive voice of Form I *yufᶜalu,* is *yuysaru* that becomes *yuwsaru* > *y(u)ūsaru* "is pleased".

The same change of the *y* into *w* is carried out in the active voice of Form IV of the imperfect yuysiru that becomes *yuwsiru* > *y(u)ūsiru* "is well off" (cf. Wright, II, 50, for the sequence see par. 9.1.5.; for the substitution see 10.1.9. 2). Thus *yuysiru* with the vowelless *y* preceded by a ḍamma becomes *yuwsiru* with the *y* changed into a *w.* As *yuwsiru* has its vowelless *w* preceded by a ḍamma, it becomes *y(u)ūsiru* with the *w* changed into an *ū.*

The same applies for the active participle Form IV *muysirun* that becomes *muwsirun* > *m(u)ūsirun* "is prosperous" (cf. Åkesson, *Ibn Masᶜūd* 286: fol. 28a-28b; for the sequence see this study par. 9.1.5.; for the substitution see 10.1.9.2). Thus *muysirun* with the vowelless 1st radical *y* preceded by a ḍamma becomes *muwsirun* with the *y* changed into a *w.* As *muwsirun* has its vowelless *w* preceded by a ḍamma it becomes *m(u)ūsirun* with the *w* changed into an *ū.* The reason of the change of the vowelless *y* into a *w* is the influence of the ḍamma of the segment preceding the *y* and the faintness of the nature of the vowelless segment in relation to the vowelled segment (cf. Åkesson, *Ibn Masᶜūd* 286: fol. 28b).

5.4.1.2. Form VIII of the perfect: the sequence in which the 1st vowelless radical y is preceded by a kasra and followed by the vowelled infixed t: the assimilation of the y to the vowelled infixed t:

In the Form VIII of the perfect *ʾiftaʿala,* e.g. *ʾiytasara* "to play at hazard", the *y* is assimilated to the infixed *t,* resulting in *ʾittasara* (for this assimilation see par. 2.4.1.1.3.1.: 5).

5.5. Conclusion

I have presented and discussed the verb with 1st *w* or *y* radical and some of its derivatives in this chapter. The verb with 1st radical *w* is generally more submitted to phonological changes than the verb with 1st radical *y*. The reason is that the *w* is considered as heavy in some specific combinations involving the kasra. In other combinations, the *w* is mostly retained as sound, e.g. in the perfect (cf. 5.2.1.1.), e.g. *waʿada* "he promised". It can be elided in the verbal noun with the prefixation of the *tāʾ marbūṭa* to compensate for the elision (cf. 5.2.1.2.), e.g. *wiʿdun* > *ʿidatun* "a promise". It is elided in the imperfect of the conjugation *yafʿilu* (cf. 5.2.1.3.), e.g. *yawʿidu* > *yaʿidu* "he promises", and is either maintained, e.g. *wağila yawğalu* "to be afraid", changed into a *y,* e.g. *yawğalu* > *yayğalu,* an *ā,* e.g. *yawğalu* > *y(a)āğalu,* or elided, e.g. *yawhabu* > *yahabu* "to give" in the conjugation *yafʿalu* (cf. 5.2.1.4.). It is either changed into a *y* in the imperative, e.g. *ʾiwğal* > *ʾiyǧal* "be scared!" or is elided together with the connective hamza to prevent a disliked combination, e.g. *ʾiwʿid* > *ʾiyʿid* > *ʾid* "promise /masc sing." (cf. 5.2.1.5.). It is maintained, e.g. *w(a)āʿidun* "promising", or anomalously transposed and then elided, e.g. *w(a)āḥidun* > *āḥidwun* > *ḥ(a)ādiwun* > *ḥ(a)ādin* in the active participle when it is followed by the vowelless *ā* (cf. 5.2.1.6.). It is maintained in the noun of time and place as it is preceded by a fatḥa, e.g. *mawᶜidun* "time or place of a promise or appointment" (cf. 5.2.1.7.) and it is changed into a *y* in Form VIII of the perfect as it is preceded by a kasra, e.g. *ʾiwtaᶜada* > *ʾiytaᶜada* "to accept a promise" (cf. 5.2.1.8.).

The verb with 1st radical *y* has in most forms the *y* sound, except in some cases when it occurs vowelless and preceded by a ḍamma, as it is changed into a *w* (cf. 5.4.1.1.), e.g. *yuysaru* > *yuwsaru* > *y(u)ūsaru* "is pleased" and *muysirun* > *muwsirun* > *m(u)ūsirun* "is prosperous", or in Form VIII of the perfect *ʾiftaᶜala,* in which it occurs vowelless, preceded by the kasra and followed by the vowelled infixed *t,* as it is assimilated to the *t* (cf. 5.4.1.2.), e.g. *ʾiytasara* > *ʾittasara* "to play at hazard".

In the next chapter I shall study the verb with 2nd *w* or *y* radical.

CHAPTER SIX

6. The verb with 2nd radical *w* or *y*

The verb with 2nd radical *w* or *y, al-muᶜtall al-ᶜayn,* is also termed *al-ˀağwaf* "the hollow verb". Another less known nomination is *ḏū l-ṯalāṯat* "the one with three segments" (cf. Åkesson, *Ibn Masᶜūd* 282: fol. 26b), which is given to it because it loses its 2nd weak radical in the perfect when the vowelled suffixed agent pronoun, namely the *-tu* "/1st person of the sing.", *-ta* "2nd person of the masc. sing.", *-ti* "2nd person of the fem. sing.", *-tumā* "2nd person of the dual", *-tum* "2nd person of the masc. pl.", *-tunna* "2nd person of the fem. pl.", or *-na* "3rd person of the fem pl., is attached to it. It comprehends three segments instead of four in these perfect forms, which distinguishes it from the other classes of verbs. I illustrate this theory with the following examples:

a- verb with 2nd radical w

An example of a verb with 2nd radical *w* is *qul-tu* "I said" underlyingly *qawal-tu* (for the phonological change see 6.5.2.1.: 1) that loses the *w* radical, and hence *qul-ta* "you said /masc.

sing." underlyingly *qawal-ta, qul-ti* "you said /fem. sing." underlyingly *qawal-ti, qul-tumā* "you said /dual" underlyingly *qawal-tumā, qul-tum* "you said /dual." underlyingly *qawal-tum, qawal-na* "they said /fem. pl." underlyingly *qawal-na,* etc.

The underlying form that comprehends four segments can be distinguished from the form in which a phonological change due to the unsound glide is carried out, resulting in three segments. Hence I illustrate this as follows:

The underlying form:

qawal-tu	=	*fa^{c}al-tu*
qa+wa+l+tu	=	*fa+^{c}a+l+tu*
1 + 2 + 3 + 4 segments	=	1 + 2 + 3 + 4 segments

The form in which a phonological change is carried out is:

qu+l+tu	=	*fu+l+tu*
1 + 2 + 3 segments	=	1 + 2 + 3 segments

b- verb with 2nd radical y

An example of a verb with 2nd radical *y* is *bi^c-tu* "I sold" underlyingly *baya^c-tu* (for the phonological change see par. 6.5.1.2.: 1) that loses the *y* radical, and hence *bi^c-ta* "you said /masc. sing." underlyingly *baya^c-ta, bi^c-ti* "you said /fem. sing." underlyingly *baya^c-ti, bi^c-na* "they said /fem. pl." underlyingly *baya^c-na,* etc.

The underlying form is:

baya^c-tu	=	*fa^{c}al-tu*
ba+ya+^{c}+tu	=	*fa+^{c}a+l+tu*
1 + 2 + 3 + 4 segments	=	1 + 2 + 3 + 4 segments

The form in which a phonological change is carried out is:

bi+^{c}+tu	=	*fi+l+tu*
1 + 2 + 3 segments	=	1 + 2 + 3 segments

6.1. The conjugations of the verb with 2nd radical *w*

The conjugations of the verb with 2nd radical *w* can be grouped into the following:

1- *faᶜala yafᶜulu,* e.g. *qawala yaqwulu* that becomes after the phonological change *qāla yaqūlu* "to say".

2- *faᶜila yafᶜalu,* e.g. *ḫawifa yaḫwafu* that becomes after the phonological change *ḫāfa yaḫāfu* "to fear".

3- *faᶜula yafᶜulu,* e.g. *ṭawula yaṭwulu* that becomes after the phonological change *ṭāla yaṭūlu* "to become long".

6.2. Examples of some derivatives of the verb with 2nd radical *w*

An example of a verb with 2nd radical *w* in the perfect is *qāla* "to ask". It becomes *yaqūlu* in the imperfect of the indicative active. Its imperative is *qul,* its active participle is *qāʾilun,* its *maṣdar* is *qawlun,* its perfect passive is *qīla,* its imperfect is *yuqālu* and its passive participle is *maqūlun.*

6.3. The conjugations of the verb with 2nd radical *y*

The conjugations of the verb with 2nd radical *y* can be grouped into the following:

1- *faᶜala yafᶜilu,* e.g. *bayaᶜa yabyiᶜu* that becomes after the phonological change *bāᶜa yabīᶜu* "to sell".

2- *faᶜila yafᶜalu,* e.g. *hayiba yahyabu* that becomes after the phonological change *hāba yahābu* "to fear".

6.4. Examples of some derivatives of the verb with 2nd radical *y*:

An example of a verb with 2nd radical *y* in the perfect is *bāᶜa* "to buy". It becomes *yabīᶜu* in the imperfect of the indicative active. Its imperative is *biᶜ*, its active participle is *bāʾiᶜun,* its *maṣdar* is *bayᶜun,* its perfect passive is *bīᶜa,* its imperfect is *yubāᶜu* and its passive participle is *mabīᶜun.*

6.5. Remarks concerning the phonological procedures in some of the forms of the verb with 2nd radical *w* or *y:*

Before embarking upon establishing the rules of the phonological changes due to the glide, it can be remarked that most of the procedures concerning the sequences of the verb with 2nd radical *w* concern as well the sequences of the verb with 2nd radical *y*. It shall be observed in this analysis that three usual changes can be applied concerning the verb with 2nd radical *w* or *y*. In some of its forms, it can have its glide changed into another segment, have it elided or retained. Another change that can affect the glide is as well the transfer of its vowel to the segment preceding it, but this occurs only on the condition that this segment is vowelless or that it has a vowel that is deemed heavy on it. I shall devote my attention to the following forms, sequences and rules:

6.5.1. The 3rd persons of the perfect of the verb with 2nd radical *w* or *y:* the sequence of the vowelled 2nd weak radical preceded by a fatḥa: the change of the vowelled weak radical into an *ā*.

6.5.2. The persons in the perfect of the verb with 2nd radical *w* or *y* in which the vowelled pronoun of the agent is suffixed: the sequence of the vowelless 2nd radical *ā* (that is substituted for the 2nd weak radical) preceded by a fatḥa and followed by the vowelless 3rd radical: the elision of the *ā* and the change of the 1st radical's fatḥa into another vowel.

6.5.3. The imperfect of the verb with 2nd radical *w* or *y* of the conjugation *yafᶜalu:* the sequence of the 2nd weak radical vowelled by a fatḥa and preceded by a sukūn: the transfer of the fatḥa to the vowelless segment preceding it and the change of the vowelled weak radical into an *ā* in all forms with the remark that the *ā* is elided in the imperfect forms of the fem. pl. in which the vowelled *–n, the -na*, is suffixed to.

6.5.4. The imperfect of the verb with 2nd radical *w* of the conjugation *yafᶜulu:* the sequence of the 2nd radical *w* vowelled by a ḍamma and preceded by a sukūn: the transfer of the ḍamma to the vowelless segment preceding it, the change of the *wu* into an *ū* with the remark that the *-ū* is elided in the forms of the fem. pl. in which the vowelled *–n, the -na*, is suffixed to.

6.5.5. The imperfect of the verb with 2nd radical *y* of the conjugation *yafᶜilu:* the sequence of the 2nd radical *y* vowelled by a kasra and preceded by a sukūn: the transfer of the kasra to the vowelless segment preceding it and the change of the *yi* into an *ī* in all forms with the remark that the *ī* is elided in the imperfect forms of the fem. pl. in which the vowelled *–n, the -na*, is suffixed to.

6.5.6. The passive participle of the verb with 2nd radical *w* *mafᶜ(u)wlun/ mafᶜ(u)ūlun:* the sequence of the 2nd radical *w* vowelled by a ḍamma, preceded by a sukūn and followed by the infixed vowelless *ū:* the transfer of the ḍamma to the vowelless segment preceding it, the change of the *wu* into an *ū* and the elision of one of the wāws.

6.5.7. The passive participle of the verb with 2nd radical *y* *mafᶜ(u)wlun/ mafᶜ(u)ūlun:* the sequence of the 2nd radical *y* vowelled by a ḍamma, preceded by a sukūn and followed by the infixed vowelless *ū:* the transfer of the ḍamma to the vowelless segment preceding it, the change of the ḍamma into a kasra, the elision of the infixed *ū* or the 2nd radical *y,* and the change of the *y* into an *ī* or the *ū* into an *ī* respectively.

6.5.8. The imperative of the verb with 2nd radical *w* or *y:* the sequence of the 2nd vowelled radical *w* or *y* that is preceded by a sukūn: the transfer of the vowel to the vowelless segment preceding it, the lengthening of the vowel into an *ū* or an *ī* respectively, and the elision of the *ū* or *ī* in both the 3rd person of the masc. sing. and the 3rd person of the fem. pl. and its retaining in the remaining persons.

6.5.9. The active participle of the verb with 2nd radical *w* or *y:* the sequence of the 2nd radical *w* or *y* vowelled by a kasra and preceded by a vowelless *ā:* the change of the *wi* or *yi* into *ʾi* respectively.

6.5.10. Anomalous cases of active participles of the verb with 2nd radical *w:* the sequence of the 2nd radical *w* vowelled by a kasra and preceded by a vowelless *ā* in them: the elision of the *w* or the transposition of segments together with the elision of the glide.

6.5.11. The verbal noun of Form I of the verb with 2nd radical *w* or *y:* the sequence in which the 2nd radical *w* or *y* is vowelless and preceded by a fatḥa: the soundness of the *w* or *y.*

6.5.12. The verbal nouns of Form IV *ʾifᶜ(a)ālun* and Form X *ʾistifᶜ(a)ālun* of the verb with 2nd radical *w:* the sequence in which the *w* is vowelled by a fatḥa and preceded by a sukūn: the transfer of the *w's* fatḥa to the segment preceding it, the change of the *w* into an *ā,* the elision of one of the alifs and the compensation with the *tāʾ marbūṭa.*

6.5.13. The passive voice of the perfect of the verb with 2nd radical *w* or *y:* the sequence of the 2nd radical *w* or *y* vowelled by a kasra and preceded by a ḍamma: the transfer of the kasra to the 1st radical and hence the change of the 1st radical's ḍamma into a kasra, the change of the *w* into a *y* or the *y* into an *ī* respectively, or the elision of the 2nd radical *w's* or *y's* kasra and the lengthening of the ḍamma preceding it into an *ū*.

6.5.14. The passive voice of the imperfect of the verb with 2nd radical *w* or *y:* the sequence of the 2nd radical *w* or *y* vowelled by a fatḥa and preceded by a sukūn: the transfer of the fatḥa to the 1st vowelless radical and the change of the *w* or the *y* into an *ā*.

6.5.15. The noun of place of the verb with 2nd radical *w:* the sequence of the 2nd radical *w* vowelled by a fatḥa and preceded by a sukūn: the transfer of the fatḥa to the vowelless segment preceding it and the change of the *wa* into an *ā*

6.5.1. The 3rd persons of the perfect with 2nd radical w or y: the sequence of the vowelled 2nd weak radical preceded by a fatḥa: the change of the vowelled weak radical into an ā:

I shall discuss at first the verb with 2nd radical *w* and then the verb with 2nd radical *y*.

6.5.1.1. The verb with 2nd radical *w:*

The verb with 2nd radical *w* is divided in the perfect between the conjugation *faᶜala* in which the 2nd radical is vowelled by a fatḥa and the conjugation *faᶜula* in which it is vowelled by a ḍamma. In both these cases the vowelled *w* is changed into an *ā*.

1- The conjugation faᶜala:

In the conjugation *faᶜala* the 2nd radical *w* is vowelled by a fatḥa and preceded by one, which results in the change of *wa* into an *ā* (cf. Ibn Ğinnī, *Munṣif I,* 247, Åkesson, *Ibn Masᶜūd* 282-284: fol. 27a-27b; and for discussions see par. 9.1.2.1. and 10.1.12.1.). It is remarked that *qawala* with the 2nd radical *w* vowelled by a fatḥa and preceded by one becomes *q(a)āla* "to say" with the *wa* changed into an *ā*.

The 3rd person of the fem. sing. is *q(a)āla-t* and the 3rd person of the masc. pl. *q(a)āl(u)-ū.*

2- The conjugation faᶜula:

In the conjugation *faᶜula* the 2nd radical *w* is vowelled by a ḍamma and is preceded by a fatḥa, which results in the change of the *wu* into an *ā* (cf. Ibn Ǧinnı, *Munṣif I,* 247, Åkesson, *Ibn Masᶜūd* 282-284: fol. 27a-27b, and for this sequence see par. 9.1.4.). It is noted as an example that *ṭawula* with the 2nd radical *w* vowelled by ḍamma and preceded by a fatḥa becomes *ṭ(a)āla* "to become long" with the *wu* changed into an *ā*.

The 3rd person of the fem. sing. is *ṭ(a)āla-t* and of the 3rd person of the masc. pl. *ṭ(a)āl(u)-ū.*

3- The conjugation faᶜila:

In the conjugation *faᶜila* the 2nd radical *w* is vowelled by a kasra and is preceded by fatḥa, which results in the change of the *wi* into an *ā* (cf. Ibn Ǧinnī, *Munṣif I,* 247, and for a discussion concerning the sequence of a glide vowelled by a kasra and preceded by a fatḥa see par. 9.1.3.). It is observed as an example that *ḫawifa* with the 2nd radical *w* vowelled by kasra and preceded by a fatḥa becomes *ḫ(a)āfa* "to be afraid" with the *wi* changed into an *ā*.

The 3rd person of the fem. sing. is *ḫ(a)āfa-t* and of the 3rd person of the masc. pl. *ḫ(a)āf(u)-ū.*

6.5.1.2. The verb with 2nd radical y:

The verb with 2nd radical *y* is divided in the perfect between the conjugation *faᶜala* in which the 2nd radical is vowelled by a fatḥa and the conjugation *fa*^{c}*ila* in which it is vowelled by a kasra. In both these cases the vowelled *y* is changed into an *ā*.

1- The conjugation fa^{c}*ala:*

The same phonological change that is carried out in the verb with 2nd radical *w* of the conjugation *fa*^{c}*ala* (cf. par. 6.5.1.1.: 1) is carried out in the verb with 2nd radical *y* of the same conjugation. In this case, the *y*, which is vowelled by a fatḥa and preceded by one, is changed into an *ā* (cf. Ibn Ǧinnı, *Munṣif I,* 247, Åkesson, *Ibn Mas*^{c}*ūd* 282-284: fol. 27a-27b; and for discussions see par. 9.1.2.1. and 10.1.12.2.). An example is *baya*^{c}*a* with the 2nd radical *y* vowelled by a fatḥa and preceded by one, which becomes *b(a)ā*^{c}*a* "to buy" with the *ya* changed into an *ā*.

The 3rd person of the fem. sing. is *b(a)ā*^{c}*a-t* and of the 3rd person of the masc. pl. *b(a)ā*^{c}*(u)-ū*.

2- The conjugation *fa*^{c}*ila:*

In the conjugation *fa*^{c}*ila* the 2nd radical *y* is vowelled by a kasra and preceded by a fatḥa (for discussions concerning this sequence see par. 9.1.3.), which results in the change of the *yi* into an *ā*. An example is *hayiba* with the 2nd radical *y* vowelled by a kasra and preceded by a fatḥa, which becomes *h(a)āba* "to be afraid" with the *yi* changed into an *ā*.

The 3rd person of the fem. sing. is *h(a)āba-t* and of the 3rd person of the masc. pl. *h(a)āb(u)-ū*.

6.5.2. The persons in the perfect of the verb with 2nd radical w or y in which the vowelled pronoun of the agent is suffixed: the sequence of the vowelless 2nd radical ā (that is substituted for the 2nd weak radical) preceded by a fatḥa and fol-

lowed by the vowelless 3rd radical: the elision of the ā and the change of the 1st radical's fatḥa into another vowel:

In the 1st persons of the sing. and pl. and the 2nd persons of the masc. and fem. sing. and pl. of perfect verbs with 2nd radical *w* or *y,* the vowelled pronoun of the agent, namely the *-tu* "1st sing.", the *-nā* "1st pl.", the *-ta* "2nd masc. sing.", the *-ti* "2nd fem. sing.", the *-tumā* "2nd /dual", the *-tum* "2nd masc. pl." and the *-tunna* "2nd fem. pl."., are suffixed to the form. As already mentioned, the 2nd weak radical, whether it is a *w* or *y,* is changed into a vowelless *ā* on account of the influence of the fatḥa preceding it and of its vowelling (cf. par. 6.5.1.). The vowelless *ā* becomes in these mentioned persons connected to the vowelless 3rd radical. This combination of two vowelless segments gives rise to the following procedures: the first is the elision of the 2nd changed radical *ā* and the second is the change of the 1st radical's vowel, namely the fatḥa, into another vowel that can in some cases give notice in its nature of the elided 2nd weak radical, whether it is a *w* or *y,* or of the underlying vowel of the 2nd radical that marks the conjugation. I shall discuss these cases in the following paragraphs.

6.5.2.1. The verb with 2nd radical w:

The conjugations that I take up are *faᶜala* and *faᶜila.*

1- The conjugation *faᶜala:*

An example is *qawala* "he said" that belongs to the conjugation *faᶜala yafᶜulu* and not to the conjugation *faᶜula yafᶜulu* (cf. Ibn Ǧinnī, *Munṣif I,* 236-237, Bakkūš, *Taṣrīf* 142-143, Bohas/Kouloughli, *Linguistic* 79) to which one of the pronouns of the agent, e.g. the *-na* of the 3rd person of the fem. pl. is suffixed to. The procedure is the following (cf. Åkesson, *Ibn*

Masᶜūd 288: fol. 29b, Bakkūš, *Taṣrīf* 136): *qawal-na* with the 2nd radical *w* vowelled by a fatḥa and preceded by one becomes *q(a)āl-na* with the *wa* changed into an *ā*. As there is in *q(a)āl-na* a cluster of two vowelless segments, the *ā* and the *l*, the *ā* is elided so that it becomes *qal-na*. It can be observed that what seems peculiar is that the fatḥa of the 1st radical *q* in *qal-na* is replaced by a ḍamma to give notice of the elided 2nd radical *w*, namely *qul-na*.

The same procedure is carried out when the remaining pronouns of the agent are suffixed, namely *qawal-tu* "I said" resulting in *qul-tu, qawal-nā* "we said" resulting in *qul-nā, qawal-ta* "you said /masc. sing." resulting in *qul-ta, qawal-ti* "you said /fem. sing." resulting in *qul-ti, qawal-tumā* "you said /dual" resulting in *qul-tumā, qawal-tum* "you said /masc. pl." resulting in *qul-tum* and *qawal-tunna* "you said /fem. pl." resulting in *qul-tunna*.

2- The conjugation faᶜila:

An example is *ḫawifa* "he was afraid". In the case of the suffixation of the agent pronoun to it, e.g. the *-na* of the 3rd person of the fem. pl., namely *ḫawif-na*, the following procedure is carried out (cf. Åkesson, *Ibn Masᶜūd* 288: fol. 29b): *ḫawif-na* with the 2nd radical *w* vowelled by a kasra and preceded by a fatḥa becomes *ḫ(a)āf-na* after that its *wi* is changed into an *ā*. As there is in *ḫ(a)āf-na* a cluster of two vowelless segments: the *ā* and the *f*, the *ā* is elided so that it becomes *ḫaf-na*. Then what is special for it is that the fatḥa of the 1st radical is replaced by a kasra, which is underlyingly the vowel of the 2nd radical *w* marking the conjugation *faᶜila*, so that it becomes *ḫif-na*.

6.5.2.2. The verb with 2nd radical y:

The conjugation that I discuss is *faᶜala*, e.g. *bayaᶜa* "he sold". In the case of the suffixation of the agent pronoun, e.g. the

-na of the 3rd person of the fem. pl., the following procedure is carried out: *baya^{c}-na* with the 2nd radical *y* vowelled by a fatḥa and preceded by one becomes *b(a)ā^{c}-na* after that its *ya* is changed into an *ā.* As there is in *b(a)ā^{c}-na* a cluster of two vowelless segments: the *ā* and the ^{c}, the *ā* is elided so that it becomes *ba^{c}-na.* The fatḥa of the 1st radical is then replaced by a kasra to give notice that the verb is with 2nd radical *y*, so it becomes *bi^{c}-na.*

The same concerns the remaining pronouns with the agent suffixes, namely *baya^{c}-tu* "I bought" resulting in *bi^{c}-tu, baya^{c}-nā* "we bought" resulting in *bi^{c}-nā, baya^{c}-ta* "you bought /masc. sing." resulting in *bi^{c}-ta, baya^{c}-ti* "you bought /fem. sing." resulting in *bi^{c}-ti, baya^{c}-tumā* "you bought /dual" resulting in *bi^{c}-tumā, baya^{c}-tum* "you bought /masc. pl." resulting in *bi^{c}-tum* and *baya^{c}-tunna* "you bought /fem. pl." resulting in *bi^{c}-tunna.*

Another example with the suffixation of the agent pronoun in the 2nd person of the masc. sing., the *-ta, is sayar-ta > s(a)ār-ta > sar-ta > sir-ta* "you moved on" (cf. Bakkūš, *Taṣrīf* 139).

6.5.3. The imperfect of the verb with 2nd radical w or y of the conjugation yaf^{c}alu: the sequence of the 2nd weak radical vowelled by a fatḥa and preceded by a sukūn: the transfer of the fatḥa to the vowelless segment preceding it and the change of the vowelled weak radical into an ā in all forms with the remark that the ā is elided in the imperfect forms of the fem. pl. in which the vowelled –n, the -na, is suffixed to:

I shall discuss at first the verb with 2nd radical *w* and then the verb with 2nd radical *y*.

6.5.3.1. The verb with 2nd radical w:

An example of a verb that is formed according to this conjugation is *yaḫwafu* "he is afraid". The phonological change involves two steps: the first is the transfer of the *w's* fatḥa to the vowelless 1st radical *ḫ* preceding it, which results in *yaḫawfu,* and the second one is the change of the vowelless *w* into an *ā* on account of the influence of the fatḥa preceding it, which results in *yaḫ(a)āfu.* These two steps answer to two different principles: the first is that when the glide is vowelled and follows a sukūn its vowel is shifted to the vowelless segment preceding it (for discussions see par. 9.1.12.) and the second is that when the glide is vowelless and is preceded by a fatḥa it can be changed into an *ā* (for discussions see par. 9.1.1.).

It can be remarked concerning the 2nd person and 3rd person of the fem. pl. to which the vowelled *–n, the –na,* is suffixed to, namely *taḫ(a)āf-na* "you are afraid /fem. pl." and *yaḫ(a)āf-na* "they are afraid /fem. pl.", that the 3rd radical becomes vowelless through the suffixation. This entails a cluster of two vowelless segments, the *ā* and the *f,* which is the reason why the *ā* is elided resulting in *taḫaf-na* and *yaḫ(a)f-na.*

6.5.3.2. The verb with 2nd radical y:

An example of a verb that is formed according to this conjugation is *yahyabu* "he is afraid". A study of the phonological changes shows the following: *yahyabu* with the 2nd radical *y* vowelled by a fatḥa preceded by a sukūn becomes *yahaybu* after that the *y's* fatḥa is shifted to the 1st radical. In *yahaybu* we have the vowelless *y* preceded by a fatḥa which forces the change of the *y* into an *ā* so that it becomes *yaḫ(a)ābu.*

Alike the verb with 2nd radical *w* of the same conjugation (cf. par. 6.5.3.: 1.), the *ā* is elided in the 2nd and 3rd person of the fem. pl. of the verb of this conjugation for the same reason. Hence *tahab-na* "you are afraid /fem. pl." is said instead of *tah(a)āb-na* and *yahab-na* "they are afraid /fem. pl." instead of *yah(u)āb-na.*

6.5.4. The imperfect of the verb with 2nd radical w of the conjugation yaf^{c}ulu: the sequence of the 2nd radical w vowelled by a ḍamma and preceded by a sukūn: the transfer of the ḍamma to the vowelless segment preceding it, the change of the wu into an ū with the remark that the -ū is elided in the forms of the fem. pl. in which the vowelled –n, the -na, is suffixe to:

In the imperfect that is formed according to *yaf^{c}ulu,* the 2nd radical *w* is vowelled by a ḍamma and preceded by a sukūn, e.g. *yaqwulu* "he says". The phonological procedure that is carried out implies the transfer of the ḍamma of the 2nd radical *w* to the 1st vowelless radical, and the change of the *w* into an *ū* on account of the influence of the ḍamma (cf. Ibn Ǧinnī, *Munṣif I,* 247 and this study par. 9.1.15.). An example is *yaqwulu* that has the 2nd radical *w* vowelled by a ḍamma and preceded by a sukūn. It becomes *yaquwlu* after that the *w's* ḍamma is shifted to the vowelless *q*. As the vowelless *w* is preceded by a ḍamma in it, the *w* is changed into an *ū* so that it becomes *yaq(u)ūlu.*

It is observed that as with *taḫ(a)āf-na* which results in *taḫaf-na* "you are afraid /fem. pl." and *yaḫ(a)āf-na* which results in *yaḫaf-na* "they are afraid /fem. pl." with the elision of the *ā* (cf. par. 6.5.3.: 1), the *ū* is elided in the 2nd and 3rd person of the fem. pl. of the verb of this conjugation for the same reason. Hence *taqul-na* "you say /fem. pl." is said instead of *taq(u)ūl-na* and *yaqul-na* "they say /fem. pl." instead of *yaq(u)ūl-na.* The procedure that is carried out form the underlying form *yaqwul-na* to the result *yaqul-na* is the following (cf. Åkesson, *Ibn Mas^{c}ūd* 290: fol. 30a): *yaqwul-na* with the 2nd radical *w* vowelled by a ḍamma and preceded by a sukūn becomes *yaquwl-na* after that the *w's* ḍamma is shifted to the vowelless *q*. As there is in it a cluster of two vowelless segments, the *w* and the *l*, the *w* is elided so that it becomes *yaqul-na.*

According to a modern theory, the *w* in *yaquwl-na* is said to be shortened into a ḍamma, which is the case when the *w* is followed by a sukūn (cf. Bakkūš, *Taṣrīf* 136).

6.5.5. The imperfect of the verb with 2nd radical y of the conjugation yaf^{c}ilu: the sequence of the 2nd radical y vowelled by a kasra and preceded by a sukūn: the transfer of the kasra to the vowelless segment preceding it and the change of the yi into an ī in all forms with the remark that the ī is elided in the imperfect forms of the fem. pl. in which the vowelled –n, the -na, is suffixed is suffixed to:

In the conjugation *yaf^{c}ilu,* the 2nd radical *y* is vowelled by a kasra and is preceded by a sukūn. An example is *yabyi^{c}u* "he sells" (cf. Åkesson, *Ibn Mas^{c}ūd* 286: fol. 29a, Bakkūš, *Taṣrīf* 62). The phonological change that is carried out in it implies the transfer of the kasra of the 2nd radical *y* to the 1st vowelless radical resulting in the lengthening of the *y*. This phonological procedure answers to a principle that when the glide is vowelled and follows a sukūn, its vowel is shifted to the vowelless segment preceding it (cf. par. 9.1.13.). I illustrate it as follows: *yabyi^{c}u* with the 2nd radical *y* vowelled by a kasra and preceded by a sukūn becomes *yabiy^{c}u* after that the *y's* kasra is shifted to the *b*. As the vowelless *y* is preceded by a kasra in it, the *y* is changed into an *ī* so that it becomes *yab(i)ī^{c}u.*

The *ī* is elided in the 2nd and 3rd person of the fem. pl. of the verb of this conjugation. Hence *tabi^{c}-na* "you sell /fem. pl." is said instead of *tab(i)ī^{c}-na* and *yabi^{c}-na* "they sell /fem. pl." instead of *yab(i)ī*ᶜ*-na*. Hence *yabyi*ᶜ*-na* with the 2nd radical *y* vowelled by a kasra and preceded by a sukūn becomes *yabiy*ᶜ*-na* after that the *y's* kasra is shifted to the *b*. As there is in it a cluster of two vowelless segments, the *y* and ᶜ, the *y* is elided so that it becomes *yabi*ᶜ*-na*.

6.5.6. The passive participle of the verb with 2nd radical w mafᶜ(u)wlun / mafᶜ(u)ūlun: the sequence of the 2nd radical w vowelled by a ḍamma, preceded by a sukūn and followed by the infixed vowelless ū: the transfer of the ḍamma to the vowelless segment preceding it, the change of the wu into an ū and the elision of one of the wāws:

In the pattern of the passive participle form *maf*ᶜ*uwlun / maf*ᶜ*(u)ūlun*, e.g. *maqwuwlun / maqw(u)ūlun* "what is said", the first step of the phonological change is that the ḍamma of the 2nd radical *w* is shifted to the vowelless segment preceding it (cf. Åkesson, *Ibn Mas*ᶜ*ūd* 292: fol. 31a and this study par. 9.1.15.). Thus *maqw(u)ūlun* with the 2nd radical *w* vowelled by a ḍamma and preceded by a sukūn becomes *maquwūlun* after that the *w's* ḍamma is shifted to the *q*.

At this point in the treatment, two different analyses can be mentioned which lead *maquwūlun* to the result *maq(u)ūlun*. The steps that are involved in them refer to Sībawaihi's and al-Aḫfaše's different theories (for discussions see Zamaḫšarī, 180-181, Ibn Yaᶜīš, X, 78-81, Åkesson, *Ibn Mas*ᶜ*ūd* 292: fol. 31a, Howell, IV, fasc. I, 1498-1501).

According to the theory of Sībawaihi, *maquwūlun* which presents a cluster of two vowelless wāws, the *w* preceded by a ḍamma and the *ū*, becomes *maquwlun* after that the infixed wāw, i.e. the *ū*, is elided. According to him, *maquwlun* is formed according to the pattern *mafu*ᶜ*lun*. As the vowelless *w* is preceded by a ḍamma, the *w* is changed into an *ū* so that it becomes *maq(u)ūlun.*

According to Sībawaihi it is the infixed wāw: the *ū,* that is elided from *maquwūlun* on account of the principle that the elision of the added segment, - by which he means the infix in this form -, is more prior than the elision of a radical.

Al-Aḫfaš's approach is different as he considers that in *maquwūlun* it is the 2nd radical *w* that is elided and not the infixed wāw as Sībawaihi believes it to be. So according to him *maquwlun* > *maq(u)ūlun* is formed according to the pattern *maf(u)ūlun,* and not *mafu*^{c}*lun* as according to Sībawaihi's theory. Al-Aḫfaš considers that it is 2nd radical *w* that is elided because he adheres to the principle that the added segment, the *ū,* is an infix marking the passive participle and the marker is not to be elided. Sībawaihi's answer to this argument is that the marker is not to be elided if it is the only marker in the form, but it can be elided if there is another marker in the word, which is the case here, as we have the *m* prefix.

6.5.7. The passive participle of the verb with 2nd radical y maf^{c}***(u)wlun / maf***^{c}***(u)ūlun: the sequence of the 2nd radical y vowelled by a ḍamma, preceded by a sukūn and followed by the infixed vowelless ū: the transfer of the ḍamma to the vowelless segment preceding it, the change of the ḍamma into a kasra, the elision of the infixed ū or the 2nd radical y, and the change of the y into an ī or the ū into an ī respectively:***

An example of a passive participle of a verb with 2nd radical *y* is *maby(u)ū*^{c}*un* "sold" (cf. par. 9.1.16.). The 1st step of the phonological procedure that is carried out in it is the following (cf. Åkesson, *Ibn Mas*^{c}*ūd* 292: fol. 31a): *maby(u)w*^{c}*un* > *maby(u)ū*^{c}*un* with the 2nd radical *y* vowelled by a ḍamma and preceded by a sukūn becomes *mabuywᶜun* and then *mabuyūᶜun* after that the *y's* ḍamma is shifted to the *b*.

As with the passive participle with 2nd radical *w* *maqw(u)ūlun* (cf. par. 6.5.6.), both Sībawaihi's and al-Aḫfaše's differences of opinions concerning the phonological changes that are carried out from *mabuyūᶜun* to the result *mab(i)īᶜun,* are applied (for discussions see Zamaḫšarī, 180-181, Ibn Yaᶜīš, X, 78-81, Åkesson, *Ibn Masᶜūd* 292: fols. 31a-31b, Howell, IV, fasc. I, 1498-1501). They can be illustrated as follows:

According to Sībawaihi, *mabuyūᶜun* that has a cluster of a vowelless *y* and *ū* becomes *mabuyᶜun* after the elision of the infixed *ū*. As there is in it a vowelless *y* preceded by a ḍamma, the ḍamma is changed into a kasra so that it becomes *mabiyᶜun.* So according to his theory, *mabiyᶜun* is formed according to *mafiᶜlun.* It can be observed that in *mabiyᶜun,* the vowelless *y* is preceded by a kasra, which is the reason why the *y* is changed into an *ī*, namely *mab(i)īᶜun.*

According to al-Aḫfaš, *mabuyūᶜun* which has a cluster of a vowelless *y* and *ū* becomes *mabu(ū)ᶜun* after that its 2nd radical *y* is elided. Then the ḍamma of the *b* is replaced by a kasra as an indication of the elided *y* so that it becomes *mabiūᶜun.* As there is in it a disliked combination of an *ū* preceded by a kasra, the *ū* is changed into an *ī* so that it becomes *mab(i)īᶜun.* So according to his theory, *mab(i)īᶜun* is formed according to *maf(i)īlun.*

An analysis of both these theories shows that according to Sībawaihi's, it is the infixed *ū* that is elided from *mabuyūᶜun* before that the other changes are carried out in it whereas according to al-Aḫfaš it is the 2nd radical *y* that is elided. As for the reasons why the infixed segment is elided in the first case and the radical in the other, they are the same as those concerning *maqwuwlun* / *maqw(u)ūlun* (cf. 6.5.6.).

6.5.8. The imperative of the verb with 2nd radical w or y: the sequence of the 2nd vowelled radical w or y that is preceded by a sukūn: the transfer of the vowel to the vowelless segment preceding it, the lengthening of the vowel into an ū or an ī respectively, and the elision of the ū or ī in both the 3rd person of the masc. sing. and the 3rd person of the fem. pl. and its retaining in the remaining persons:

I shall discuss at first the verb with 2nd radical *w* and then the verb with 2nd radical *y*.

6.5.8.1. The verb with 2nd radical w:

In the case of the 3rd person of the masc. sing. of the imperative that is formed according to *ʾufwul (ufᶜul),* the 2nd radical *w* is vowelled by a ḍamma and preceded by a sukūn. The phonological changes that are carried out imply the transfer of the 2nd radical *w's* vowel to the vowelless 1st radical preceding it, the elision of the connective hamza of the imperative on account that the 1st radical is now vowelled and hence the hamza that is prefixed to hinder the word from beginning with a vowelless segment is not more needed, the change of the *w* into an *ū* and the elision of the *ū* to avoid the cluster of two vowelless segments.

An example is *ʾuqwul* that becomes *qul* "say!" (cf. Åkesson, *Ibn Masᶜūd* 290: fol. 30a, ᶜAbd al-Raḥīm, *Ṣarf* 31, and for this sequence see par. 9.1.15). The procedure is the following: *ʾuqwul* with the 2nd radical *w* vowelled by a ḍamma and preceded by a sukūn becomes *ʾuquwl* after that the *w's* ḍamma is shifted to the vowelless *q*. As the 1st radical *q* is vowelled, the connective hamza of the imperative is elided because it is not more needed, so it became *quwl.* The vowelless *w* is here preceded by a ḍamma which is why it is changed into an *ū* so it becomes *q(u)ūl.* As there is now a cluster of two vowelless segments, the *ū* and *l,* the *ū* is elided so it becomes *qul.*

The *ū* is as well elided in the 3rd person of the fem. pl. *qul-na* "Say /fem. pl." which is not said *q(u)ūl-na* to avoid the combination of the vowelless *ū* and the 3rd vowelless radical *l.*

However in the forms of the imperative to which the vowelless agent pronoun is suffixed to, namely the 2nd person of the fem. sing. with the *-ī* suffix, e.g. *q(u)ūl(i)-ī,* the dual with the *ā* suffix, e.g. *q(u)ūl(a)-ā* and the 2nd person of the masc. pl., with the *-ū* suffix, e.g. *q(u)ūl(u)-ū,* the 2nd radical *ū* is maintained. The reason is that the 3rd radical of the verb, the *l,* is not more vowelless due to the suffixation of the pronoun, but vowelled with a vowel that agrees with the nature of the suffix, and hence the situation of having two vowelless segments which would force the elision is not actual in this case.

6.5.8.2. The verb with 2nd radical y:

The phonological changes are the same as those concerning the 3rd person of the masc. sing. of the imperative of verbs with 2nd radical *w* that are formed according to *ʾufʿul* (cf. above), except that conjugation is instead *ʾifʿil,* e.g. *ʾibyiʿ* "sell!". Hence the kasra of the *y* is shifted to the vowelless segment preceding it, namely *ʾibiyʿ*, the connective hamza is elided, namely *biyʿ*, the *y* is changed into an *ī,* namely *b(i)īʿ*, and is then elided, namely *biʿ*.

The *ī* is as well elided in the 3rd person of the fem. pl. *biʿ-na* "sell /fem. pl." which is not said *b(i)īʿ-na* to avoid the combination of the vowelless ī and the 3rd vowelless radical ʿ.

In the forms of the imperative to which the vowelless agent pronoun is suffixed to, namely the 2nd person of the fem. sing. with the *-ī* suffix, e.g. *b(i)yʿ(i)-ī* > *b(i)īʿ(i)-ī,* the dual with the ā suffix, e.g. *b(i)y^c(a)-ā* > *b(i)ī^c(a)-ā* and the 2nd person of the masc. pl., with the *-ū* suffix, e.g. *b(i)y^c(u)-ū* > *b(i)ī^c(u)-ū*, the 2nd radical *y* is maintained.

6.5.9. The active participle of the verb with 2nd radical w or y: the sequence of the 2nd radical w or y vowelled by a kasra and preceded by a vowelless ā: the change of the wi or yi into ʾi respectively:

I shall discuss at first the verb with 2nd radical *w* and then the verb with 2nd radical *y*.

6.5.9.1. The verb with 2nd radical w:

The active participle's form of the verb with 2nd radical *w* is *f(a)ā^{c}ilun*. In this form the 2nd radical *w* is vowelled by a kasra and preceded by a vowelless *ā*. The phonological procedure that is carried out in it implies that the *wi* is changed into *ʾi* (cf. ^{c}Abd al-Raḥīm, *Ṣarf* 80, this study par. 9.1.14. and par. 10.1.1.2.: 3). An example is *q(a)āwilun* that becomes *q(a)āʾilun* "a sayer".

The phonological procedure is different according to Ibn Mas^{c}ūd (cf. Åkesson, *Ibn Mas^{c}ūd* 290: fol. 30b). He adheres to the theory that *q(a)āwilun* with the 2nd radical *w* vowelled by a kasra is influenced by the fatḥa preceding the *ā*, and the *ā* is not taken into account because of its vowellessness. So the *wi* is changed into an *ā* on account of the influence of the fatḥa preceding it, so that it becomes *q(a)āālun*. The reason why one of the alifs is not dropped resulting in *q(a)ālun*, is to prevent that the active participle is mixed up with the perfect *q(a)āla* "he said". The 2nd *ā* is therefore changed into a hamza to prevent the combination of two vowelless alifs, so it became *q(a)āʾilun*.

6.5.9.2. The verb with 2nd radical y:

Alike the active participle of the verb with 2nd radical *w* that is formed according to *fā^{c}ilun* (cf. par. 6.5.9.: 1), the active participle of the verb with 2nd radical *y*, has its *yi* changed into *ʾi* instead (cf. par. 9.1.14, 10.1.1.3.: 2). An example is *b(a)āyiᶜun* with the 2nd radical *y* vowelled by a kasra and preceded by an *ā* that becomes *b(a)āʾiᶜun* "a seller" after that the *yi* is changed into an *ʾi*.

6.5.10. Anomalous cases of active participles of the verb with 2nd radical w: the sequence of the 2nd radical w vowelled by a kasra and preceded by a vowelless ā in them: the elision of the w or the transposition of segments together with the elision of the glide:

The cases that I will discuss are those that imply the elision of the 2nd radical *w* and the transposition of the segments together with the elision.

1- The elision of the 2nd radical w:

In some cases of active participles, the 2nd weak radical is elided (cf. Åkesson, *Ibn Masᶜūd* 290-292: fol. 30b). Some examples are *h(a)āᶜun* "vomitting" used instead of *h(a)āʾiᶜun* underlyingly *h(a)āwiᶜun* from *hawaᶜa* "to vomit", *l(a)āᶜun* "suffering" used instead of *l(a)āʾiᶜun* underlyingly *l(a)āwiᶜun* from *lawaᶜa* "to suffer, burn" and *h(a)ārun* "undermined" used instead of *h(a)āʾirun* underlyingly *h(a)āwirun* from *hawara* "to demolish". The variant *h(a)ārun* (instead of *h(a)āʾirun)* with the elision of the *ʾi* occurs in the genetive in the sur. 9: 109 *(ᶜalā šafā ǧurufin hārin)* "On an undermined sand-cliff". Hence these examples of active participles are formed according to the pattern *fālun* and not *fāᶜilun*. The phonological changes concerning one of these examples, e.g. *h(a)āwiᶜun* that becomes *h(a)āᶜun* "vomitting", are the following: *h(a)āwiᶜun* with the 2nd radical *w* vowelled by a kasra and preceded by an *ā* becomes *h(a)āʾiᶜun* after that the *wi* is changed into an *ʾi.* The procedure resulting in the elision of the 2nd weak radical is that the 2nd radical *w* vowelled by a kasra in *h(a)āwiᶜun* is influenced by the fatḥa of the *h* preceding the *ā,* on account of the principle that the *ā* is not taken into account because of its vowellessness. So the *wi* is changed into an *ā* so that it becomes *h(a)āāᶜun.* As there is in it a cluster of two vowelless alifs, one of them is elided so that it becomes *h(a)āᶜun.*

2- *The transposition of segments together with the elision of the glide*

The transposition of the segments is carried out in some examples (for an example concerning the active participle of a verb with 1st radical *w,* e.g. *w(a)āḥidun* > *ḥ(a)ādin* see par. 5.2.1.6.).

An example is *š(a)āwikun* "sharp" in which the 2nd radical *w* changes place with the 3rd radical (cf. Ibn Manẓūr, IV, 2362-2363). It becomes at first *š(a)ākiwun* formed according to the pattern *f(a)āliᶜun* instead of *f(a)āᶜilun.* As the form ends with a weak radical, it resembles the active participle of verbs with 3rd weak radical, e.g. the underlying forms *r(a)āmiyun* for the nominative and *r(a)āmiyin* for the genitive which becomes *r(a)āmin* "one who is throwing" for both the nominative and the genitive (cf. Wright, II, 90). This is how it is understood that the variant *š(a)ākiwun* has its last radical elided and the *tanwin* "nunation" is given to its 2nd radical on the analogy of this category of forms, so that it becomes *š(a)ākin.* It occurs in this verse recited by Ṭarīf b. Tamīm al-ᶜAmbarī al-Tamīmi, cited by Sībawaihi, II, 419, Ibn Ǧinnī, *Munṣif II,* 53, III, 66, Howell, IV, fasc. I, 1494, Åkesson, *Ibn Masᶜūd* 317: (292):

> *"Fa-taᶜarrafūnī ʾinnanī ʾanā ḏākumu*
> *šākin silāḥī fī l-ḥawādiṯi muᶜlimu".*Then seek to know me: verily that I, this one, [am such that]

sharp is my weapon in mishaps, am a bearer of the cognizance, or badge, or device, of the valiant".

6.5.11. The verbal noun of Form I of the verb with 2nd radical w or y: the sequence in which the 2nd radical w or y is vowelless and preceded by a fatḥa: the soundness of the w or y:

The verbal noun of Form I of the verb with 2nd radical *w* or *y* is *faᶜlun.* In both these forms the 2nd weak radical is vowelless and preceded by a fatḥa (cf. par. 9.1.1.), which is the reason why it remains sound. An example of a verbal noun with 2nd radical *w* is *qawlun* "a saying" and with 2nd radical *y* *bayᶜun* "a selling".

6.5.12. The verbal nouns of Form IV ˀifᶜ(a)ālun and Form X ˀistifᶜ(a)ālun of the verb with 2nd radical w: the sequence in which the w is vowelled by a fatḥa and preceded by a sukūn: the transfer of the w's fatḥa to the segment preceding it, the change of the w into an ā, the elision of one of the alifs and the compensation with the tāˀ marbūṭa:

In some examples of verbal forms of Form IV *ˀīfᶜ(a)ālun,* e.g. *ˀiqw(a)āmun* "the act of being constant (in prayer)", the 2nd radical *w* is vowelled by a fatḥa and preceded by a sukūn. The phonological changes that are carried out in it resulting in *ˀiq(a)āmatun* are the following: *ˀiqw(a)āmun* with the 2nd radical *w* vowelled by a fatḥa and preceded by a sukūn becomes at first *ˀiqawāmun* after that the fatḥa is shifted to the vowelless *q* and then *ˀiq(a)āāmun* after that the *w* is changed into an *ā.* As there is in it a cluster of two vowelless segments, the alifs, one of them is elided resulting in *ˀiq(a)āmun,* and the *tāˀ marbūṭa* is suffixed to compensate for this elision so that it becomes

ʾiq(a)āmatun. It can be mentioned that the *tāʾ marbūṭa* is elided from *wa-ʾiq(a)āmatu* (cf. Sībawaihi, II, 260-261, Zamaḫšarī, 179, de Sacy, I, 294, Howell, I, fasc. III 1126, fasc. IV, 1571-1572, IV, fasc. I 1424, Wright, II, 120-121), in the sur. 21: 73 *(wa-ʾiqāmu l-ṣalāti)* "to establish regular prayers", the reason being that *l-ṣalāti,* which is the second element of the construct state, is considered as a substitute that compensates for the elided *tāʾ marbūṭa* (compare the case of *ᶜida l-ʾamri* in par. 5.2.1.2.).

The same phonological changes apply for Form X of the verbal noun that is formed according to *ʾistifᶜ(a)ālun,* e.g. *ʾistiqw(a)āmun* that becomes *ʾistiq(a)āmatun* "the act of walking uprightly in the paths of religion". The 2nd radical *w* in *ʾistiqw(a)āmun,* which is vowelled by a fatḥa, is changed into an *ā* after that its fatḥa is shifted to the *q,* so that it becomes *ʾistiq(a)āāmun,* then one of the alifs is elided to avoid the cluster of two vowelless alifs, and the *tāʾ marbūṭa* is suffixed to the word as a compensation for this elision.

6.5.13. The passive voice of the perfect of the verb with 2nd radical w or y: the sequence of the 2nd radical w or y vowelled by a kasra and preceded by a ḍamma: the transfer of the kasra to the 1st radical and hence the change of the 1st radical's ḍamma into a kasra, the change of the w into a y or the y into an ī respectively, or the elision of the 2nd radical w's or y's kasra and the lengthening of the ḍamma preceding it into an ū:

I shall discuss at first the verb with 2nd radical *w* and then the verb with 2nd radical *y.*

6.5.13.1. The verb with 2nd radical w:

An example of a verb in the passive voice *fu^cila* is *quwila* "was said". The *w* is vowelled by a kasra in it and preceded by a ḍamma, which is deemed as a heavy combination. The usual following phonological changes that are carried out in it resulting in *q(i)īla* are the following (cf. Åkesson, *Ibn Mas^cūd* 294: fol. 31b, Bakkūš, *Taṣrīf* 146, ^cAbd al-Raḥīm, *Ṣarf* 31-32, this study par. 9.1.6.):

quwila with the 2nd radical *w* vowelled by a kasra and preceded by a ḍamma becomes *qiwla* after that the kasra of the *w* is shifted to the 1st radical and hence replaces the ḍamma. As the vowelless *w* is preceded by a kasra in it, the *w* is changed into a *y* resulting in *qiyla.* Then the vowelless *y* preceded by a kasra is lengthened into an *ī* so that it became *q(i)īla.*

According to another dialectal variant which is deemed as feeble, the *w* of *quwila* is made vowelless for the purpose of alleviation, and the variant *quwla* resulting in *q(u)ūla* occurs (cf. Åkesson, *Ibn Mas^cūd* 294: fol. 31b, par. 9.1.6.). This is the dialectal variant of the Banū Asad (for discussions see Bakkūš, *Taṣrīf* 146-147). I illustrate the changes with the following:

quwila with the 2nd radical *w* vowelled by a kasra and preceded by ḍamma becomes *quwla* after that the *w's* kasra is elided to alleviate. As the vowelless *w* is preceded by a ḍamma in it, the *w* is lengthened into an *ū,* or in other words the *w* is assimilated to the ḍamma resulting in *q(u)ūla.*

According to another dialectal variant, the *^ɔišmām,* i.e. "giving the vowel preceding the glide a flavour of the ḍamma so that it notifies of the underlying form", is carried out: *q(i)īla* is said *quila* (cf. ibid).

Hence I can mention the following variants with the vowelled pronoun of the agent in the perfect (cf. Sībawaihi, II, 398,

Ibn Ǧinnī, *Munṣif I,* 293-295, Åkesson, *Ibn Mas^{c}ūd* 294: fol. 31b, Howell, IV, fasc. I, 1476-1484):

Form I *quwil-na* with the *-na* /fem. → 1- *qil-na* "were said pl."
→ 2- *qu(u)ūl-na*
→ 3- *ʾišmām: quil-na*

6.5.13.2. The verb with 2nd radical y:

An example of a passive voice of a verb with 2nd radical *y* that I take up is *buyi^{c}a* "was sold" that is formed according to *fu^{c}ila.* As with *quwila* (cf. above) the three variants can be applied for it. The usual phonological changes concerning the first variant (cf. par. 9.1.6.) are the following:

buyi^{c}a with the 2nd radical *y* vowelled by a kasra and preceded by ḍamma becomes *biy^{c}a* after that the kasra of the *y* is shifted to the 1st radical and hence replaces the ḍamma. As the 2nd radical vowelless *y* is preceded by a kasra in it, the *y* is lengthened into an *ī* so that it becomes *bi(ī)^{c}a.*

The two other possibilities are *b(u)ū^{c}a* (cf. par. 9.1.6.) and with the *ʾišmām* carried out in it *bui^{c}a.*

Hence the following variants with the vowelled pronoun of the agent in the perfect can be mentioned:

Form I *buyi^{c}-na* with the *-na* /fem. → 1- *bi^{c}-na* "were sold pl.".
→ 2- *b(u)ū^{c}-na*
→ 3- *ʾišmām: bui^{c}-na*

6.5.14. The passive voice of the imperfect of the verb with 2nd radical w or y: the sequence of the 2nd radical w or y vowelled by a fatḥa and preceded by a sukūn: the transfer of

the fatḥa to the 1st vowelless radical and the change of the w or the y into an ā:

The imperfect of the passive voice of the verb with 2nd radical *w* or *y* is formed according to *yufᶜalu.* The sequence in this form is that of a glide vowelled by a fatḥa and preceded by a sukūn (for discussions see par. 9.1.12.). The first rule that is taken into account is that the fatḥa of the glide is shifted to the vowelless segment preceding it. This in its turn leads to a second rule that is the change of the glide into an *ā*.

An example of a verb with 2nd radical *w* is *yuqwalu* which becomes *yuq(a)ālu* "is said". On examination, the phonological changes are the following:

yuqwalu with the 2nd radical *w* vowelled by a fatḥa preceded by a sukūn becomes *yuqawlu* after that the *w's* fatḥa is shifted to the 1st radical *q*. As *yuqawlu* has its vowelless *w* preceded by a fatḥa, it becomes *yuq(a)ālu* with the *w* changed into an *ā*. This change of the vowelless *w* into an *ā* may be said to be triggered by the fatḥa preceding the *w*.

An example of a verb with 2nd radical *y* is *yubyaᶜu* which becomes *yub(a)āᶜu* "is sold". On examination, *yubyaᶜu* with its 2nd radical *y* vowelled by a fatḥa preceded by a sukūn becomes *yubayᶜu* with the *y's* fatḥa shifted to the 1st radical *b*.

And *yubayᶜu* with the vowelless *y* preceded by a fatḥa becomes *yub(a)āᶜu* with the *y* changed into an *ā*.

6.5.15. The noun of place of the verb with 2nd radical w: the sequence of the 2nd radical w vowelled by a fatḥa and preceded by a sukūn: the transfer of the fatḥa to the vowelless segment preceding it and the change of the w into an ā:

The pattern of the noun of place of the verb with with 2nd radical *w* is *mafᶜalun.* An example is *maqwalun* resulting in *maq(a)ālun* "speech" (cf. Åkesson, *Ibn Masᶜūd* 292: fol. 31b). The sequence is that of a *w* vowelled by a fatḥa and preceded by a sukūn (cf. par. 9.1.12.). Alike the cases analysed in par. 6.5.14., the first rule that is taken into account is the transfer of the glide's fatḥa to the vowelless segment preceding it, and the second rule is the change of the glide into an *ā*.

Thus *maqwalun* with the 2nd radical *w* vowelled by a fatḥa and preceded by a sukūn becomes at first *maqawlun* with the *w's* fatḥa shifted to the 1st radical *q*. As *maqawlun* has its vowelless *w* preceded by a fatḥa, it becomes *maq(a)ālun* with the *w* changed into an *ā*.

6.6. A few remarks concerning some homonymous forms

One form can be common for two different forms, and it is only by *al-farq al-taqdīrī* "the theoretical difference" existing between both their underlying forms that it is possible to separate the forms from each other (for an example of a verb form with 3rd radical *w*, *yaᶜf(u)ūna* "he remits it, or they remit it /fem. pl., respectively" see par. 7.6).

An example of such a form referring to a verb with 2nd radical *w* is *qul-na* which is common for both the 3rd person of the fem. pl. of the perfect "they said, fem. pl." and the 2nd person of the fem. pl. of the imperative "say! fem. pl.". The Arab grammarians seemed satisfied with the underlying forms of both these tenses which differenciate them from one another. As a matter of fact, the form *qul-na* referring to the 3rd person of the fem. pl. of the perfect is underlyingly *qawal-na* (for the phonological change carried out in it see par. 6.5.2.: 1) and the form *qul-na* referring to the 2nd person of the fem. pl. of the imperative is underlyingly *ʾuqwul-na* (cf. par. 6.5.8.1.).

Another example of such a form referring to a verb with 2nd radical *y* is *bi*^{c}*-na* "they sold, or they were sold /fem. pl.", which is common for the active and the passive voice. The underlying form of the active voice is *baya*^{c}*-na* with the *b* and the *y* vowelled by a fatḥa (for the phonological change that is carried out in it see par. 6.5.2.2.) and that of the passive voice is *buyi*^{c}*-na* (with the *b* vowelled by a ḍamma and the *y* vowelled by a kasra (for the phonological change see 6.5.13.2.).

6.7. Conclusion

I have presented the verb with 2nd *w* or *y* radical and some of its derivatives in this chapter. I have also briefly discussed the soundness or the unsoundness of the middle radical.

It has been observed that the glide is maintained in the verbal noun of Form I as it is vowelless and preceded by a fatḥa (cf. 6.5.11.), e.g. *qawlun* "a saying" and *bay*^{c}*un* "a selling". It is changed into an *ā* in the 3rd persons of the perfect as it is vowelled and preceded by a fatḥa (cf. 6.5.1.), e.g. *qawala* > *q(a)āla* "he said" and *baya*^{c}*a* > *b(a)ā*^{c}*a* "to buy".

The *ā* preceding the vowelless 3rd radical is elided in the persons of the perfect to which the vowelled pronoun of the agent is suffixed to and the vowel of the 1st radical is changed into another vowel, e.g. *q(a)āl-na* (from *qawal-na)* that becomes *qal-na* and then *qul-na* "they said /fem. pl." (cf. 6.5.2.).

The vowel of the 2nd radical is shifted to the vowelless segment preceding it together with other changes that are carried out in many forms. This shifting is found in the imperfect of the conjugation *yaf*^{c}*alu,* e.g. *yaḫwafu* > *yaḫawfu* > *yaḫ(a)āfu* "he is afraid" (cf. 6.5.3.), *yaf*^{c}*ulu,* e.g. *yaqwulu* > *yaquwlu* > *yaq(u)ūlu* "he says" (cf. 6.5.4.), *yaf*^{c}*ilu,* e.g. *yabyi*^{c}*u* > *yabiy*^{c}*u* > *yab(i)ī*^{c}*u* "he sells" (cf. 6.5.5.), in the passive participle of the verb with 2nd radical *w,* e.g. *maqw(u)ūlun* > *maquwūlun* > *maq(u)ūlun* "what is said" (cf. 6.5.6.) or 2nd radical *y,* e.g. *maby(u)ūʿun* > *mabuyūʿun* > *mabuyʿun* "what is sold" (cf. 6.5.7.), in the imperative, e.g. *ʾuqwul* > *ʾuquwl* > *quwl* > *q(u)ūl* > *qul* "say!" and *ʾibyiʿ* > *ʾibiyʿ* > *biyʿ* > *b(i)īʿ* > *biʿ* "sell!" (cf. par. 6.5.8.), in the passive voice of the imperfect, e.g. *yuqwalu* > *yuqawlu* > *yuq(a)ālu* "is said" and *yubyaʿu* > *yubayʿu* > *yub(a)āʿu* (cf. 6.5.14.), in the noun of place of the verb with 2nd radical *w,* e.g. *maqwalun* > *maqawlun* > *maq(a)ālun* "speech" (cf. 6.5.15.) and in the passive voice of the perfect, e.g. *quwila* > *qiwla* > *qiyla* > *q(i)īla* and *buyiʿa* > *biyʿa* > *bi(ī)ʿa* (cf. 6.5.13.).

The *w* or *y* that is vowelled by a kasra and preceded by an *ā* in the active participle is changed into a hamza, e.g. *q(a)āwilun* > *q(a)āʾilun* "a sayer" and *b(a)āyiʿun* > *b(a)āʾiʿun* "a seller" (cf. 6.5.9.).

In somes anomalous cases of active participles of the verb with 2nd radical *w,* the *wi* that is changed into *ʾi* is elided, e.g. *h(a)āwiʿun* > *h(a)āʾiʿun* > *h(a)āʿun* "vomitting", or the segments are transposed and the *wi* is elided, e.g. *š(a)āwikun* > *s(a)ākiwun* > *š(a)ākin* "sharp" (cf. 6.5.10).

The *w* of the verbal nouns of Form IV *ʾifʿ(a)ālun* and Form X *ʾistifʿ(a)ālun* of the verb with 2nd radical *w* is changed into an *ā,* then one of the alifs is elided and the elision is compensated by the *tāʾ marbūṭa,* e.g. *ʾiqw(a)āmun* > *ʾiq(a)āāmun* > *ʾiq(a)āmun* > *ʾiq(a)āmatun* "the act of being constant (in prayer)" (cf. 6.5.12.).

In the next chapter I shall study the verb with 3rd *w* or *y* radical and some of its forms.

CHAPTER SEVEN

7. The verb with 3rd radical *w* or *y*

The verb with 3rd radical *w* or *y* or the defective verb is generally termed as *mu*ᶜ*tal al-lām or al-nāqiṣ*.

A less well-known nomination is *ḏū l-*ʾ*arba*ᶜ*a* "the one with four segments" that is given to it by Ibn Masᶜūd (Åkesson, *Ibn Mas*ᶜ*ūd* 326: fol. 32a), because it maintains its 3rd weak radical when the vowelled suffixed agent pronoun, namely the *-tu* "/1st person of the sing.", *-ta* "2nd person of the masc. sing.", *-ti* "2nd person of the fem. sing.", *-tumā* "2nd person of the dual", *-tum* "2nd person of the masc. pl." or *-na* "3rd person of the fem pl., is attached to it, by contrast to the verb with 2nd *w* or *y* radical that loses its 2nd weak radical in these cases (cf. par. 6.). Hence it comprehends four segments in these perfect forms. For the sake of concreteness, I illustrate it with the following examples:

a- verb with 3rd radical w

An example of a verb with 3rd radical *w* in the 1st person of the sing. is *da*ᶜ*aw-tu* "I called", and hence *da*ᶜ*aw-ta* "you called

/masc. sing.", *da*^{c}*aw-ti* "you called /fem. sing." and *da*^{c}*aw-na* "they called /fem. pl.". Thus:

da^{c}*aw-tu*	=	*fa*^{c}*al-tu*
da+^{c}*a+w+tu*	=	*fa+*^{c}*a+l+tu*
1 + 2 + 3 + 4 segments	=	1 + 2 + 3 + 4 segments

b- verb with 3rd radical y

An example of a verb with 3rd radical *y* in the 1st person of the sing. is *ramay-tu* "I threw", and hence *ramay-ta* "you threw /masc. sing.", *ramay-ti* "you threw /fem. sing." and *ramay-na* "they called /fem. pl.". Thus:

ramay-tu	=	*fa*^{c}*al-tu*
ra+ma+y+tu	=	*fa+*^{c}*a+l+tu*
1 + 2 + 3 + 4 segments	=	1 + 2 + 3 + 4 segments

7.1. The conjugations of the verb with 3rd radical *w*

The verb with 3rd radical *w* falls into the following conjugation:

1- *fa*^{c}*ala yaf*^{c}*ulu,* e.g. *ġazawa yaġzuwu* "to attack" that becomes after the phonological change *ġazā yaġzū.*

7.2. Examples of some derivatives of the verb with 3rd radical *w*

An example of a verb with 3rd radical *w* in the perfect is *ġazā* "to attack" (with final *alif mamdūda).* It becomes *yaġzū* in the imperfect of the indicative active. Its imperative is ˀ*uġzu,* its active participle is *ġāzin,* its *maṣdar* is *ġazwun,* its perfect passive is *ġuziya,* its imperfect is *yuġzā* and its passive participle is *maġzīyun.*

7.3. The conjugations of the verb with 3rd radical *y*

The verb with 3rd radical *y* falls into the following conjugations:

1- *fa^cala yaf^cilu,* e.g. *ramaya yarmiyu* "to throw" that becomes after the phonological change *ramā yarmī.*

2- *fa^cala yaf^calu,* e.g. *nahaya yanhayu* "to forbid" that becomes after the phonological change *nahā yanhā.*

3- *fa^cila yaf^calu,* e.g. *raḍiya yarḍayu* "to consent" that becomes after the phonological change *raḍā yarḍā.*

7.4. Examples of some derivatives of the verb with 3rd radical *y*

An example of a verb with 3rd radical *y* in the perfect is *ramaya* "to throw". It becomes *yarmī* in the imperfect of the indicative active. Its imperative is *ʾirmi,* its active participle is *rāmin,* its *maṣdar* is *ramyun,* its perfect passive is *rumiya,* its imperfect is *yurmā,* its passive participle is *marmīyun* and the nouns of time and place are *marman.*

7.5. Remarks concerning the phonological procedures in some of the forms of the verb with 3rd radical *w* or *y*

Most of the phonological changes that are carried out in the verb with 3rd radical *w* and some of its derivatives are similar to those that are carried out in the verb with 3rd radical *y* and some of its derivatives. The *w* or the *y* can be changed in some forms into another segment, be elided or retained. Its vowel can as well be shifted to the segment preceding it after the elision of the *w* or the *y* or its vowel can be elided and the vowel preceding it can be changed into another vowel (cf. 7.5.5.).

Thus I present and study the following forms and sequences:

7.5.1. The 3rd person of the masc. sing. of the perfect: the sequence of the vowelled *w* or *y* preceded by a fatḥa: its change into an *ā.*

7.5.2. The 3rd person of the fem. sing. and fem. dual of the perfect: the sequence in which the vowelless *ā* (that is substituted for the glide vowelled by a fatḥa) is followed by the *-t* that marks the fem.: the elision of the *ā*.

7.5.3. The persons in the perfect to which the vowelled agent pronoun is suffixed to: the sequence of the 3rd vowelless weak radical preceded by a fatḥa: the retaining of the *w* or *y*.

7.5.4. The 3rd person of the masc pl. of the perfect of the conjugation *faᶜala:* the sequence of the 3rd radical *w* or *y* vowelled by a ḍamma (on account that it is followed by the vowelless *ū* / *w* marker of the pl.), and preceded by a fatḥa: the change of the *wu* or *yu* into an *ā* and the elision of the *ā*.

7.5.5. The 3rd person of the masc pl. of the perfect of the verb with 3rd radical *y* of the conjugation *faᶜila:* the sequence of the 3rd radical *y* vowelled by a ḍamma (on account of the vowelless *ū* / *w* marker of the pl. following it), and preceded by a kasra: the transfer of the ḍamma before the *y* and hence the change of the kasra into a ḍamma, the elision of the *y* and the lengthening of the ḍamma into an *ū* according to a theory, or the elision of the *y's* ḍamma, the elision of the *y* and the change of the kasra into a ḍamma according to another theory.

7.5.6. The persons in which no suffix is attached to the imperfect: the sequence in which the glide is vowelled by the ḍamma of the indicative and preceded by a vowel: the elision of the ḍamma.

7.5.7. The duals of the imperfect: the sequence in which the glide is vowelled by a fatḥa and preceded by a vowel: the glide's retaining.

7.5.8. The 2nd person of the fem. sing. of the imperfect of a verb with 3rd radical *y:* the sequence in which the 3rd radical *y* is vowelled by a kasra and is followed by the vowelless *ī* marker of the fem. sing.: the elision of the vowel of the *y* together with the *y*.

7.5.9. The 2nd and 3rd persons of the masc. pl. of the imperfect of a verb with 3rd radical *y:* the sequence in which the 3rd radical *y* is vowelled by a ḍamma, preceded by a kasra and followed by the vowelless *ū* marker of the masc. pl.: the elision of the ḍamma of the *y* together with the *y* and the change of the kasra into a ḍamma.

7.5.10. Form IV and other derived forms of the perfect of verbs with 3rd *w* radical to which the vowelled agent pronoun is suffixed to: the sequence of the 3rd vowelless weak radical preceded by a fatḥa: the change of the *w* into a *y*.

7.5.11. Form IV and other derived forms of the imperfect of the verbs with 3rd *w* radical: the sequence of the 3rd vowelled weak radical preceded by a kasra in them: the change of the *w* into a *y*.

7.5.12. The active participle of the verb with 3rd radical *y:* the sequence of the vowelled *y* preceded by a kasra in the definite and indefinite forms: the elision of the vowel of the *y* in the definite form, and the elision of the vowel together with the 3rd radical *y* in the nominative and genitive cases with the *tanwīn* replacing the kasra of the 2nd radical in the indefinite form.

7.5.13. The passive participle of the verb with 3rd radical *y:* the sequence of the vowelless infixed *ū* preceding the *y:* the change of the vowelless infixed *ū* into a *y*, the change of the ḍamma preceding the changed *y* into a kasra and the assimilation of the *y* to the *y*.

7.5.14. The noun of place of the verb with 3rd radical *y:* the sequence of the vowelled *y* preceded by a kasra: the change of the kasra into a fatḥa and of the *y* into an *alif maqṣūra*.

7.5.15. The jussive of the verb with 3rd radical *w* or *y:* the sequence of the vowelless *w* or *y* preceded by a vowel: the elision of the *w* or *y*.

7.5.1. The 3rd person of the masc. sing. of the perfect: the sequence of the vowelled w or y preceded by a fatḥa: its change into an ā:

I shall discuss at first the verb with 2nd radical *w* and then the verb with 2nd radical *y*.

7.5.1.1. The verb with 3rd radical w:

The verb with 3rd radical *w* occurs in the 3rd person of the masc. sing. of the perfect according to the conjugation *faᶜala.* In this sequence the *w* is vowelled by a fatḥa and is preceded by one, which results in its change into an *ā* namely an *alif mamdūda* (cf. Åkesson, *Ibn Masᶜūd* 326: fol. 32a; and for discussions concerning the sequence formed of a glide vowelled by a fatḥa and preceded by one see par. 9.1.2.).

An example of a verb with a 3rd radical *w* is *ġazawa* with the 3rd radical *w* vowelled by a fatḥa and preceded by one that becomes *ġaz(a)ā* "to raid" with the *wa* changed into *ā* [sc. *alif mamdūda].*

7.5.1.2. The verb with 3nd y radical:

The verb with 3rd radical *y* occurs according to *faᶜala* or *faᶜila.* The *ya* in both these conjugations is changed into *ā,* namely an *alif maqṣūra* (cf. Åkesson, *Ibn Masᶜūd* 326: fol. 32a; for discussions concerning the sequence formed of a glide vowelled by a fatḥa and preceded by one see par. 9.1.2.).

An example of a verb with a 3rd radical *y* formed according to *fa^cala* is *ramaya* with the 3rd radical *y* vowelled by a fatḥa and preceded by a fatḥa that becomes *ram(a)ā* "to throw" with the *ya* changed into an *ā* [sc. *alif maqṣūra]*.

An example of a verb with a 3rd radical *y* formed according to *fa^cila* is *raḍiya* with the 3rd radical *y* vowelled by a fatḥa and preceded by a kasra that becomes *raḍ(a)ā* "to consent" with the *ya* changed into *ā* [sc. *alif maqṣūra]* and the kasra changed into a fatḥa.

7.5.2. The 3rd person of the fem. sing. and fem. dual of the perfect: the sequence in which the vowelless ā (that is substituted for the glide vowelled by a fatḥa) is followed by the -t that marks the fem.: the elision of the ā:

It has been asserted earlier that in the case of the 3rd person of the fem. sing. of the verb with 3rd *w* or *y* radical to which the vowelless suffix *-t* that marks the fem. is suffixed to, the 3rd weak radical is at first changed into *ā* on account of the fatḥa preceding it (for this sequence see par. 7.5.1.1., 7.5.1.2.) and the *ā* is then elided to avoid the cluster of two vowelless segments: the vowelless *ā* and the vowelless fem. marker *-t*. The *ā* is as well elided in the 3rd person of the fem. dual when the vowelled fem. marker *-t(a)ā* is suffixed to it.

Thus I illustrate this with the following:

7.5.2.1. The verb with 3rd radical w:

An example of a verb with a 3rd radical *w* is *ġazawa-t* that results in *ġaza-t* "she raided". The phonological procedure is complex as it involves more than two steps: *ġazawa-t* with the 3rd radical *w* vowelled by a fatḥa and preceded by one, becomes at first *ġaz(a)ā-t* with the *wa* changed into *ā,* and as *ġaz(a)ā-t* involves the cluster of the vowelless *ā* and *t*, it becomes *ġaza-t* with the *ā* elided.

The same principle is in operation in the dual of the 3rd person of the fem., e.g. *ġaza-t(a)ā*. It can be observed that the *ā* that is changed from the 3rd radical vowelled by a fatḥa, namely the *wa*, is as well elided in it. Hence the procedure from the base form to the derived form is the following: *ġazawa-t(a)ā* > *ġaz(a)ā-t(a)ā* > *ġaza-t(a)ā*. This elision of the *ā* is carried out in it spite of the fact that the *-t(a)ā* ending in *ġaz(a)ā-t(a)ā* that marks the fem. dual, has its *-t* vowelled by a fatḥa, implying that there does not occur a cluster of two vowelless letters which would trigger off the elision, as in the case of the 3rd person of the fem. sing. *ġaz(a)ā-t* resulting in *ġaza-t* after the necessary elision of the *ā*. However according to a theory propounded by Ibn Masᶜūd (cf. Åkesson, *Ibn Masᶜūd* 326 fol. 32a) it is assumed that there is such a combination theoretically on account that the *-t(a)* of the *-t(a)ā* that marks the fem. sing. is underlyingly vowelless, i.e. *-t*, and is only given the fatḥa when it is connected to the vowelless *-ā* suffix of the dual.

7.5.2.2. The verb with 3rd radical y:

The reasoning is the same as the one I introduced concerning the verb with 3rd radical *w* (cf. par. 7.5.2.1.), except that it is the *ya* that is changed into *ā*, and then is elided. An example is *ramaya-t* "she threw" which has the 3rd radical *y* vowelled by a fatḥa and preceded by one. It becomes *ram(a)ā-t* with the *ya* changed into *ā*, and then as there is a cluster of two vowelless segments: the *ā* and *t*, its *ā* is elided so that it becomes *rama-t* (cf. Åkesson, *Ibn Masᶜūd* 326: fol. 32a).

The procedure is the same concerning the dual of the 3rd person of the fem. as the one of the verb with 3rd radical *w*. An example is *ramaya-t(a)ā* that becomes *ram(a)ā-t(a)ā* and then *rama-t(a)ā*. Some people however who use a defective dialectal variant maintain the *ā* and say *ram(a)ā-t(a)ā* instead (cf. ibid 56: fols. 5a-5b, Zamaḫšarī 154, Ibn Yaᶜīš, IX, 27-29, Wright, II, 89, Åkesson, *Conversion* 28).

7.5.3. The persons in the perfect to which the vowelled agent pronoun is suffixed to: the sequence of the 3rd vowelless weak radical preceded by a fatḥa: the retaining of the w or y:

In the forms of the perfect in which the vowelled agent pronouns are suffixed to, e.g. the *-tu* of the 1st person of the sing., the *-n(a)ā* of the 1st person of the pl., the *-ta* of the 2nd person of the masc. sing., the *-tum* of the 2nd person of the masc. pl., the *-na* of the 3rd person of the fem. pl., etc., the 3rd vowelless radical *w* or *y* is maintained.

An example of a verb with 3rd radical *w* is *ġazaw-tu* "I attacked /1st person of the sing.", *ġazaw-n(a)ā* "/1st person of the pl.", *ġazaw-ta* "/2nd person of the masc. sing.", *ġazaw-tum* "/2nd person of the masc. pl.", *ġazaw-na* "/3rd person of the fem. pl.", etc.

An example of a verb with 3rd radical *y* is *ramay-tu* "I threw /1st person of the sing.", *ramay-n(a)ā* "/1st person of the pl.", *ramay-ta* "/2nd person of the masc. sing.", *ramay-tum* "/2nd person of the masc. pl.", *ramay-na* "/3rd person of the fem. pl.", etc.

The reason of the maintaince of the *w* or *y* in these forms is that the glide is made vowelless on account of the suffixation of the vowelled pronoun suffix of the agent, and thus is preceded by a fatḥa. The sequence of the vowelless glide preceded by a fatḥa has in most cases its glide retained (cf. par. 9.1.1.).

7.5.4. The 3rd person of the masc pl. of the perfect of the conjugation fa^cala: the sequence of the 3rd radical w or y vowelled by a ḍamma (on account that it is followed by the vowelless ū / w marker of the pl.), and preceded by a fatḥa: the change of the wu or yu into an ā and the elision of the ā:

The verb with 3rd radical *w* or *y* of the conjugation *fa*[c]*ala* that occurs in the 3rd person of the masc. pl., has the vowelless agent pronoun marking the pl., namely the *-ū,* suffixed to it, and hence has its 3rd radical vowelled with a ḍamma. The vowelled 3rd radical *w* or *y* that is preceded by a fatḥa is changed into an *ā* (cf. par. 9.1.4.) and the *ā* is then elided.

An example of a verb with 3rd radical *w* is *ġazaw(u)-ū* that becomes *ġaza-w* "they attacked". The procedure is the following: *ġazaw(u)-ū* / *ġazaw(u)-w* with the 3rd radical *w* vowelled by a ḍamma and preceded by a fatḥa becomes *ġaz(a)ā-w* after that the *w(u)* is changed into an *ā.* As there is a cluster of the vowelless *ā* and *w* in it, the *ā* is elided so that it becomes *ġaza-w.*

An example of a verb with 3rd radical *y* is *ramay(u)-w* that becomes *rama-w* "they threw" (cf. Åkesson, *Ibn Mas*[c]*ūd* 326: fol. 32a). The procedure is the following: *ramay(u)-w* with the 3rd radical *y* vowelled by a ḍamma and preceded by a fatḥa becomes *ram(a)ā-w* after that the *y(u)* is changed into an *ā.* As there is a cluster of the vowelless *ā* and *w* in it, the *ā* is elided so that it becomes *rama-w.*

7.5.5. The 3rd person of the masc pl. of the perfect of a verb with 3rd radical y of the conjugation faᶜila: the sequence of the 3rd radical y vowelled by a ḍamma (on account of the vowelless ū / w marker of the pl. following it), and preceded by a kasra: the transfer of the ḍamma before the y and hence the change of the kasra into a ḍamma, the elision of the y and the lengthening of the ḍamma into ū according to a theory, or the elision of the y's ḍamma, the elision of the y and the change of the kasra into a ḍamma according to another theory:

In the case of the 3rd person of the masc. pl. of the verb with 3rd radical *y* of the conjugation *faᶜila,* e.g. *raḍiya* "to consent" to which the vowelless agent pronoun namely the *-ū,* is suffixed to, namely *raḍiy(u)-ū,* the 3rd radical *y* is elided (for discussions see Wright, II, 89) resulting in *raḍi(u)-ū,* except that the 2nd radical *ḍ* becomes vowelled with a ḍamma, namely *raḍ(u)-ū,* to hinder the combination of the ḍamma followed by the kasra (cf. Åkesson, *Ibn Masᶜūd* 326: fol. 32a), which is deemed as heavy, and also so that the ḍamma accords with the suffixed *ū* (cf. Daqr, *Muᶜǧam* 390-391).

The phonological procedure is carried out by eliding the 3rd weak radical and changing the vowel of the 2nd radical into another. There exist two different theories concerning the phonological procedure resulting in the vowelling of the 2nd radical by a ḍamma.

According to the theory of Ibn Ǧinnī, *Munṣif II,* 126, *raḍiy(u)-ū* with the 3rd radical *y* vowelled by a ḍamma and preceded by a kasra becomes *raḍuy-ū* after that the ḍamma of the *y* is shifted to the segment preceding it, the *ḍ,* for the sake of alleviation, which implies that the *ḍ's* kasra is changed into a ḍamma. As there is in it a cluster of a vowelless *y* and *ū,* the *y* is elided so that it becomes *raḍ(u)-ū.*

According to the theory of Ibn Masᶜūd (cf. Åkesson, *Ibn Masᶜūd* 286: fol. 28b), there does not forecome any transfer of the ḍamma of the *y* of *raḍiy(u)-ū* to the segment before it, but the ḍamma is however elided for the sake of alleviation, namely *raḍiy-ū,* then the vowelless *y* is elided to hinder the cluster of two vowelless segments, the *y* and the *ū,* namely *raḍi-ū,* and then the *ḍ's* kasra is changed into a ḍamma resulting in *raḍ(u)-ū.*

7.5.6. The persons in which no suffix is attached to the imperfect: the sequence in which the glide is vowelled by the ḍamma of the indicative and preceded by a vowel: the elision of the ḍamma:

In the cases of the verb with 3rd *w* or *y* radical in the persons to which no suffix is attached to, as the 1st person of the sing., e.g. *ʾaġzuwu* "I attack" with 3rd radical *w, ʾarmiyu* "I throw" with 3rd radical *y,* the 1st person of the pl., e.g. *naġzuwu* "we attack", *narmiyu* "we throw", the 2nd person of the masc. sing., e.g. *taġzuwu* "you attack", *tarmiyu* "you throw" and the 3rd person of the fem. sing., e.g. *taġzuwu* "she attacks", *tarmiyu* "she throws", the ḍamma of the indicative that vowels the 3rd radical is elided because it is considered as heavy on the *w* or *y* (cf. Åkesson, *Ibn Masᶜūd* 326: fol. 32b and this study par. 9.1.7.). I illustrate the phonological changes as follows:

Concerning the verb with 3rd radical *w,* I take up the case of *yaġzuwu* which has the *w* vowelled by a ḍamma and preceded by one, that becomes *yaġzuw* > *yaġz(u)ū* after the elision of the ḍamma and the assimilation of the *w* to the ḍamma resulting in the lengthened *w: ū.*

Concerning the verb with 3rd radical *y,* I take up the case of *yarmiyu* which has the *y* vowelled by a ḍamma and preceded by a kasra, which becomes *yarmiy* > *yarm(i)ī* after the elision of the ḍamma and the assimilation of the *y* to the kasra resulting in the lengthened *y: ī.*

7.5.7. The duals of the imperfect: the sequence in which the glide is vowelled by a fatḥa and preceded by a vowel: the glide's retaining:

The weak radical of the verb with 3rd radical *w* or *y* is maintained in the cases of the duals of the 2nd persons, e.g. *taġzuw(a)-āni* "you raid /2nd dual", *tarmiy(a)-āni* "you throw /2nd dual" and the 3rd persons of the pl., e.g. *yaġzuw(a)-āni* "/3 masc. dual" and *yarmiy(a)-āni* "/3 masc. dual". As for the reason of its retaining, it is because the fatḥa that vowels the glide and precedes the infix *-ā* of the dual is counted as light (cf. Åkesson, *Ibn Mas*ᶜ*ūd* 326: fol. 32b).

7.5.8. The 2nd person of the fem. sing. of the imperfect of a verb with 3rd radical y: the sequence in which the 3rd radical y is vowelled by a kasra and is followed by the vowelless ī marker of the fem. sing.: the elision of the vowel of the y together with the y:

The underlying form of the 2nd person of the imperfect sing. of a verb with 3rd weak radical *y,* e.g. *ramaya* "to throw" is *tarmiy(i)-īna* "/2 fem. sing.". The phonological changes are carried out in the following manner (cf. Åkesson, *Ibn Mas*ᶜ*ūd* 286: fol. 28b): *tarmiy(i)-īna* with the 3rd radical *y* vowelled by a kasra and preceded by one becomes *tarmiy-īna* after the elision of the kasra of the 3rd weak radical *y* due to the heaviness of the combination. As there is in it a cluster of two vowelless segments: the *y* and the *ī,* the 3rd radical *y* is elided so that it becomes *tarm(i)-īna.*

This elision of the weak 3rd radical is usual in the defective verb in which the agent pronoun of the 2nd person of the fem. sing. of the imperfect, *-īna,* is suffixed to (cf. Wright, II, 89, Daqr, *Muʿǧam* 391).

7.5.9. The 2nd and 3rd persons of the masc. pl. of the imperfect of a verb with 3rd radical y: the sequence in which the 3rd radical y is vowelled by a ḍamma, preceded by a kasra and followed by the vowelless ū marker of the masc. pl.: the elision of the ḍamma of the y together with the y and the change of the kasra into a ḍamma:

The underlying form of the 2nd person of the imperfect sing. of a verb with 3rd weak radical *y*, e.g. *ramaya* "to throw" is *tarmiy(u)-ūna* "/2 masc. pl." and of the 3rd person of the masc. pl. *yarmiy(u)-ūna* "/3 masc. pl." The phonological changes in them both are carried out by eliding the ḍamma of the 3rd weak radical *y* due to the heaviness of the combination, namely *tarmiy-ūna* and *yarmiy-ūna.* As there results a cluster of two vowelless segments: the *y* and the *ū,* the *y* is elided and then the kasra is changed into a ḍamma to prevent that the *ū* is changed into a *y* due to its sukūn and the influence of the kasra preceding it, so they became *tarm(u)-ūna* and *yarm(u)-ūna.*

7.5.10. Form IV and other derived forms of the perfect of verbs with 3rd w radical to which the vowelled agent pronoun is suffixed to: the sequence of the 3rd vowelless weak radical preceded by a fatḥa: the change of the w into a y:

An example of a Form IV of a verb with 3rd radical *w* is *ʾaġzaw-tu* that occurs in the perfect with the pronoun of the agent suffixed to it, which becomes *ʾaġzay-tu* "I raided". The procedure is the following: *ʾaġzaw-tu* with the vowelless 3rd radical *w* preceded by a fatḥa becomes *ʾaġzay-tu* after that the *w* is changed into a *y*.

This change of the *w* into a *y* is on the analogy of the one that is carried out in its imperfect *yuġziwu* > *yuġz(i)yu* > *yuġz(i)ī* "he raids" (cf. Åkesson, *Ibn Masᶜūd* 282: 27a; and for discussions see 7.5.11.).

Some other examples of derived forms in which this phonological change is carried out on the analogy of the one that is carried out in their imperfects, are Form II *ġazzawa* that becomes *ġazzaya* and then *ġazz(a)ā* [with final *alif maqṣūra]* "to raid" and Form X *ʾistarḍawa* that becomes *ʾistarḍaya* and then *ʾistarḍ(a)ā* "to consent" (cf. Wright, II, 91).

7.5.11. Form IV and other derived forms of the imperfect of the verbs with 3rd w radical: the sequence of the 3rd vowelled weak radical preceded by a kasra: the change of the w into a y:

An example of a Form IV of a verb with 2nd radical *w* in the imperfect is *yuġziwu* in which the vowelled *w* is preceded by a kasra which is why it is changed into a *y*, namely *yuġz(i)yu* that becomes *yuġz(i)ī* "he raids". The procedure is the following: *yuġziwu* with the vowelless 3rd radical *w* preceded by a kasra becomes *yuġz(i)yu* after that the *w* is changed into a *y*. As in it the *y* is preceded by a kasra and vowelled by a ḍamma, the *y's* ḍamma is elided and the *y* is assimilated to the kasra resulting in the lengthened *y: ī*, so that it becomes *yuġz(i)ī*.

Some other examples of derived forms in which this phonological change is carried out are Form II *yuġazziwu* that becomes *yuġazziyu* "he raids" and then *yuġazz(i)ī* and Form X *yastarḍiwu* that becomes *yastarḍiyu* and then *yastarḍ(i)ī*.

7.5.12. The active participle of the verb with 3rd radical y: the sequence of the vowelled y preceded by a kasra in the definite and indefinite forms: the elision of the vowel of the y in the definite form, and the elision of the vowel together with the 3rd radical y in the nominative and genitive cases with the tanwīn replacing the kasra of the 2nd radical in the indefinite form:

The active participle's form of verbs with *w* and *y* 3rd radical is *f(a)āᶜilun.* An example of an active participle with 3rd radical *y* in the definite form in the underlying form *al-r(a)ām(i)yu* "the one who throws" that becomes *al-r(a)ām(i)ī* in the cases of the nominative, accusative and genitive with the vowelless *ī,* because of the dislike of vowelling the *y* after the kasra. Its underlying form as an indefinite noun is *r(a)āmiyun* for the nominative and *r(a)āmiyin* for the genetive. The 3rd radical together with the vowel is elided and the *tanwīn* replaces the kasra of 2nd radical, namely *r(a)āmin* which is used for both the nominative and the genitive (cf. Åkesson, *Ibn Masᶜūd* 328: fol 33a, Wright, II, 90). The reason why the *y* is made vowelless and is then elided in both these cases is the heaviness of both the ḍamma and the kasra vowelling it. It is not elided in the accusative *r(a)āmiyan* because the nunation with the fatḥa is considered as light.

7.5.13. The passive participle of the verb with 3rd radical y: the sequence of the vowelless infixed ū preceding the y: the change of the vowelless infixed ū into a y, the change of the ḍamma preceding the changed y into a kasra and the assimilation of the y to the y:

The passive participle of verbs with 3rd radical *y* is formed according to *mafᶜ(u)wlun / mafᶜ(u)ūlun.* An example is the underlying form *marm(u)wyun* / *marm(u)ūyun* that becomes *marmiyyun* "what is thrown" (cf. Åkesson, *Ibn Mas^cūd* 328: fol 33a, Howell, IV, fasc. I, 1543, de Sacy, I, 108, Wright, II, 91, Vernier, I 340-341). The procedure is the following: *marm(u)wyun* / *marm(u)ūyun* with the vowelless infixed *w* / *ū* preceding the *y* and preceded by a ḍamma becomes *marm(u)yyun* after that the *w* is changed into a *y* due to the *y's* influence. As there is in it a heavy combination of a ḍamma preceding the yāʾs, the ḍamma is changed into a kasra so that it becomes *marm(i)yyun*.

7.5.14. The noun of place of the verb with 3rd radical y: the sequence of the vowelled y preceded by a kasra: the change of the kasra into a fatḥa and of the y into an alif maqṣūra:

The pattern of the noun of place of the verb with 3rd radical *y* is *maf^calun* and not *maf^cilun* (cf. Åkesson, *Ibn Mas^cūd* 88: fol. 17a, Zamaḫšarī, 104, Wright, II, 127-128, Vernier, I, 188). The reason why the kasra is changed into a fatḥa is to avoid having a vowelled *y* following a kasra that is deemed as heavy. Hence *al-marmiyu* becomes *al-marm(a)ā* "a place of throwing or shooting arrows", with the kasra of the *m* changed into a fatḥa and the *y* changed into an *alif maqṣūra*.

7.5.15. The jussive of the verb with 3rd radical w or y: the sequence of the vowelless w or y preceded by a vowel: the elision of the w or y:

As a rule the 3rd radical *w* or *y* of the verb that takes the sukūn as a marker of the jussive mood is elided (cf. Åkesson, *Ibn Mas^cūd* 328: fol 32b).

The reason of this elision is that the weak 3rd radical holds the same position as the vowel of the strong verb. As the strong verb's 3rd radical loses its vowel and takes the sukūn as a marker of the jussive mood, e.g. *lam yaḍrib* "he did not hit", the verb with weak 3rd radical loses its weak radical, e.g. *lam yaġzu* that is said instead of *lam yaġz(u)ū* "he did not attack" and *lam yarmi* that is said instead of *lam yarm(i)ī* "he did not throw".

7.6. A few remarks concerning some homonymous forms

An example that applies for both the 3rd person of the masc. sing. and the 3rd person of the fem. pl. is *yaᶜf(u)ūna* "he remits it, or they remit it /fem. pl., respectively", from *ᶜaf(a)ā* [with final alif mamdūda] underlyingly *ᶜafawa* "to be obliterated", a verb with 3rd *w* radical. It is only by referring to the underlying forms of the intended persons that it possible to differenciate them from each other (cf. Åkesson, *Ibn Masᶜūd* 326: fol. 32b; and for some examples of verb forms with 2nd *w* or *y* radical see par. 6.6).

The underlying form of the 3rd person of the masc. pl. is *yaᶜfuw(u)-ūna* (formed according to *yafᶜul(u)-ūna)* of which the 3rd radical *w* vowelled by a ḍamma is elided on account of the suffixation of the vowelless agent marker of the masc. pl., the *ū,* preceding the *-na* of the indicative, resulting in *yaᶜf(u)-ūna.*

The underlying form of the 3rd person of the fem. pl. is *yaᶜf(u)w-na* > *yaᶜf(u)ū-na* (formed according to *yafᶜul-na)* with the 3rd radical *w* maintained before the suffix marker of the fem. pl., the *-na.*

The *-na,* marker of the indicative in the ending *-ūna,* is dropped in the 3rd person of the masc. pl. in the case of the subjunctive in the sur. 2: 237 *(wa-ʾan taᶜfū ʾaqrabu li-l-taqwā)*

"And the remission (of the man's half) is the nearest to righteousness" (cf. Howell, II-III, 16-17), in which *wa-ʾan taᶜf(u)-ū* is said instead *wa-ʾan taᶜf(u)-ūna,* and so as well in the case of the jussive, e.g. *lam taᶜf(u)-ū* "you did not remit" as a marker for these moods.

The *-na,* marker of the fem. pl., is not dropped in the sur. 2: 237 *(ʾillā ʾan yaᶜfūna)* "Unless they remit it" (cf. Åkesson, *Ibn Masᶜūd* 326: fol. 32b), as the *-na* in *yaᶜf(u)ū-na* is not the marker of the indicative that is elided in the subjunctive mood, but the marker of the fem. pl.

7.7. Conclusion

I have presented the verb with 3rd *w* or *y* radical and some of its derivatives in this chapter. I have studied the soundness or the unsoundness of the 3rd radical.

It has been observed that the glide is sound in the persons of the perfect to which the vowelled agent pronoun is suffixed to, as it is vowelless and preceded by a fatḥa (cf. 7.5.3.), e.g. *ġazaw-tu* "I attacked /1st person of the sing." and *ramay-tu* "I threw /1st person of the sing.", and in the duals of the imperfect, as it is vowelled by a fatḥa and preceded by a vowel (cf. 7.5.7.), e.g. *taġzuw(a)-āni, tarmiy(a)-āni* "/2nd persons of the dual" and *yaġzuw(a)-āni* and *yarmiy(a)-āni* "/3 masc. dual".

The glide is changed into an *ā* in the 3rd person of the masc. sing. of the perfect as it is vowelled by a fatḥa and preceded by a fatḥa (cf. 7.5.1.), e.g. *ġazawa* > *ġaz(a)ā* and *ramaya* > *ram(a)ā.* The *ā* that is substituted for the vowelled glide is elided in the 3rd person of the fem. sing. of the perfect as it is followed by the vowelless *-t* marker of the fem. (cf. 7.5.2.), e.g. *ġazawa-t* > *ġaz(a)ā-t* > *ġaza-t* and *ramaya-t* > *ram(a)ā-t* > *rama-t,* and in the 3rd person of the masc pl. of the perfect of the conjugation *faʿala* (cf. 7.5.4.), e.g. *ġazaw(u)-ū > ġaz(a)ā-w > ġaza-w* and *ramay(u)-w > ram(a)ā-w > rama-w*.

The 3rd weak radical *y* is elided together with other phonological changes that are carried out in the 3rd person of the masc pl. of the perfect of a verb with 3rd radical *y* of the conjugation *faʿila* (cf. 7.5.5.), e.g. *raḍiy(u)-ū > raḍi(u)-ū > raḍ(u)-ū* "they consented", in the 2nd person of the fem. sing. of the imperfect (cf. 7.5.8.), e.g. *tarmiy(i)-īna > tarmiy-īna > tarm(i)-īna* "/2 fem. sing." and in the 2nd and 3rd persons of the masc. pl. of the imperfect (cf. 7.5.9.), e.g. *tarmiy(u)-ūna > tarmiy-ūna > tarm(u)-ūna* "/2 masc. pl." and *yarmiy(u)-ūna > yarmiy-ūna > yarm(u)-ūna* "/3 masc. pl." respectively.

The 3rd vowelless *w* radical to which the vowelled agent pronoun is suffixed to and that is preceded by a vowel is changed into a *y* in Form IV and in some other derived forms of the perfect (cf. 7.5.10.), e.g. *ʾaġzaw-tu > ʾaġzay-tu,* and of the imperfect, e.g. *yuġziwu > yuġz(i)yu > yuġz(i)ī.* The ḍamma of the 3rd weak radical is elided in the persons of the imperfect in which no suffix is attached to (cf. 7.5.6.), e.g. *ʾaġzuwu > ʾaġz(u)w > ʾaġz(u)ū* "/1st person sing." and *ʾarmiyu > ʾarm(i)y > ʾarm(i)ī* "/1st person sing.".

The 3rd weak radical preceded by a vowel is elided in the jussive (cf. 7.5.15.), e.g. *lam yaġz(u)ū > lam yaġzu* "he did not attack" and *lam yarm(i)ī > lam yarmi* "he did not throw".

I shall discuss the verb that is doubly weak in the next chapter.

CHAPTER EIGHT

8. The verb that is doubly Weak

The verb that is doubly weak is named *al-lafīf* "complicated, tangled".

It is divided into two classes:

1- *mafrūq:* having a 1st and 3rd weak radical, e.g. *waq(a)ā yaq(i)y* "to guard, preserve".

2- *maqrūn:* having a 2nd and 3rd weak radical, e.g. *ṭaw(a)ā yaṭw(i)y* "to fold".

8.1. The conjugations of the verb with 1st and 3rd weak radical

The verb with 1st and 3rd weak radical falls into the following conjugations:

1- *faᶜala yafᶜilu,* e.g. *waqaya yaqiyu* that becomes after the phonological change *waq(a)ā* [with final *alif maqṣūra] yaq(i)ī* "to guard, preserve".

2- *faᶜila yafᶜilu,* e.g. *waliya yaliyu* "to be near" of which only the imperfect becomes after the phonological change *yal(i)ī.*

3- *faᶜila yafᶜalu,* e.g. *waǧiya yawǧayu* of which only the imperfect becomes after the phonological change *yawǧ(a)ā* [with final *alif maqṣūra]*.

8.2. Examples of some derivatives of the verb with 1st and 3rd weak radical

An example of a verb with 1st and 3rd weak radical in the perfect is *waq(a)ā* "he guarded". It becomes *yaqī* in the imperfect of the indicative active. Its imperative is *qi* or *qih,* its active participle is *wāqin,* its *maṣdar* is *waqyun,* its perfect passive is *wuqiya,* its imperfect is *yūqā,* its passive participle is *mawqīyun,* its noun of place is *mawqan* and its noun of instrument is *mīqan.*

8.2.1. Remarks concerning the phonological procedures in some of its forms:

The 1st weak radical of the verb with 1st and 3rd weak radical is submitted to the same rules as the 1st weak radical of the verb with 1st radical *w* or *y* (cf. chap. 5.), and its 3rd weak radical is submitted to the same rules as the 3rd weak radical of the verb with 3rd radical *w* or *y* (cf. chap. 7.).

8.3. The conjugations of the verb with 1st and 3rd weak radical

The verb with 2nd and 3rd weak radical falls into the following conjugations:

1- *faᶜala yafᶜilu,* e.g. *ṭawaya yaṭwiyu* that becomes after the phonological change ṭawā [with final *alif maqṣūra] yaṭwī* "to fold".

2- *faᶜila yafᶜalu,* e.g. *qawiya yaqwayu* "to be strong" of which only the imperfect becomes after the phonological change *yaqwā* [with final *alif maqṣūra]*.

3- *fa^cila yaf^calu,* e.g. *ḥayiya yaḥyayu* of which only the imperfect becomes after the phonological change *yaḥyā* [with final *alif mamdūda].*

8.4. Examples of some derivatives of the verb with 2nd and 3rd weak radical

An example of a verb with 2nd and 3rd weak radical in the perfect is *ṭawā* [with final *alif maqṣūra]* "he folded". It becomes *yaṭwī* in the imperfect of the indicative active. Its imperative is *ʾiṭwi,* its active participle is *ṭāwin,* its *maṣdar* is *ṭayyun,* its perfect passive is *ṭuwiya,* its imperfect is *yuṭwā,* its passive participle is *maṭwīyun,* its noun of place is *maṭwan* and its noun of instrument is *miṭwan.*

8.4.1. Remarks concerning the phonological procedures in some of its forms:

The 2nd weak radical of the verb with 2nd and 3rd weak radical is submitted to the same rules as the 2nd weak radical of the verb with 2nd radical *w* or *y* (cf. chap. 6.), and its 3rd weak radical is submitted to the same rules as the 3rd weak radical of the verb with 3rd radical *w* or *y* (cf. chap 7.).

8.4. Conclusion

I have discussed the verb that is doubly weak in this chapter. It has been observed that its glides are submitted to the same rules as the glides of the other classes of weak radicals: the 1st weak radical as the 1st weak radical of verbs with 1st weak radical, the 2nd weak radical as the 2nd weak radical of verbs with 2nd weak radical, and the 3rd weak radical as the 3rd weak radical of verbs with 3rd weak radical.

In the next chapter I shall generally study the soundness or the unsoundness of the glide.

CHAPTER NINE

9. The soundness or the unsoundness of the glide

Having discussed the weak verb in which one weak radical or more constitutes the form, I shall study the soundness of the glide or the phonological changes due to its unsoundness in a noun or in a verb in this chapter.

9.1. The soundness or the unsoundness of the glide: the sequences involved and the conditions

As it has been observed in the chapters treating the weak verbs, the glide can be sound or unsound. The sound glide is the one that is not subjected to any phonological change, e.g. *wa^{c}ada* "to promise", in which the *w* remains sound on the basis that it is not preceded by any other segment (cf. par. 5.2.1.1.). By contrast to the sound glide, the unsound one implies a change in the word structure, e.g. the imperfect *ya^{c}idu* underlyingly *yaw^{c}idu* in which the 1st radical *w* is elided (cf. par. 5.2.1.3.). These changes are termed as *$^{\circ}$i^{c}lāl*, and the most common ones are that the unsound glide is made vowelless, that it is changed into another glide, that it is elided, that its vowel is shifted, or that it itself is shifted to the position of another segment (cf. Åkesson, *Ibn Mas*ᶜ*ūd* 270: fol. 25b-26a, Rāğiḥī, *Basīṭ* 159).

The soundness of the glide or the phonological change(s) due to its unsoundness involves a sequence of two segments in which the unsound glide is the second segment and is preceded by a vowelless or by a vowelled sound segment. It goes without saying that the sequence of two vowelless segments is excluded, as it is impossible to combine two vowelless segments together.

In order to have a system of analysis that makes it possible to explore the phonological changes I propose for this study the following sequences comprising a glide preceded by a sound segment, whether strong or weak:

9.1.1. The glide is vowelless and preceded by a fatḥa: its soundness or its change into an *ā*.

9.1.2. The glide is vowelled by a fatḥa and preceded by a fatḥa: its change into an *ā*.

9.1.3. The glide is vowelled by a kasra and preceded by a fatḥa: its change into an *ā*.

9.1.4. The glide is vowelled by a ḍamma and preceded by a fatḥa: the change of the *wu* or *yu* into an *ā*.

9.1.5. The glide, the *y*, is vowelless and preceded by a ḍamma: its change into a *w*.

9.1.6. The glide is vowelled by a kasra and preceded by a ḍamma: the transfer of the kasra to the preceding segment and hence the change of the preceding segment's ḍamma into a kasra, the change of the *w* into a *y* or the *y* into an *ī* respectively, or the elision of the glide's kasra and the lengthening of the ḍamma preceding it into an *ū*.

9.1.7. The glide is vowelled by a ḍamma and preceded by a vowel: the glide's ḍamma is elided.

9.1.8. The glide is vowelled by a fatḥa and preceded by a ḍamma: its soundness.

9.1.9. The glide, the *w*, is vowelled by a fatḥa and preceded by a kasra: its change into a *y*.

9.1.10. The glide, the *y*, is vowelled by a ḍamma and preceded by a kasra: the transfer of the ḍamma before the *y* and hence the change of the preceding segment's kasra into a ḍamma, the elision of the *y* and the lengthening of the ḍamma into an *ū* according to a theory, or the elision of the *y's* ḍamma together with the elision of the *y* and the change of the preceding segment's kasra into a ḍamma according to another theory.

9.1.11. The glide, the *y*, is vowelled by a kasra and preceded by a kasra: the elision of the vowel of the *y* together with the *y*.

9.1.12. The glide is vowelled by a fatḥa and preceded by a sukūn: the transfer of the fatḥa to the segment preceding it and the change of the *w* into an *ā*.

9.1.13. The glide, the *y*, is vowelled by a kasra and preceded by a sukūn: the transfer of the kasra to the segment preceding it and the change of the *y* into an *ī*.

9.1.14. The glide is vowelled by a kasra and preceded by a vowelless *ā*: the change of the *wi* or *yi* into *ʾi*.

9.1.15. The glide, the *w*, is vowelled by a ḍamma and preceded by a sukūn: the transfer of the ḍamma to the segment preceding it and the change of the *w* into *ū*.

9.1.16. The glide, the *y*, is vowelled by a ḍamma and preceded by a sukūn: the transfer of the ḍamma to the vowelless segment preceding it, the change of the ḍamma into a kasra and the change of the *y* into *ī*.

9.1.17. The glide, the *w* or *y*, is vowelless and preceded by a kasra: its change into a *y* or *ī* respectively.

9.1.18. The transposition of segments in some nouns.

It shall be remarked concerning these sequences that some of them are affected by a change or a series of changes due to the unsoundness of the glides in them whereas others are not.

There exist as well some conditions (cf. Howell, IV, fasc. I, 1237 sqq. who discusses eleven conditions, Bohas/Kouloughli, *Linguistic* 85-86 who discuss three) that are to be followed if a phonological change is carried out due to the unsoundness of the glide. I can mention seven common ones here:

1 - the glide should be in a verb or in a noun of the verbal form of the measure *fa*^{c}*al*. This is why the phonological change is not carried out if the pattern has the *tā*^{ɔ} *marbūṭa* or the *alif maqṣūra* suffixed to it. Some examples are *ḥawakatun* "weavers" that did not become *ḥ(a)ākatun* and *Ṣawar(a)ā* "*Ṣawar(a)ā*, name of a water" that did not become *Ṣ(a)ār(a)ā* (for discussions see 9.1.2.2.1.: 1).

The phonological change is not either carried out if the word is formed according to a certain form, and hence is not formed according to *fa*^{c}*al*. Some examples are *ǧadwalun* "a rivulet" that is formed according to *fa*^{c}*walun* and *miqwalun* "loquacious, eloquent" and *miḫyaṭun* "a needle" that are formed according to the contracted form *mif*^{c}*alun* of *mif*^{c}*(a)ālun* (for discussions see 9.1.12.1.: 1).

2 - The glide should not be vowelled by a vowel that is not supplied by the basic form. An example is *da*^{c}*aw(u) l-qawma* (دَعَوُا ٱلْقَوْمَ) "they called for the people" in which the sequence *w(u)* is retained because the *u* is a vowel of juncture given to the *w* to avoid the cluster of the underlying vowelless *w* of *da*^{c}*aw* (دَعَوْا) with the vowelless *l-* following the *waṣla* in the definite article prefixed to the second word *l-qawma* (for discussions see 9.1.4.1.: 1).

Another example is *al-dalwu* "the bucket" in which the *w* remains sound as its vowel marks the declension in a certain sentence (cf. 9.1.15.1. :1) and *al-ramyu* "the throwing" in which the *y* remains sound for the same reason (for discussions see par. 9.1.16.1.: 1).

3 - The fatḥa or the kasra preceding the glide is ruled by the sukūn of another form. An example with the fatḥa vowelling the *w* is Form VIII *ʾiǧtawar(u)ū* "they became mutual neighbours" that did not become *ʾiǧt(a)ār(u)ū* because it has the meaning of Form VI *taǧ(a)āwar(u)ū* (for discussions see 9.1.2.1.1.: 2.) in which the sukūn of the *ā* prevented the sequence *wa* after it to be changed into an *ā*. Hence it is as if this *ā* rules as well the sequence *wa* in *ʾiǧtawar(u)ū*. An example with the kasra vowelling the *w* is Form I *ʿawira* "to be blind of one eye" that did not become *ʿ(a)āra*, because it is associated to Form IX *ʾiʿwarra*, in which the sukūn of the consonant *ʿ* hindered any change to affect the sequence *wa* (for discussions see 9.1.3.1.: 1.). Hence it is as if this vowelless *ʿ* rules as well the sequence *wi* in *ʿawira*, and hence hinders any change to affect it.

4 - The word refers in its meaning to intensive mobility. An example is *ḥayaw(a)ānun* "animal, much life" that did not become *ḥ(a)āw(a)ānun* (for discussions see 9.1.2.2.1.: 3.).

5- The combination of two phonological changes due to the unsound glides should be avoided. An example is *ṭawaya* that becomes *ṭaw(a)ā* [with final *alif maqṣūra]* "to fold" with one phonological change, and should not result in *ṭ(a]ā(a)ā* with a second phonological change carried out in it (for discussions see 9.1.2.1.1.: 1.).

6- The form should remain unchanged to prevent that the last glide becomes vowelled by a ḍamma in the imperfect. An example is *ḥayiya* "to live" that did not become *ḥ(a)āya,* to avoid that its imperfect becomes *yaḥ(a)āyu* (for discussions see 9.1.3.1. 2).

7- The glide is meant to give clues to the base form. Some examples are *qawadun* "retaliation" with the wa retained that refers to the root *q w d* and *ṣayadun* "a disease in a camel's head" with the *ya* retained that refers to the root *s y d* (for discussions see 9.1.2.2.1.: 2).

9.1.1. The glide is vowelless and preceded by a fatḥa: its soundness or its change into an ā:

The glide, the *w* or the *y,* which is vowelless and preceded by a fatḥa is mostly sound, and is therefore not changed into an *ā* unless in some anomalous cases. Hence the rule is the following:

-aw → *-aw*

-ay → *-ay*

Some examples are the verbal nouns of verbs with 2nd weak radical formed according to *faᶜlun,* e.g. *qawlun* "a saying" with the 2nd radical *w* retained and *bayᶜun* "a selling" with the 2nd radical *y* retained (cf. par. 6.5.11.). Some prefer however to consider the *w* in *qawlun* as unsound and change it anomalously into an *ā,* i.e. *q(a)ālun* (cf. Ibn Manẓūr, V, 3779, Åkesson, *Ibn Masᶜūd* 282: fol. 27a), but the variant pertains to the anomalies.

The reason of the soundness of the glide is that the fatḥa preceding it, which is followed by the sukūn, is not considered as a strong vowel capable of forcing a change upon it (cf. Åkesson, *Ibn Masᶜūd* 282: fol. 27a).

Another case in which the weak radical is retained is the verb with 3rd radical *w* or *y* in the perfect, in which the 3rd weak radical is vowelless and precedes the vowelled agent pronoun suffix, e.g. *ġazaw-tu* "I raided" and *ramay-tu* "I threw" respectively (cf. par. 7.5.3.).

As what concerns the case in which the vowelless *w* or the *y* preceded by a fatḥa is changed into an *ā,* it can be remarked that it is carried out as the second step of a phonological change that implies at first the transfer of a vowel. This is the case of the imperfect of the verb with 2nd radical *w* vowelled by a fatḥa that occurs formed according to the conjugation *yafᶜalu,* e.g. *yaḫwafu* > *yaḫawfu* > *yaḫ(a)āfu* "he is afraid" (cf. par. 6.5.3.1.) and of the verb with 2nd radical *y,* e.g. *yahyabu* > *yahaybu* > *yah(a)ābu* "he is afraid" (cf. par. 6.5.3.2.)

9.1.1.1. Some anomalous cases:

In spite of the fact that the *w* is preceded by a fatḥa, it can be changed into a *y* anomalously in some cases:

-aw → *-ay*

This occurs in the derived forms of perfects of some verbs with with 3rd radical *w,* e.g. Form II *ġazzawa* that becomes *ġazzaya* "to raid" and then *ġazz(a)ā* [with final alif maqṣūra], Form IV *ʾaġzaw-tu* > *ʾaġzay-tu* "I raided" and Form X *ʾistarḍawa* > *ʾistarḍaya* > *ʾistarḍ(a)ā* (cf. par. 7.5.10.).

The change of the *w* into a *y* in these forms is on the analogy of its change into a *y* in their imperfects: Form II *yuġazziwu* > *yuġazziyu* "he raids", Form IV *yuġziwu* > *yuġz(i)yu* > *yuġz(i)ī* "he raids" and Form X *yastarḍiwu* > *yastarḍiyu* > *yastarḍ(i)ī* (cf. par. 7.5.11.) respectively.

9.1.2. The glide is vowelled by a fatḥa and preceded by a fatḥa: its change into an ā:

This sequence occurs in verbs with 2nd or 3rd weak radical and in nouns and adjectives. As I shall discuss below, the glide is changed into an *ā* in verbs with 2nd weak radical (cf. 9.1.2.1) and in nouns and adjectives (cf. 9.1.2.2.), and into an *alif mam-*

dūda in verbs with 3rd radical *w* or into an *alif maqṣūra* in verbs with 3rd radical *y* (cf. 9.1.2.1). The glide remains sound in some specific cases (cf. 9.1.2.1.1.).

9.1.2.1. The phonological change that is carried out in verbs:

The cases that can be mentioned are the perfects of verbs with 2nd or 3rd weak radical in the 3rd person of the masc. sing.

In the cases of verbs with 2nd weak radical, the glide, the *w* or the *y*, is vowelled by a fatḥa and is preceded by one, which results in its change into an *ā*.

-awa → - *(a)ā*

-aya → - *(a)ā*

An example of a verb with weak 2nd radical *w* is *qawala* > *q(a)āla* "to say" (cf. par. 6.5.1.1.: 1 and 10.1.12.1.).

An example of a verb with weak 2nd radical *y* is *bayaᶜa* > *b(a)āᶜa* "to sell" (cf. par. 6.5.1.2.: 1 and 10.1.12.2.).

In the cases of verbs with 3rd weak radical, the glide, the *w* or the *y*, is vowelled by a fatḥa and preceded by one, which results in its change into an *alif mamdūda* if the glide is a *w,* e.g. *ġazawa* > *ġaz(a)ā* "to raid" [with final *alif mamdūda]* (cf. par. 7.5.1.1.) or into an *alif maqṣūra* if the glide is a *y,* e.g. *ramaya* > *ram(a)ā* "to throw" (cf. par. 7.5.1.2).

9.1.2.1.1. The soundness of the glide:

The glide remains sound in these cases that are discussed below, just to mention a few:

1- The combination of two phonological changes due to the unsound glides should be avoided.

2- The fatḥa preceding the glide is ruled by the sukūn of another form.

1- The combination of two phonological changes due to the unsound glides should be avoided:

An example that can introduce two phonological changes, which is forbidden, is *ṭawaya* in which the sequence *ya* preceded by a fatḥa is changed into an *(a)ā,* namely *ṭaw(a)ā* [with final alif maqṣūra] "to fold" (cf. Åkesson, *Ibn Mas*ᶜ*ūd* 284: fol. 28a). It is not allowed after this change to change the sequence *wa* of *ṭaw(a)ā* preceded by a fatḥa into *(a)ā* that would result in *ṭ(a)āā* as this would necessarily imply a cluster of two vowelless glides, the alifs: the *alif mamdūda* and the *alif maqṣūra.*

It can be remarked that the phonological change is not carried out as well in the dual of the masc. *ṭaway(a)ā* "/dual" in spite of the fact that the final radical *y* is vowelled, and thus there is no risk in combining two vowelless segments, by analogy with *ṭaw(a)ā* (cf. ibid, 284: fol. 28a). In other words *ṭaway(a)ā* could have become *ṭ(a)āy(a)ā,* but did not do so by analogy with *ṭaw(a)ā* that did not either become *ṭ(a)āā.*

2- The fatḥa preceding the glide is ruled by the sukūn of another form:

A factor that can hinder the change of the glide vowelled by a fatḥa and preceded by one into an *ā,* is that the fatḥa of the segment preceding the glide in a specific form can be influenced theoretically by the sukūn of another form which it resembles in meaning, and thus this fatḥa is counted as ruled by a sukūn (cf. ibid, 284: fol. 27b-28a).

This is the case of some verbs of Form VIII *ᵓifta*ᶜ*ala* with 2nd radical *w,* that have the meaning of Form VI *taf(a)ā*ᶜ*ala* denoting the reciprocity, in which the *w* is counted as sound in them (cf. Sībawaihi, II, 399-401, Zamaḫšarī, 180, Ibn Yaᶜīš, X, 74-75, Howell, II-III, 275, IV, fasc. I, 1242-1243), and thus the sequence *awa* in them is not changed into *(a)ā*. Some examples are Form VIII *ʾiǧtawar(u)ū* "they became mutual neighbours" that did not become *ʾiǧt(a)ār(u)ū* because it has the meaning of Form VI *taǧ(a)āwar(u)ū,* and Form VIII *ʾizdawaǧ(u)ū* "they intermarried" that did not become *ʾizd(a)āǧ(u)ū* because it has the meaning of Form VI *taz(a)āwaǧ(u)ū*. The change of the sequence awa into *(a)ā* is necessary otherwise, e.g. *ʾiḫtawana* that has the meaning of Form I *ḫ(a)āna,* which becomes *ʾiḫt(a)āna* "was unfaithful".

To be more explicit, in for instance the case of Form VIII *ʾiǧtawara,* the fatḥa preceding the *w* is counted as being ruled by the sukūn of the vowelless *ā* preceding the *w* in Form VI *taǧ(a)āwara* (cf. Åkesson, *Ibn Masᶜūd* 284: fol. 28a), which is the reason why the *wa* is retained and the form did not become *ʾiǧt(a)āra.* As a matter of fact, *ʾiǧtawara* is associated to *taǧ(a)āwara* on account of its similarity of meaning to it, and in *taǧ(a)āwara,* the vowelless *ā* prevented the change of the sequence *wa* into *(a)ā.* It is then as if the vowelless *ā* of *taǧ(a)āwara* rules as well the *w* of *ʾiǧtawara,* in which the fatḥa becomes counted as a sukūn, and thus hinders any change to be carried out.

9.1.2.2. The phonological change that is carried out in nouns and adjectives:

The phonological change is carried out in the noun or adjective on the condition that the noun is formed according to the verbal form *faᶜal.*

-awa → *-(a)ā*

An example is *dawarun* with the 2nd radical *w* vowelled by a fatḥa and preceded by one that becomes *d(a)ārun* "house" after that the *wa* is changed into an *ā*.

The phonological change that is carried out in this noun is not only due to the fact that its glide is vowelled by a fatḥa and is preceded by one, but also because it answers the condition of resembling the verbal form *faᶜal* (for this condition see Åkesson, *Ibn Masᶜūd* 284: fol. 27b, Bohas/Kouloughli, *Linguistic* 86). Thus no phonological change is carried out in nouns that lose their resemblance to a verbal form through the suffixation of a noun suffix (cf. 9.1.2.2.1.: 1).

9.1.2.2.1. The soundness of the glide:

The glide remains sound in the noun or in the adjective in the following cases that are discussed below, just to mention a few:

1- The noun or the adjective is not formed according to the verbal form *faᶜal* through the suffixation of the *tāʾ marbūṭa* or the *alif maqṣūra*.

2- The glide is meant to give clues to the base form.

3- The word refers in its meaning to intensive mobility.

1- The noun or the adjective is not formed according to the verbal form faᶜal through the sufixation of the tāʾ marbūṭa or the alif maqṣūra:

Some examples are *ḥawakatun* "weavers", which is the pl. of *ḥ(a)āʾikun* and *ḫawanatun* "traitors", which is the pl. of *ḫ(a)āʾinun* (cf. Zamaḫšarī, 181, Åkesson, *Ibn Masᶜūd* 284: fol. 28a, Howell, IV, fasc. I, 1510). Both these triliterals differ from their verbs' measures *ḥawaka* "to weave" and *ḫawana* "to betray" through the *tā᾽ marbūṭa* of feminization. This is the reason why the sequence *wa* is not changed into *(a)ā* in them, and serves through its retaining to give indication of their base forms.

An example of a noun to which the *alif maqṣūra* is suffixed to is *Ṣawar(a)ā* "Ṣawar(a)ā, name of a water" (cf. Åkesson, *Ibn Masᶜūd* 284: fol. 28a), which is referred to as being the name of a water in Medīna (cf. Ibn Wallād, *Maqṣūr* 74). The sequence *wa* in it is retained and not changed into an *ā*. An example of an adjective is *ḥayad(a)ā* "(a he-ass) shying at his own shadow because of his liveliness" (cf. Åkesson, *Ibn Masᶜūd* 284: fol. 28a, Howell, IV, fasc. I, 1251), that is formed according to the pattern *faᶜal(a)ā,* in which the *ya* is retained.

2- The glide is meant to give clues to the base form:

An example of a noun in which the *w* is intended to notify of the base form is *qawadun* "retaliation" that refers to the root *q w d,* and of a noun in which the *y* is intended to notify of the base form is *ṣayadun* "a disease in a camel's head" (cf. Zamaḫšarī, 173, Åkesson, *Ibn Masᶜūd* 284: fol. 28a, Howell, IV, fasc. I, 1251) that refers to *s y d.* The sequence *wa* in *qawadun* is not changed into *(a)ā,* i.e. *qa(ā)dun,* in spite of its being vowelled with a fatḥa and preceded by one, as this would cause a confusion on whether the form is from the root *qawada* "to lead" with the *w* as 2nd radical or the root *qayada* "to bind" with the *y* as 2nd radical. The same goes for the *ya* in *ṣayadun* that is not changed into *(a)ā,* i.e. *ṣa(ā)dun,* as this would cause a confusion on whether the form is from the root *ṣawada* with the *w* as 2nd radical, that is the base form of *al-ṣ(a)ādu* "the [letter] ṣād" or the root *ṣayada* "to hunt" with the *y* as 2nd radical.

3- The word refers in its meaning to intensive mobility:

This is the case of the noun *ḥayaw(a)ānun* "animal, much life" (cf. Åkesson, *Ibn Masᶜūd* 284: fol. 28a, Howell, IV, fasc. I, 1409) in which no phonological change is carried out so that the word corresponds in mobility to what it represents, which is a mobile animal. It occurs in the sur. 29: 64 *(la-hya l-ḥayawānu)* "that is Life indeed". The variant *mawt(a)ānun* is its opposite in meaning, and on this account it is formed according to its pattern (cf. Ibn Manẓūr, VI, 4296, Åkesson, *Ibn Masᶜūd* 284: fol. 28a, Lane, I, 679, 682, Howell, IV, fasc. I, 1244, 1409, 1465).

9.1.3. The glide is vowelled by a kasra and preceded by a fatḥa: its change into an ā:

The glide that is vowelled by a kasra and preceded by a fatḥa is changed into an *ā*.

-awi → *-(a)ā*

-ayi → *-(a)ā*

The cases that can be mentioned are the perfects of verbs with 2nd weak radical in the 3rd person of the masc. sing. of the conjugation *faᶜila*.

An example of a verb with weak 2nd radical *w* vowelled by a kasra is *ḫawifa* > *ḫ(a)āfa* "to fear" (cf. par. 6.5.1.1.: 3).

An example of a verb with 2nd radical *y* vowelled by a kasra is *hayiba* > *h(a)āba* "to be afraid" (cf. par. 6.5.1.2.: 2).

9.1.3.1. The soundness of the glide:

The glide remains sound in these cases that are discussed below, just to mention a few:

1- The fatḥa preceding the glide is ruled by the sukūn of another form.

2- The form should remain unchanged to prevent that the last glide becomes vowelled by a ḍamma in the imperfect.

1- The fatḥa preceding the glide is ruled by the sukūn of another form:

The same procedure is applied as the one that concerns the verb with the 2nd radical vowelled by a fatḥa and preceded by one, e.g. Form VIII *ʾiǧtawar(u)ū* "they became mutual neighbours" in which the *w* remains sound as the fatḥa preceding it is ruled by the sukūn of the *ā* of Form VI *taǧ(a)āwar(u)ū* (cf. 9.1.2.1.1.: 2).

An example with the glide vowelled by a kasra and preceded by a fatḥa is Form I *ʿawira* "to be blind of one eye". In this example the sequence *wi* did not become *a(ā)* as expected due to the influence of the fatḥa preceding it, which would result in *ʿ(a)āra,* because the verb is associated to Form IX *ʾiʿwarra* with which it shares the same meaning. As the sukūn of the consonant *ʿ* in *ʾiʿwarra* hinders any change to affect the sequence *wa,* it is as if this sukūn rules as well the *ʿa* in Form I *ʿawira,* and by doing so, hinders the change to be carried out in the sequence *wi* that could have resulted in *ʿ(a)āra.*

Another example of a verb is *ḥawila* "squinted", which has the meaning of Form IX *ʾiḥwalla,* and for the same reason as with *ʿawira* has the sequence *wi* unchanged (cf. Sībawaihi, II, 399, Zamaḫšarī, 180, Howell, IV, fasc. I, 1241-1242). It can be noted that Wright, *Comparative Grammar* 243 was perplexed by the uncontraction in *ʿawira* and *ḥawila,* as he writes:

> "I do not know why *ḫawifa* became *ḫāfa,* and *mawita, māta,* whilst *ḥawila* and *ʿawira* remained uncontracted".

2- The form should remain unchanged to prevent that the last glide becomes vowelled by a ḍamma in the imperfect:

This is the case of *ḥayiya* "to live" (cf. Åkesson, *Ibn Masᶜūd* 284: fol. 28a) in which the sequence *yi* is not changed into *(a)ā* due to the influence of the fatḥa preceding it, namely *ḥ(a)āya,* to avoid that its imperfect becomes *yaḥ(a)āyu,* with the disliked combination of the ḍamma following the *y* that is deemed as heavy (cf. Åkesson, *Conversion* 28). Instead the imperfect is *yaḥy(a)ā* [with final alif maqṣūra].

9.1.4. The glide is vowelled by a ḍamma and preceded by a fatḥa: the change of the wu or yu into an ā:

The *w* or the *y* that is vowelled by a ḍamma and preceded by a fatḥa is changed into an *ā*. Thus:

-awu → *-(a)ā*
-ayu → *-(a)ā*

This sequence occurs in the verb with 2nd radical *w* in the perfect formed according to the conjugation *faᶜula,* e.g. *ṭawula* that becomes *ṭ(a)āla* "to become long" (cf. par. 6.5.1.1.: 2), and in the verb with 3rd radical *w* or *y* of the conjucation *faᶜala* that occurs in the 3rd person of the masc. pl., e.g. *ġazaw(u)-ū / ġazaw(u)-w* that becomes at first *ġaz(a)ā-w* (cf. par. 7.5.4.) with this change, then *ġaza-w* "they attacked" with the elision of the *ā,* and *ramay(u)-ū / ramay(u)-w* that becomes at first *ram(a)ā-w* (cf. ibid) with this change, then *rama-w* "they threw" with the elision of the *ā*.

9.1.4.1. The soundness of the glide:

The glide remains sound in this case:

1- The glide should not be vowelled by a vowel that is not supplied by the basic form.

1- The glide should not be vowelled by a vowel that is not supplied by the basic form:

The *wu* that is preceded by a fatḥa is not changed into an *ā* if the ḍamma of the *w* is not supplied by the basic form (for this condition see Åkesson, *Ibn Mas*^{c}*ūd* 284: fol. 27b, Bohas/ Kouloughli, *Linguistic* 85), but by an external factor.

This is the case of the verb with 3rd radical *w da*^{c}*awa* "to call" that occurs in the 3rd person of the masc. pl. *da*^{c}*aw* AåÌä§äe with *alif mamdūda,* followed by a noun to which the *-l* of the definite article following the waṣla, is prefixed to, e.g. *da*^{c}*aw(u) l-qawma* دَعَوُا ٱلْقَوْمَ "they called for the people" (cf. Åkesson, *Ibn Mas*^{c}*ūd* 284: fol. 28a). As remarked the suffixed pronoun of the agent, namely the *w* of the pl. of *da*^{c}*aw,* is underlyingly vowelless, but becomes vowelled by the ḍamma that is a vowel of juncture (for discussions concerning the vowel of juncture see Roman, *Étude II,* 747-755), to avoid the cluster of two vowelless segments, namely the vowelless *w* that is the pronoun of the agent of دَعَوْا and the vowelless *l-* following the waṣla of the definite article prefixed to the second word *l-qawma.* As the ḍamma in *da*^{c}*aw(u)* is not supplied by the basic form, but is due to an external reason that has to do with the second word following it, the *wu* of *da*^{c}*aw(u)* remains sound and is not changed into an *ā*.

9.1.5. The glide, the y, is vowelless and preceded by a ḍamma: its change into a *w*.

The weak vowelless *y* that is preceded by a ḍamma is usually changed into a w (cf. Åkesson, *Ibn Mas*^{c}*ūd* 282: 27a, Wright, II, 80). Thus:

-uy → *-uw* > *(u)ū*

This sequence occurs in verbs with 1st radical *y* in the imperfect of the passive voice of Form I *yuf^{c}alu,* e.g. *yuysaru* "is pleased" that becomes *yuwsaru > y(u)ūsaru,* the active voice of Form IV of the imperfect *yuf^{c}ilu,* e.g. *yuysiru* that becomes *yuwsiru > y(u)ūsiru* "is well off" (cf. par. 5.4.1.1.; for the substitution see par. 10.1.9.2) and the active participle of Form IV *muf^{c}ilun,* e.g. *muysirun* that becomes *muwsirun > m(u)ūsirun* "is prosperous" (cf. par. 5.4.1.1.; for the substitution see par. 10.1.9.2).

9.1.6. The glide is vowelled by a kasra and preceded by a ḍamma: the transfer of the kasra to the preceding segment and hence the change of the preceding segment's ḍamma into a kasra, the change of the w into a y or the y into an ī respectively, or the elision of the glide's kasra and the lengthening of the ḍamma preceding it into an ū:

The *w* that is vowelled by a kasra and preceded by a ḍamma is considered as unsound and gives hand to two possibilities.

1st possibility: *-uwi* with the *w* vowelled by a kasra and preceded by a ḍamma becomes *-iw* after that the *w's* kasra is shifted before the *w* and hence the ḍamma is changed into a kasra. As in it the vowelless *w* is preceded by a kasra, the *w* is changed into an *ī:* lengthened *ī,* namely *-iy / (i)ī.*

An example of this sequence is found in a verb with 2nd radical *w* in the passive voice formed according to *fu^{c}ila,* e.g. *quwila* "it was said" (cf. par. 6.5.13.1.). According to this theory *quwila > qiwla > q(i)yla > q(i)īla* can be mentioned.

2nd possibility: *-uwi* with the *w* vowelled by a kasra and preceded by a ḍamma becomes *–uw* after that the *w's* kasra is elided for the sake of alleviation. As in it the vowelless *w* is preceded by a ḍamma, the *w* is changed into an *ū:* lengthened *ū* so that it becomes *-(u)ū*. According to this theory the example *quwila* > *quwla* > *q(u)ūla* can be mentioned.

The *y* that is vowelled by a kasra and preceded by a ḍamma is also considered as unsound. The two possibilities concerning the phonological changes that can be carried out are the following:

1st possibility: *-uyi* with the *y* vowelled by a kasra and preceded by a ḍamma becomes *-iy* after that the *y's* kasra is shifted before the *y* and hence the ḍamma is changed into a kasra. As there is in it a vowelless *y* preceded by a kasra the *y* is changed into an *ī:* lengthened *ī,* so that it becomes *(i)ī.*

An example of this sequence is found in a verb with 2nd radical *y* in the passive voice formed according to *fu*^{c}*ila,* e.g. *buyi*^{c}*a* "it was sold" (cf. par. 6.5.13.2.). According to this theory, the changes are the following: *buyi*^{c}*a* > *biy*^{c}*a* > *b(i)ī*^{c}*a.*

2nd possibility: *-uyi* with the *y* vowelled by a kasra and preceded by a ḍamma becomes *-uy* after that the *y's* kasra is elided for the sake of alleviation. As there is in it a vowelless *y* preceded by a ḍamma, the *y* is changed into a *w,* so that it becomes *-uw.* As there is in it a vowelless *w* preceded by a ḍamma, the *w* is changed into an *ū:* lengthened *ū,* so that it becomes *-(u)ū.* According to this theory the example *buyi*^{c}*a* > *buy*^{c}*a* > *b(u)ū*^{c}*a* can be mentioned.

9.1.7. The glide is vowelled by a ḍamma and preceded by a vowel: the glide's ḍamma is elided:

The glide that is vowelled by a ḍamma and preceded by a vowel is considered as unsound, and the phonological change that is carried out in this sequence results in the elision of the glide's ḍamma to alleviate, because the combination is deemed as heavy.

If the glide is a *w* vowelled by a ḍamma and preceded by one, the procedure is the following: *-uwu* with the *w* vowelled by a ḍamma and preceded by one becomes *-uw* > *-(u)ū* after that the ḍamma is elided and the *w* is changed into an *ū:* lengthened *ū*. An example of such a sequence is found in the verb in the imperfect of the 3rd person of the masc. sing. *yaġzuwu* "he attacks" that becomes *yaġzuw* / *yaġz(u)ū* (for discussions see 7.5.6.).

If the glide is a *y* vowelled by a ḍamma and preceded by a kasra, the procedure is the following: *-iyu* with the *y* vowelled by a ḍamma and preceded by a kasra that becomes *iy* > *(i)ī* after that the ḍamma is elided and the *y* is changed into an *ī:* lengthened *ī*.

An example of such a sequence is found in the verb in the imperfect of the 3rd person of the masc. sing. *yarmiyu* "he throws" that becomes *yarmiy* > *yarm(i)ī* (for discussions see 7.5.6.).

9.1.8. The glide is vowelled by a fatḥa and preceded by a ḍamma: its soundness:

The glide that is vowelled by a fatḥa and preceded by a ḍamma remains sound. The reason of its soundness is the lightness of the fatḥa (cf. Åkesson, *Ibn Mas*ᶜ*ūd* 286: fol. 28b).

-uwa → *-uwa*

-uya → *-uya*

An example in which such a sequence is found is a verb with 3rd radical *w* that occurs in the subjunctive of the 3rd person of the masc. sing., e.g. *lan yad*ᶜ*uwa* "he shall not call", in which the

3rd radical *w* of the verb is vowelled by the fatḥa, as a marker of the subjunctive, and is preceded by a ḍamma. This *w* remains sound in spite of the fact that it is preceded by a ḍamma, which could have resulted in the assimilation of the *w* to the ḍamma and thus in the lengthened *w: ū,* i.e. *lan yadᶜ(u)ū.* The reason why the phonological change is not carried out in it is that the fatḥa is considered as light on the *w* (for other examples see Ibn Ǧinnī, *Munṣif II,* 114). So there is no need to alleviate more by having *lan yadᶜ(u)ū* instead of *lan yadᶜuwa.* We can remark as well that if this was to occur the subjunctive would be mixed up with the jussive.

In line with this theory that the glide vowelled by a fatḥa and preceded by a ḍamma remains sound, the *w* vowelled by a fatḥa and preceded by a ḍamma in *nuwamatun* "one who sleeps much" and the *y* vowelled by a fatḥa and preceded by a ḍamma in *ᶜuyabatun* "one who reproaches people much" (cf. Zamaḫšarī, 181, Ibn Yaᶜīš, X, 82-83, Åkesson, *Ibn Masᶜūd* 286: fol. 28b) remain sound.

9.1.9. The glide, the w, is vowelled by a fatḥa and preceded by a kasra: its change into a y:

The *w* that is vowelled by a fatḥa and preceded by a kasra is usually changed into a *y.*

-iwa → *-iya*

An example in which such a sequence occurs is the active participle *dāᶜiwatun* "the one who invites /fem." (cf. Åkesson, *Ibn Masᶜūd* 286: fol. 28b) with the 3rd radical *w* from the verb *daᶜawa* "to call", which occurs in the fem. sing., and thus with the fatḥa preceding the *tāʾ marbūṭa.* Hence *d(a)āᶜiwatun* with the 3rd radical *w* vowelled by a fatḥa and preceded by a kasra becomes *d(a)āᶜiyatun* after the change of the *wa* into a *ya.* The reason why the *w* vowelled by a fatḥa is changed in this sequence into a *y* is the influence of the kasra preceding it and the faintness of the nature of the fatḥa.

9.1.9.1. Some anomalous cases:

An anomalous case in which the *w* is changed into a *y* is *siw(a)āṭun* that becomes *siy(a)āṭun* "whips". The phonological change is carried out in it in spite of the fact that it is not formed according to the verbal pattern *fa^c^al* (for the conditions see 9.1.). The reason of the unsoundness of the *w(a)* in it is that it is compared to the vowelless *w* of its sing. *sawṭun* (cf. Åkesson, *Ibn Mas^c^ūd* 284: fol. 28a). Zamaḫšarī, 182 compares the vowelless *w* as well with the vowelless alif of *d(a)ārun* "house". Being then compared with a vowelless segment, the vowelled w in *siw(a)āṭun* is treated as being so, and as it is preceded by a kasra it is changed into the *y*, namely *siy(a)āṭun* (cf. Howell, IV, fasc. I, 1264-1265).

Another example is the broken pl. *diw(a)ārun* with 2nd radical *w* that becomes *diy(a)ārun* (cf. Åkesson, *Ibn Mas^c^ūd* 284: fol. 28a, Howell, IV, fasc. I, 1264). One of the reasons why the phonological change is carried out in it is so that it is on the analogy of the change that is carried out in its sing. *dawarun* that becomes *d(a)ārun* in which the *wa* is changed into an *ā* because the *w* is vowelled by a fatḥa and preceded by one (cf. Åkesson, *Ibn Mas^c^ūd 284:* fol. 28a, this study par. 10.1.8.2.). Another example is the verbal noun Form I *qiw(a)āmun* that becomes *qiy(a)āmun* "standing" (cf. par. 10.1.8.2.). The reason of this change according to Ibn Mas^c^ūd (Åkesson, *Ibn Mas^c^ūd* 284: fol. 28a), is that there should be an analogy with the change that is carried out in its verb *qawama* that became *q(a)āma* with the *wa* changed into an *ā*.

9.1.10. The glide, the y, is vowelled by a ḍamma and preceded by a kasra: the transfer of the ḍamma before the y and hence the change of the preceding segment's kasra into a ḍamma, the elision of the y and the lengthening of the ḍamma into an ū according to a theory, or the elision of the y's ḍamma together with the elision of the y and the change of the preceding segment's kasra into a ḍamma according to another theory:

An example in which the *y* is vowelled by a ḍamma and preceded by a kasra is the verb with 3rd weak *y raḍiya* "to be pleased" in the perfect of the 3rd person of the masc. pl. to which the suffix marking the pl., the *ū,* is attached to, namely *raḍiy(u)-ū* "they were pleased /masc. pl." (cf. Åkesson, *Ibn Mas*ᶜ*ūd* 286: fol. 28b).

There are two theories concerning the phonological changes. The first theory is that *-iy(u)-ū* with the *y* vowelled by a ḍamma and preceded by a kasra becomes *-uy-ū* after that the *y's* ḍamma is shifted backwards, and hence the preceding segment's kasra is changed into a ḍamma. As there is in it a cluster of two vowelless segments, the *y* and *ū,* the *y* is elided so that it becomes *(u)-ū.*

This procedure goes back to Ibn Ǧinnī's theory (cf. Ibn Ǧinnī, *Munṣif II,* 126). An example that he mentions is *raḍiy(u)-ū >raḍuy-ū > raḍ(u)-ū* (for discussions see par. 7.5.5.).

According to Ibn Masᶜūd (cf. Åkesson, *Ibn Mas*ᶜ*ūd* 286: fol. 28b) the phonological changes are the following:

raḍiy(u)-ū> raḍiy-ū > raḍi-ū > raḍ(u)-ū (for discussions see par. 7.5.5.).

The second theory is that *-iy(u)-ū* with the *y* vowelled by a ḍamma and preceded by a kasra becomes *iy-ū* after that the *y's* ḍamma is elided for the sake of alleviation. As there is in it a cluster of a vowelless *y* and *ū*, the *y* is elided so that it becomes *i-ū*. As the vowelless *ū* is preceded by a kasra, the kasra is changed into a ḍamma so that it becomes *(u)-ū*.

9.1.11. The glide, the y, is vowelled by a kasra and preceded by a kasra: the elision of the vowel of the y together with the y:

The phonological changes involve the elision of the *y's* kasra and the elision of the *y*. Thus I illustrate this with the following: the sequence *iy(i)-ī* that occurs in the 2nd person of the fem. sing. of a verb with the 3rd radical *y* vowelled by a kasra and preceded by one becomes *iy-ī* after that the *y's* kasra is alleviated. As there is in it a cluster of two vowelless segments: the *y* and the *ī*, the 3rd radical *y* is elided so that it becomes *(i)-ī*.

This sequence occurs in the verb in the imperfect of the 2nd person of the fem. sing. *tarmiy(i)īna* that becomes *tarm(i)-īna* "you throw" The phonological changes are the following: *tarmiy(i)-īna* > *tarmiy-īna* > *tarm(i)-īna* (cf. par. 7.5.8.).

9.1.12. The glide is vowelled by a fatḥa and preceded by a sukūn: the transfer of the fatḥa to the segment preceding it and the change of the w into an ā:

The phonological changes involve the transfer of the glide's fatḥa to the vowelless segment preceding it and the change of the vowelless *w* or *y* into an *ā* on account of the influence of the fatḥa preceding it.

Thus if the glide is a *w*, the procedure is the following: - *°wa* (*°* stands for vowelless segment) with the *w* vowelled by a fatḥa and preceded by a sukūn becomes *-aw* after that the *w's* fatḥa is shifted to the vowelless segment preceding it. As in it the *w* is preceded by a fatḥa, the *w* is changed into an *ā* so that it becomes *(a)ā.*

If the glide is a *y,* the procedure is the following: - ^{o}*ya* with the *y* vowelled by a fatḥa and preceded by a sukūn becomes *-ay* after that the *y's* fatḥa is shifted to the vowelless segment preceding it.

Some examples in which such a sequence occurs are the verb with 2nd radical *w* formed according to the conjugation *yaf*^{c}*alu* that occurs in the imperfect, e.g. *yaḫwafu* that becomes *yaḫawfu* and then *yaḫ(a)āfu* "he is afraid" (cf. par. 6.5.3.1.), the imperfect of the passive voice of the verb with 2nd radical *w* or *y* formed according to *yuf*^{c}*alu,* e.g. *yuqwalu* that becomes *yuqawlu* and then *yuq(a)ālu* "is said" and *yubya*^{c}*u* that becomes *yubay*^{c}*u* and then *yub(a)ā*^{c}*u* "is sold" (cf. par. 6.5.14.) and the noun of place of a verb with 2nd radical *w,* e.g. *maqwalun* that becomes *maqawlun* and then *maq(a)ālun* "speech" (cf. par. 6.5.15.).

9.1.12.1. The soundness of the glide:

The glide remains sound in the noun or in the adjective in the following case that is discussed below, just to mention one:

1- The noun or the adjective is not formed according to the verbal form *fa*^{c}*al.*

1- The noun or the adjective is not formed according to the verbal form fa^{c}*al:*

An example is the noun *ğadwalun* "a rivulet" (cf. Åkesson, *Ibn Mas*^{c}*ūd* 286: fol. 29a, Howell, IV, fasc. I, 1524), in which the *w* is vowelled by a fatḥa and preceded by a sukūn, from *ğadala* "to make firm".

The reason of the *w's* soundness in it is that the noun is quasi-coordinate to the measure *faᶜwalun* and hence is not formed according to the verbal *faᶜal.* So the *w* could not be changed into an *ā* after that its fatḥa is shifted to the *ğ* preceding it, i.e. *ğad(a)ālun,* as this would cancel the formation.

Other examples are *miqwalun* that is contracted from the base form *miqw(a)ālun* "loquacious, eloquent" with 2nd radical *w,* and *miḫyaṭun* that is contracted from the base form *miḫy(a)āṭun* "a needle" (cf. Åkesson, *Ibn Masᶜūd* 288: fol. 29a) with 2nd radical *y.* So their pattern *mifᶜalun* is the contracted form of *mifᶜ(a)ālun.*

9.1.12.2. Some anomalous cases:

An anomalous case that can be taken up, which is due to a sequence of two glides instead of a glide preceded by a consonantal segment, is the verbal noun *kaywan(u)ūnatun* (that is on the pattern *fayᶜal(u)ūlatun,* cf. Ibn Ğinnī, *Munṣif II,* 10), in which the 2nd radical *w* is vowelled by a fatḥa and preceded by a vowelless *y.* The phonological changes that are carried out are the change of the *w* into a *y* and the assimilation of the *y* to the *y* resulting in *kayyan(u)ūnatun* "being" (cf. par. 10.1.8.2.). Thus *kaywan(u)ūnatun* with the 2nd radical *w* vowelled by a fatḥa and preceded by a vowelless *y* becomes *kayyan(u)ūnatun* after the change of the *wa* into a *ya* and the assimilation of the yāʾs.

The base form *kayyan(u)ūnatun* is used mostly in poetic licence. It occurs in this verse said by al-Nahšalī, cited by Ibn Ğinnī, *Munṣif II,* 15, Ibn al-Anbārī, *Inṣāf* Q. 115, 334, Suyūṭī, *Ašbāh III,* 335, Ibn Manzūr, V, 3926, Howell, IV, fasc. I, 1461, Åkesson, *Ibn Masᶜūd* 300: (263):

> *"Yā layta ʾannā ḍammanā safīnah*
> *ḥattā yaᶜūda l-waṣlu kayyanūnah".*
> "O would that we and the beloved were so placed that a boat held us,
> to the end that union might return in being!".

An alleviated form exists as well, namely *kayn(u)ūnatun* (cf. Åkesson, *Ibn Masᶜūd* 282: fol. 27a-27b) that is from *kayyan(u)ūnatun* after that the 2nd *y* vowelled by a fatḥa is elided.

An analysis of *kayn(u)ūnatun* shows that it occurs with a *y* following the 1st radical, and not with a *w*, - in spite of the fact that it is a verbal noun of a verb with 2nd radical *w* namely *kawana* "to be". The reason of that is that it is made formed according to the verbal nouns of verbs with 2nd radical *y* (cf. ibid 282: fol. 27b, Wright, II, 120) on the basis that they are much more numerous. I can mention that only four words of patterns of verbal nouns with *w* as 2nd radical seem to occur formed according to *fayᶜal(u)ūlatun* (cf. Ibn Manẓūr, V, 3959, Åkesson, *Ibn Masᶜūd* 282-284: fol. 27b): namely: 1- *kayn(u)ūnatun* from *k(a)āna yak(u)ūnu* "to be", 2- *daym(u)ūmatun* from *d(a)āma yad(u)ūmu* "to continue", 3- *sayd(u)ūdatun* from *s(a)āda yas(u)ūdu* "to rule" and 4- *hayᶜ(u)ūᶜatun* from *h(a)āᶜa yah(u)ūᶜu* "to vomit". Some examples of verbal nouns of verbs with 2nd radical *y* to which *kayn(u)ūnatun* is formed according to, are: *ṣayr(u)ūratun* from *ṣ(a)āra yaṣ(i)īru* "to become", *ġayb(u)ūbatun* from *ġ(a)āba yaġ(i)ību* "to be unconscious" and *qayl(u)ūlatun* from *q(a)āla yaq(i)īlu* "to take a midday nap".

Another anomalous example that can be taken up in which the phonological change is carried out in spite of the fact that two phonological changes due to the unsound glides should be avoided and not combined, is the verbal noun Form IV *ʾiqw(a)āmun* (cf. Åkesson, *Ibn Masʿūd* 288: fols. 29a-29b) that becomes *ʾiq(a)āmatun* "performance". The changes that we observe are the following: *ʾiqw(a)āmun* > *ʾiq(a)āāmun* (with the forbidden combination of two vowelless *ā*) > *ʾiq(a)āmun* (with the elision of one *ā*) > *ʾiq(a)āmatun* (with the compensation of the elided *ā* by the suffixed *tāʾ marbūṭa*) (for discussions see 6.5.12.).

If I take up *ʾiq(a)āāmun* with the combination of the forbidden vowelless glides in this process, I can mention that some grammarians believed that it is the 1st *ā* that is substituted for the 2nd *w* radical vowelled by a fatḥa from *ʾiqw(a)āmun* that is elided, whereas others believed that it is the 2nd one which is the infixed *ā* of *ʾifʿ(a)ālatun* (cf. Ibn Yaʿīš, VI, 58). Concerning it and its likes, Ibn Ǧinnī, *Munṣif I*, 291-292 remarks:

> "The base forms of *ʾiq(a)āmatun* "erecting", *ʾiḫ(a)āfatun* "frightening" and *ʾib(a)ānatun* "explanation" are: *ʾiqw(a)āmatun, ʾiḫw(a)āfatun* and *ʾiby(a)ānatun.* They intended to carry out a phonological change due to the unsoundness of the glide in the *maṣdar* in conformity with the phonological change that is carried out in [their verbs] *ʾaq(a)āma* "to erect" and *ʾab(a)āna* "to explain". So they shifted the fatḥa from the *w* [of *ʾiqw(a)āmatun]* and from the *y* [of *ʾiby(a)ānatun]* to the segment preceding them [i.e. *ʾiqawāmatun* and *ʾibayānatun],* then they changed them [i.e the *w* and the *y* respectively] into an *ā* preceding the infixed *ā* of *ʾifʿ(a)ālatun,* so they became as you remark *ʾiq(a)āāmatun* and *ʾib(a)āānatun.* Abū l-Ḥasan believed that the elided *ā* is the 1st *ā* whereas al-Ḫalīl believed that it is the 2nd one, which is the infixed one, according to what has been presented among both their teachings -".

9.1.13. The glide, the y, is vowelled by a kasra and preceded by a sukūn: the transfer of the kasra to the segment preceding it and the change of the y into an ī:

The phonological changes involve the transfer of the *y's* kasra to the vowelless segment preceding it and the change of the *y* into an *ī*. Thus:

- *°yi* → -*iy*

(*°* stands for vowelless segment)

An example in which such a sequence occurs is the verb with 2nd radical *y* that is formed according to the conjugation *yafᶜilu* in the imperfect, e.g. *yabyiᶜu* > *yabiyᶜu* > *yab(i)īᶜu* "he sells" (for discussions see par. 6.5.5.).

9.1.13.1. Anomalous cases:

An anomalous case due to a sequence of two glides following each other instead of a glide preceded by a consonantal segment, is *mawyitun* "a dead man", in which the *y* vowelled by a kasra is preceded by the vowelless 2nd radical *w*. The result is the change of the *w* into a *y* (cf. 10.1.8.2.) and the assimilation of the *y* to the *y*.

Thus *mawyitun* with the *y* vowelled by a kasra and preceded by a vowelless *w* becomes *mayyitun* after that the *w* is changed into a *y* and the yāʾs are assimilated.

An alleviated form exists as well, namely *maytun* (cf. Åkesson, *Ibn Masᶜūd* 282: fol. 27b) from *mayyitun* in which the 2nd *y* vowelled by a kasra is elided. It occurs in this verse said by an unknown poet, cited by Carter, *Linguistics* [Širbīnī, *Āǧurrūmīya]* 376, Åkesson, *Ibn Masᶜūd* 301: (263):

"ʾInnamā l-maytu man yaᶜīšu kaʾīban
kāsifan bāluhu qalīla l-raǧāʾi".

"The dead man is simply he who lives grieving,
wretched his plight and small of hope".

Both variants *maytun* and *mayyitun* are combined in this verse said by ᶜAdī b. al-Raᶜlā, cited by Muʾaddib, *Taṣrīf* 113, 268, Ibn Yaᶜīš, X, 69, *Mulūkī* 466, Ibn Manẓūr, VI, 4295, Howell, IV, fasc. I, 1461, Åkesson, *Ibn Masᶜūd* 301: (264):

"Laysa man māta fa-starāḥa bi-maytin
ʾinnamā l-maytu mayyitu l-ʾaḥyāʾi".
"He who has died, and taken his rest, is not really dead: the really dead is only the dead of the living, [i.e. is only he that is living, while his state is like that of the dead]".

9.1.14. The glide is vowelled by a kasra and preceded by a vowelless ā: the change of the wi or yi into ʾi:

Such a sequence occurs in the cases of active participles of verbs with 2nd radical *w* and *y* that are formed according to *f(a)āᶜilun,* in which the *w* or *y* is vowelled by a kasra and preceded by the vowelless *ā*.

The phonological change implies the change of the *wi* or the *yi* into *ʾi.* I take up at first the sequence - *āwi* with the *w* vowelled by a kasra and preceded by an *ā* that becomes *-āʾi* after that the *wi* is changed into *ʾi.* An example is *q(a)āwilun* > *q(a)āʾilun* "a sayer" (cf. par. 6.5.9.1. and 10.1.1.2.:3).

Also the sequence *-āyi* with the *y* vowelled by a kasra and preceded by an *ā* that becomes *-āʾi* after that the *yi* is changed into *ʾi.*

An example is *b(a)āyiun* > *b(a)āʾiᶜun* "a seller" (cf. par. 6.5.9.2 and 10.1.1.3.: 2).

9.1.15. The glide, the w, is vowelled by a ḍamma and preceded by a sukūn: the transfer of the ḍamma to the segment preceding it and the change of the w into ū:

The phonological changes concerning this sequence are the following: *-^{o}wu* (^{o} stands for vowelless segment) with the *w* vowelled by a ḍamma and preceded by a sukūn becomes *-uw* after that the *w's* ḍamma is shifted to the vowelless segment preceding it. As the ḍamma precedes the *w*, the *w* is changed into an *ū* or lengthened *u: ū,* so that it becomes *(u)ū.*

Such a sequence is found in the verb with 2nd radical *w* of the conjugation *yafʿulu* that occurs in the imperfect, e.g. *yaqwulu* "he says" > *yaquwlu* > *yaq(u)ūlu* (cf. par. 6.5.4.), in the imperative, e.g. *ʾuqwul* "say!" > *ʾuquwl* > *uq(u)ūl,* and then after the elision of the connective hamza and the *ū* > *qul* (cf. par. 6.5.8.1.) and in the passive participle *maqwuwlun* > *maqw(u)ūlun* "what is said" > *maq(u)ūlun* (cf. par. 6.5.6.).

9.1.15.1. The soundness of the glide:

The glide remains sound in the noun or in the adjective in the following case:

1- The glide should not be vowelled by a vowel that is not supplied by the basic form.

1- The glide should not be vowelled by a vowel that is not supplied by the basic form:

The *w* remains sound if it is the 3rd radical of a noun that carries the marker of the declension, and thus its vowel is not supplied by the basic form but by an external reason having to do with syntax (for this condition see 9.1. and compare the case of *al-ramyu* "the throwing" that ends with the 3rd radical *y*, see par. 9.1.16.1.: 1). An example is *al-dalwu* "the bucket" with the 3rd radical sound *w*.

9.1.16. The glide, the y, is vowelled by a ḍamma and preceded by a sukūn: the transfer of the ḍamma to the vowelless segment preceding it, the change of the ḍamma into a kasra and the change of the y into ī:

The phonological changes concerning this sequence are the following: -^{o}*yu* (^{o} stands for vowelless segment) with the *y* vowelled by a ḍamma and preceded by a sukūn becomes -*uy* after that the *y's* ḍamma is shifted to the vowelless segment preceding it. As the ḍamma precedes the vowelless *y*, the ḍamma is changed into a kasra so that it becomes *iy*. As the kasra precedes the *y*, the *y* is changed into *ī* or lengthened *i: ī*, so that it becomes *(i)ī*.

Such a sequence occurs in the passive participle of the verb with 2nd radical *y* of the conjugation *yaf^{c}ilu*, e.g. *yabyi^{c}u* "he sells", namely *maby(u)u^{c}un* "sold" which becomes *mab(i)ī^{c}un*. The steps are *maby(u)ū^{c}un* > *mabuyū^{c}un* of which the *ū* is elided to hinder the succession of two vowelless segments resulting in *mabuy^{c}un* of which the *u* is changed into *i*, namely *mabiy^{c}un* > *mab(i)ī^{c}un* of which the *i* is lengthenened (cf. par. 6.5.7.).

9.1.16.1. The soundness of the glide:

The glide remains sound in the noun or in the adjective in the following case:

1- The glide should not be vowelled by a vowel that is not supplied by the basic form.

1- The glide should not be vowelled by a vowel that is not supplied by the basic form:

The *y* remains sound if it is the 3rd radical of a noun that carries the marker of the declension, and thus the vowel is not supplied by the basic form but by an external reason having to do with syntax (for this condition see 9.1. and compare the case of *al-dalwu* with the 3rd radical *w* par. 9.1.15: 2.).

An example is *al-ramyu* "the throwing" (cf. Åkesson, *Ibn Mas*ᶜ*ūd* 286: fol. 29a) in which the *y* is vowelled and preceded by a sukūn. If a phonological change is to be carried out in it, it would imply the transfer of its various vowels of declension: the ḍamma in the case of the nominative, the fatḥa in the case of the accusative and the kasra in the case of the genitive to the vowelless segment preceding this vowel. In the case of the ḍamma, *al-ramyu* would become *al-ramuy* and then the *y* would have to be changed into a vowelless *w* to accord with the ḍamma preceding it, namely *al-ram(u)ū.* In the case of the fatḥa, *al-ramya* would become *al-ramay* and then the *y* would have to be changed into a vowelless *ā* to accord with the fatḥa preceding it, namely *al-ram(a)ā.* In the case of the kasra, *al-ramyi* would become *al-ramiy* and the vowelless *y* would be changed into *ī,* namely *al-ram(i)ī.* In all the three cases, the declinable noun would have to end with a vowelless segment without any marker of declension, which is the reason why it is preferred that in order to safeguard the marker of the declension, the *y,* remains sound.

Another example of a declinable substantive is *al-ẓabyu* "the gazelle" with the 3rd radical sound *y.*

9.1.17. The glide, the w or y, is vowelless and preceded by a kasra: its change into a y or ī respectively:

The general rule is that the vowelless glide that is preceded by a vowel is changed into a segment of the nature of the vowel preceding it. The reason of this change is the weakness of the state of the glide, which is vowelless, and the influence of the vowel, whether it is a kasra or a ḍamma, preceding it, on it (cf. Åkesson, *Ibn Mas^c^ūd* 282: 27a).

If the glide is a vowelless *w* preceded by a kasra it is changed into a lengthened *y:*

-iw → *-Iy* > *(i)ī*

An example is *miwzānun* that becomes *m(i)yzānun* > *m(i)īzānun* "balance" (cf. par. 10.1.8.2.).

If the glide is a vowelless y preceded by a kasra it is changed into a lengthened *y* (cf. Wright, II, 80).

-iy → *-(i)ī*

An example is the imperative *ʾiysir* that becomes *ʾ(i)īsir* "be well off!".

9.1.18. The transposition of segments in some nouns:

An example is *qisiyyun* underlyingly *quw(u)ūsun* which is the pl. of *qawsun* "bow" (cf. Åkesson, *Ibn Mas^c^ūd* 292: fols. 30b-31a, Howell, I, fasc. III, 930, IV, fasc. I, 1583-1585, de Sacy, I, 108, Vernier, I, 340-341).

It is so that *quw(u)ūsun* is formed according to the pattern *fu^c^(u)ūlun* in which the radicals are transposed resulting in *qusuwwun* formed according to *ful(u)ū^c^un* and not *fu^c^(u)ūlun,* as if it is the pl. of *qaswun* and not of *qawsun.* In *qusuwwun* the wāws are changed into yāʾs because they occur at the extremity of the word, which is deemed as heavy, resulting in *qusuyyun,* then the ḍamma of the *s* is changed into a kasra because of the *y's* influence, resulting in *qusiyyun.* The *q* becomes then vowelled with a kasra on the analogy of the kasra and of the *y* following it, so that it became *qisiyyun.*

The same phenomenon occurs with *ᶜiṣiyyun* or *ᶜuṣiyyun* pl. of *ᶜaṣā* "stick" (cf. ibid). Another example in which the transposition of segments occurs is the pl. of *n(a)āqatun* namely *ˀanwuqun.* As the ḍamma is deemed heavy upon the *w,* the *w* is transposed made to precede the *n* resulting in *ˀawnuqun,* then the *y* is substituted for the *w* resulting in *ˀaynuqun* (cf. Åkesson, *Ibn Masᶜūd* 292: fol. 31a, Howell, I, fasc. III, 1074). This change of the *w* into a *y* does not follow the analogy as the *w* is vowelless and is preceded by fatḥa, but it is carried out for the sake of alleviation.

9.2. Conclusion

I have studied in this chapter the various sequences that are constituted of a glide preceded by a sound segment, whether it is a consonant or a glide, in which the glide remains sound or is unsound for different reasons.

Generally, the glide remains sound if it is vowelless and preceded by a fatḥa, e.g. *qawlun* "a saying" and *bayᶜun* "a selling" (cf. 9.1.1.), or if it is vowelled by a fatḥa and preceded by a ḍamma, e.g. *nuwamatun* "one who sleeps much" (cf. 9.1.8.).

It is changed into an *ā* if it is vowelled by a fatḥa, kasra or ḍamma and preceded by a fatḥa, e.g. *qawala* > *q(a)āla* "to say" and *bayaᶜa* > *b(a)āᶜa* "to sell" (cf. 9.1.2)., *ḫawifa* > *ḫ(a)āfa* "to fear" and *hayiba* > *h(a)āba* "to be afraid" (cf. 9.1.3.) and *ṭawula* > *ṭ(a)āla* "to become long" (cf. 9.1.4.).

It has its vowel shifted to the vowelless segment preceding it and is then changed into a lenghtened *ā*, e.g. *yaḫwafu* > *yaḫawfu* > *yaḫ(a)āfu* "he is afraid" and *yubya*^{c}*u* > *yubay*^{c}*u* > *yub(a)ā*^{c}*u* "is sold" (cf. 9.1.12.), an *ū*, e.g. *yaqwulu* "he says" > *yaquwlu* > *yaq(u)ūlu* (cf. 9.1.15) or an *ī*, e.g. *maby(u)ū*^{c}*un* "sold" > *mabuyū*^{c}*un* > *mabuy*^{c}*un* > *mabiy*^{c}*un* > *mab(i)ī*^{c}*un* (cf. 9.1.16).

Its vowel is elided if the glide is vowelled by a ḍamma and preceded by a vowel, e.g. *yaġzuwu* "he attacks" > *yaġzuw* / *yaġz(u)ū* and *yarmiyu* "he throws" > *yarmiy*> *yarm(i)ī* (cf. 9.1.7.) and in the latter case, the *y* is elided together with its vowel if it is vowelled by a kasra and preceded by one, e.g. *tarmiy(i)-īna* > *tarmiy-īna* > *tarm(i)-īna* "you throw" (cf. 9.1.11.).

The *y* is changed into *w* if it is vowelless and preceded by a ḍamma, e.g. *yuysaru* "is pleased" > *yuwsaru* > *y(u)ūsaru* (cf. 9.1.5.).

The *w* is changed into a *y* if it is vowelled by a fatḥa and preceded by a kasra, e.g. *d(a)ā*^{c}*iwatun* > *d(a)ā*^{c}*iyatun* "the one who invites /fem." (cf. 9.1.9.).

The combination of the *y* vowelled by a ḍamma and preceded by a kasra, or the *w* vowelled by a kasra and preceded by a ḍamma is deemed as heavy and leads to certain phonological changes, among them the transfer of the vowel to the segment preceding it, the change of the ḍamma into a kasra or the kasra into a ḍamma together with the change of the *y* into a *w* or the *w* into a *y*, e.g. *raḍiy(u)-ū* > *raḍuy-ū* > *raḍ(u)-ū* "they were pleased /masc. pl." (cf. 9.1.10.), *quwila* > *qiwla* > *q(i)yla* > *q(i)īla* "it was said" and *buyi*^{c}*a* > *biy*^{c}*a* > *b(i)ī*^{c}*a* (cf. 9.1.6.).

I shall treat the substitution in the next chapter.

CHAPTER TEN

10. The substitution

In this chapter I shall study the phonological change known as substitution. The segments of substitution are at first presented and then the substitution of each one of them into another is discussed. The substitution is usually carried out in a word to alleviate the pronunciation if there exists in it a combination of two sounds which is deemed as heavy, or if both these segments' points of articulation are close to each other, or if the segments are akin in character (for the segments see 2.2.; for the assimilation see chapt. 2.). Other more unusual reasons relate to the peculiarity of a dialectal variant, to a verse's metrical exigency or to the exigency of the pause.

10.1. The segments of substitution

There exist special segments which are recognized as segments that can be substituted for other segments (for a study of the substitution see Ibn Ǧinnī, *de Flexione* 19-30, Ibn ᶜUṣfūr, I, 319-415, Zamaḫšarī, 172-177, Ibn Yaᶜīš, X, 7-54, Howell, IV, fasc. I, 1182-1203). These segments are termed as *ḥurūf al-ibdāl* "segments of substitution". They are comprised in different phrases, among them *ʾistanǧadahu yawma ṣāla Zuṭṭa* "he asked him for help on the day some Zuṭṭ [sc. a race of Hindus] attacked" (cf. Zamaḫšarī, 172, Ibn Yaᶜīš, X, 7-8, Åkesson, *Ibn Masᶜūd* 330, fol. 33b, Howell, IV, fasc. I, 1192-1193), which starts with the ʾ and ends with the *ṭ*. According to their order in this phrase these segments are: 1- the ʾ, 2- the *s*, 3- the *t*, 4- the *n*, 5- the *ǧ*, 6- the *d*, 7- the *h*, 8- the *y*, 9- the *w*, 10- the *m*, 11- the *ṣ*, 12- the *ā*, 13- the *l*, 14- the *ẓ*, and 15- the *ṭ*.

In what follows in this chapter, I shall study the segments, starting with the ʾ and ending with the *ṭ*.

10.1.1. The substitution of the hamza

The ʾ can be substituted for the following segments: 1- the alif of feminization, 2- the *w*, 3- the *y*, 4- the *h*, 5- the *ā* and 6- the ᶜ.

10.1.1.1. The substitution of the hamza for the alif of feminization, the ā (alif maqṣūra):

An example is *ṣaḥr(a)āʾ* in which the hamza is substituted for the alif of feminization (cf. Ibn Ǧinnī, *de Flexione* 25, *Sirr I,* 83-84, Ibn ᶜUṣfūr, I, 329-331, Zamaḫšarī, 172, Ibn Yaᶜīš, X, 9, Åkesson, *Ibn Masᶜūd* 330: fol. 33b, Howell, IV, fasc. I, 1205). The base form *is ṣahr(a)āā* with a final *alif maqṣūra* preceded by an *alif mamdūda,* suggesting a forbidden combination of two vowelless segments, namely the *alif mamdūda* and the *alif maqṣūra*. The reason of replacing the *alif maqṣūra* by a hamza is to prevent this combination.

10.1.1.2. The substitution of the hamza for the w:

The *w* that is substituted by the hamza can be vowelled by any of the three vowels: the fatḥa, the ḍamma or the kasra.

1- The hamza vowelled by a fatḥa:

An example is *ʾawāṣilu* (cf. Zamaḫšarī, 172, Ibn Yaᶜīš, X, 10, Ibn ᶜAqīl, II, 552, Åkesson, *Ibn Masᶜūd* 330: fol. 34a, Howell, IV, fasc. I, 1218-1222, Fleisch, *Traité I,* 152, ᶜAbd al-Tawwāb, *Taṭawwur* 41), the pl. of *wāṣilatun* "joining", that is conformable to the measure *fawāᶜilu,* in which the *ʾa* is necessarily substituted for the 1st radical *w* vowelled by a fatḥa, the *wa,* of the base form *wawāṣilu.* The *wa* is changed into an *ʾa* to prevent the heavy combination of both the wāws.

Another example is the imperative *ʾaḥḥid ʾaḥḥid* in which the *ʾa* is substituted for the 1st radical *w* vowelled by a fatḥa, the *wa,* of the base form *waḥḥid waḥḥid* "make the sign with one, one" (cf. Rāzī in Ḫalīl b. Aḥmad ..., *Ḥurūf* 137 in the note, Zamaḫšarī, 172, Ibn Yaᶜīš, X, 14-15, Ibn Manẓūr, VI, 4782, Åkesson, *Ibn Masᶜūd* 330: fol. 34a, Howell, IV, fasc. I, 1230). A tradition relates that Muḥammad has said this phrase to a man when he saw him making the sign with his two forefingers in reciting the creed.

2- The hamza vowelled by a ḍamma:

An example is *ʾuǧūhun* (cf. Sībawaihi, II, 341, Ibn Ǧinnī, *de Flexione* 25, *Sirr I,* 92, Ibn ᶜUṣfūr, I, 332, Zamaḫšarī, 172, Ibn Yaᶜīš, X, 10-11, Åkesson, *Ibn Masᶜūd* 330: fol. 34a, Howell, IV, fasc. I, 1224-1225), the pl. of *waǧhun* "face" from *waǧuha* "to be a man of distinction" which is a verb with 1st radical *w.* In *ʾuǧ(u)ūhun* the *ʾu* is possibly substituted for the 1st radical *w* vowelled by a ḍamma, the *wu,* of the base form *wuǧ(u)ūhun.* The reason of this substitution is the dislike of having the *w* vowelled by a ḍamma (cf. Sībawaihi, II, 391), which is deemed as heavy.

Another example is *ʾadʾurun* "houses" (cf. Sībawaihi, II, 341, Ibn Ǧinnī, *Sirr I,* 98, *de Flexione* 25, Zamaḫšarī, 172, Ibn ᶜUṣfūr, I, 335-336, Ibn Yaᶜīš, X, 10-11, Åkesson, *Ibn Masᶜūd* 330: fol. 34a, Howell, IV, fasc. I, 1224-1225), the pl. of *d(a)ārun,* in which the *ʾu* is necessarily substituted for the 2nd radical *w* that is vowelled by a ḍamma, the *wu,* of the base form *ʾadwurun.*

Another example is *kisāʾun* "a wrapper" in which the *ʾu* is necessarily substituted for the 3rd radical *w* (cf. Zamaḫšarī, 172, Ibn Yaᶜīš, X, 9-10, Åkesson, *Ibn Masᶜūd* 330: fol. 34a, Howell, IV, fasc. I, 1203-1204, Mokhlis, *Taṣrīf* 195) that is vowelled by a ḍamma, the *wu,* of the base form *kisāwun.* This substitution is carried out to prevent that the original *w* becomes vowelled by any of the three vowels marking the declension, namely *kisāwun* for the nominative, *kisāwan* for the accusative and *kisāwin* for the genitive, which is deemed as heavy (cf. Åkesson, *Ibn Masᶜūd* 330: fol. 34a).

3- The hamza vowelled by a kasra:

An example is *ʾišāḥun* "baldric" in which the *ʾi* is possibly substituted for the 1st radical *w* (cf. Sībawaihi, II, 341) that is vowelled by a kasra, the *wi,* of the base form *wišāḥun.* Zamaḫšarī, 172-173 notes that al-Māzinī considered this substitition of the *w* vowelled by the kasra as *qiyās* "analogy".

Another example is the active participle *q(a)āʾilun* "saying" underlyingly *q(a)āwilun* from the verb *q(a)āla* "to say" underlyingly *qawala* with 2nd radical *w.* In it, the *ʾi* is necessarily substituted for the 2nd radical *w* vowelled by a kasra, the *wi* (cf. Zamaḫšarī, 172, 180, Ibn Yaᶜīš, X, 10, Ibn ᶜUṣfūr, I, 327-329, Åkesson, *Ibn Masᶜūd* 330: fol. 34a, Howell, IV, fasc. I, 1209-1210, par. 6.5.9.1., this study par. 9.1.14.).

10.1.1.3. The substitution of the hamza for the y:

The hamza can be substituted for the *y* vowelled by a fatḥa or with a kasra.

1- The hamza vowelled by a fatḥa:

An example is *ᵓadayhi* in which the ᵓ is possibly substituted for the initial *y* vowelled by a fatḥa of the base form *yadayhi* "his hands" (cf. Zamaḫšarī, 173, Ibn Yaᶜīš, X, 15, Ibn Manẓūr, VI, 4951, Åkesson, *Ibn Masᶜūd* 330: fol. 34a, Vernier, I 346). According to Ibn Masᶜūd (Åkesson, *Ibn Masᶜūd* 330: fol. 34a), the reason of this substitution is the heaviness of the fatḥa vowelling the *y*.

2- The hamza vowelled by a kasra:

An example is the active participle *b(a)āᵓiᶜun* "selling" (cf. Zamaḫšarī, 172, 180, Ibn Yaᶜīš, X, 10, Ibn ᶜUṣfūr, I, 327-329, Åkesson, *Ibn Masᶜūd* 330: fol. 34a, Howell, IV, fasc. I, 1209-1210, Mokhlis, *Taṣrīf* 195), from the verb *b(a)āᶜa* "to sell" underlyingly *bayaᶜa* with 2nd radical *y*. The ᵓ is necessarily substituted for the 2nd radical *y* vowelled by a kasra of the base form *b(a)āyiᶜun* (cf. par. 6.5.9.2. and 9.1.14.).

10.1.1.4. The substitution of the hamza for the h:

An example is *māᵓun* in which the ᵓ is substituted for the 3rd radical *h* of the base form *māhun* "water" (cf. Ibn Ǧinnī, *Sirr I,* 100-101, Ibn ᶜUṣfūr, I, 348-351, Zamaḫšarī, 173, Ibn Yaᶜīš, X, 15-16, Åkesson, *Ibn Masᶜūd* 330: fol. 34a, Howell, IV, fasc. I, 1232-1235), from *mawaha* "to mix", a verb with 2nd radical *w*. The pl. form of *māᵓun* is *miyāhun* with the 3rd radical *h* and its diminutive is *muwayhun* (cf. Ibn Manẓūr, VI, 4302).

Another pl. form is *ʾamwāhun* in which the *h* is as well substituted by the ʾ so that it became *ʾamwāʾun*. The reason of this substitution is the oneness of the point of articulation of the ʾ and the *h* as they both originate from the farthest part of the throat, and are laryngals (for the segments see par. 2.2.1.). The example *ʾamwāʾuhā* occurs in this verse cited by Ibn Ǧinnī, *Sirr I,* 100, *Munṣif II,* 151, Zamaḫšarī, 173, Ibn Yaᶜīš, X, 15, Ibn ᶜUṣfūr, I, 348, Ibn Manẓūr, VI, 4302, Howell, IV, fasc. I, 1233, Åkesson, *Ibn Masᶜūd* 347: (325)):

> *"Wa-baldatin qāliṣatin ʾamwāʾuhā*
> *māṣiḥatin raʾda l-ḍuḥā ʾafyāʾuhā".*
> "And many a land, whose waters were exhausted,
> and whose shades were passing away in the part of the noon
> when the sun was hight".

10.1.1.5. The substitution of the hamza for the ā:

An example is the active participle of Form VIII *l-muštaʾiq* (in pause) in which the *ʾi* is substituted for the *ā* of *l-muštāq* "the yearner" from *šawaqa* "to desire", a verb with 2nd radical *w,* that occurs in a verse cited by Ibn Ǧinnī, *Sirr I,* 91, *Ḫaṣāʾiṣ III,* 145, Zamaḫšarī, 172, Ibn Yaᶜīš, X, 12-13, Ibn Manẓūr, II, 1405, IV, 2361, Howell, IV, fasc. I, 1227, Åkesson, *Ibn Masᶜūd* 347: (326)):

> *"Yā dāra Mayya bi-l-dakādīki l-buraq*
> *ṣabran fa-qad hayyağti šawqa l-muštaʾiq".*
> "O abode of Mayya [sc. a woman's name] in the low-lying
> sands, sands mixed with stones and earth,
> give me patience, for you have excited the yearning of the
> yearner".

10.1.1.6. The substitution of the hamza for the ᶜ:

An example is the substantive *ʾubābun* in which the ʾ is substituted for the ᶜ of the base form *ᶜubābun* "billow". The reason of this substitution is the closeness of the points of articulation of the ˀ and the ᶜ as the ˀ originates from the farthest part of the throat and is a laryngal and the ᶜ originates from the middle of the throat and is a pharyngal (for the segments see par. 2.2.). This theory about the substitution that concerns *ˀubābun* is however criticized by Ibn Ǧinnī, *Sirr I,* 106, who does not consider the ˀ to be substituted for the ᶜ, but that the form is *fuᶜālun,* namely *ˀub(a)ābun* from *ˀabba* "to prepare itself". His remark is also mentioned by Ibn Manẓūr, I, 4. The example *ˀubābu* occurs in this verse cited by Ibn Ǧinnī, *Sirr I,* 106, Zamaḫšarī, 173, Ibn Yaᶜīš, X, 15, Ibn ᶜUṣfūr, I, 352, Howell, IV, fasc. I, 1235, Åkesson, *Ibn Masᶜūd* 349: (328):

> *"Wa-māǧa sāᶜātin malā l-wadīqi*
> *ˀubābu baḥrin ḍāḥikin zahūqi"*
> "And the deserts of intense heats were agitated at times,
> like a billow of a laughing, far-extending sea".

10.1.2. The substitution of the *s*

The *s* can be substituted for the *t.*

10.1.2.1. The substitution of the s for the t:

An example is *ˀistaḫaḏa* in which the *s* is substituted for the *t* of the base form Form VIII *ˀittaḫaḏa* "to take for one's self" (cf. Sībawaihi, II, 480, Åkesson, *Ibn Masᶜūd* 330: fol 34a, Howell, IV, fasc. I, 1192), from *ˀaḫaḏa* "to take". The verb *ˀistaḫaḏa* referring to Form VIII should not be confounded with Form X *ˀistaḫaḏa* which looks exactly the same as it. The reason why the *t* is changed into the *s* in it is that they both are among the surd segments (for them see par. 2.2.2.).

10.1.3. The substitution of the *t*

The *t* can be substituted for the following segments: 1- the *w*, 2- the *y*, 3- both the *d* and the *s*, 4- the *ṣ* and 5- the *b*.

10.1.3.1. The substitution of the t for the w:

This substitution can affect the initial segment or the ultimate segment of a word.

An example that concerns the initial segment is *tuḫamatun* in which the *t* is substituted for the initial *w* of the base form *wuḫamatun* "a malady like cholera" (cf. Ibn Yaᶜīš, X, 37-38, Åkesson, *Ibn Masᶜūd* 330: fol 34a). Some other examples (for them see Ibn Yaᶜīš, X, 38-39) are *tuǧāha* "in front of" for *wuǧāha, tayqūrun* for *wayqūrun* "grave", *tuklānun* for *wuklānun* "incapacity and reliance upon others", *tukalatun* for *wukalatun* "a man incapable, committing his affair to another", *tuhamatun* for *wuhamatun* "suspicion", *taqīyatun* for *waqīyatun* "fear", *turāṯun* for *wurāṯun* "inheritance" that occurs in the sur. 89:19 *(wa-taᵓkulūna l-turāṯa ᵓaklan lammā)* "And ye devour Inheritance - All with greed" and *tilādun* for *wilādun* "old property, what was born in your possession".

An example that concerns the ultimate segment of the word is *ᵓuḫtun* "sister" in which the *t* is substituted for the 3rd radical *w* of the base form *ᵓuḫwun* (cf. Zamaḫšarī, 175, Ibn Yaᶜīš, X 39-40, Åkesson, *Ibn Masᶜūd* 330: fol 34b, Howell, I, fasc. III, 1370-1372, IV, fasc. I, 1347-1348, ᶜAbd al-Tawwāb, *Taṭawwur* 91), that is from the root *ᵓa ḫ w* with 3rd radical *w*.

10.1.3.2. The substitution of the t for the y:

An example is *ṯintāni* in which the t is substituted for the 3rd radical *y* of *ṯanayānī* "the second to the one" (cf. Zamaḫšarī, 175, Ibn Yaᶜīš, X, 40, Ibn ᶜUṣfūr, I, 388, Åkesson, *Ibn Masᶜūd* 330-332: fol 34b, Howell, IV, fasc. I, 1349-1350), from the expression *ṯanaytu l-wāḥida* "I was a second to the one", and in Form IV *ᵓasnatū* for *ᵓasnayū* "they experienced drough or barrenness" with 3rd radical *y*. Referring to *ᵓasnatū,* Sībawaihi, II,

341 notes that the substitution of the *t* for the *y* as a 3rd radical is rare. It can be mentioned that *ṯintāni* is used in the dialectal variant of Tamīm (cf. Daqir, *Muᶜǧam* 2 in the notes, 338) and *ʾiṯnāni* and *ʾiṯnatāni* are used by the Ḥiǧāzīs (cf. ibid 338). The reason of this substitution is to avoid vowelling the *y* (cf. Åkesson, *Ibn Masᶜūd* 332: fol 34b), which is deemed as heavy.

10.1.3.3. The substitution of the t for the d and the s:

An example is *sittun* "six" in which the doubled *t* is substituted for the *d* and the *s* of the base form *sudusun* (cf. Sībawaihi, II, 479, Åkesson, *Ibn Masᶜūd* 332: fol. 34b, Zamaḫšarī, 175, 196). This substitution of the *t* for both the *d* and the *s* in *sudusun* is considered as rare by Sībawaihi, II, 341.

Other examples in which the *t* is substituted for the *s* are *l-nāti,* underlyingly *l-nāsi,* and *ʾakyāti* underlyingly *ʾakyāsi* which occur in these verses, which are believed to have been said by ᶜIlbāʾ b. Arqam al-Yaškarī. This substitution pertains to a dialectal variant that is known to be of the usage of the Yemenites, and is called *al-watmu.* The verses are cited by Rāzī in Ḫalīl b. Aḥmad ..., *Ḥurūf* 150, Ibn Fāris, *Ṣāḥibī* 109, Ibn Ǧinnī, *Sirr I,* 155, *Ḫaṣāʾiṣ II,* 53, Zamaḫšarī, 175, Ibn Yaᶜīš, X, 36, Ibn ᶜUṣfūr, I, 389, Ibn Manẓūr, I, 148, Howell, IV, fasc. I, 1352-1353, Åkesson, *Ibn Masᶜūd* 352: (334)):

"Yā qātala l-lāhu banī l-siᶜlāti
ᶜAmr b. Masᶜūd širāra l-nāti
ġayra ʾaᶜiffāʾa wa-lā ʾakyāti".
"O [my people] God slay the sons of she-devils,
ᶜAmr b. Masᶜūd, the worst of men,
incontinent and not sharp-witted!".

10.1.3.4. The substitution of the t for the ṣ:

An example is *liṣtun* or *luṣtun* in which the *t* is substituted anomalously for the 2nd *ṣ* of the doubled ṣāds of the base form *liṣṣun* or *luṣṣun* "robber" (cf. Zamaḫšarī, 175, Ibn Yaᶜīš, X, 41, Åkesson, *Ibn Masᶜūd* 332: fol 34b, Howell, IV, fasc. I, 1353). The reason of this substitution is that both the *t* and the *ṣ* are among the surd segments (for the segments' characters see par. 2.2.2.), which facilitates the substitution of one for the other.

10.1.3.5. The substitution of the t for the b:

An example is *ḏaᶜālitun* in which the *t* is substituted for the *b* of the base form *ḏaᶜālibun* "worn-out rags". The example *ḏaᶜālitin* in the genitive occurs in this verse, which according to Ibn Manẓūr, II, 1504, 2100, is said by one of the Banū ᶜAwf b. Saᶜd. It is also cited by Ibn Ǧinnī, *Sirr I,* 157, Howell, IV, fasc. I, 1355, Åkesson, *Ibn Masᶜūd* 353: (336):

"Ṣafqatu ḏī ḏaᶜālitin samūli
bayᶜu mriʾin laysa bi-mustaqīli".
"The bargain of the poor needy purchaser, wearer of worn-out
rags is, in irrevocability and conclusiveness,
like a sale by a man that is not desirous of rescinding".

10.1.4. The substitution of the *n*

The *n* can be substituted for the following segments: 1- the *w* and 2- the *l*.

10.1.4.1. The substitution of the n for the w:

An example is *ṣanᶜānīyu* "someone or something from a city in Yemen" in which the *n* is substituted for the *w* of the base form *ṣanᶜāwīyu* (cf. Ibn Ǧinnī, *de Flexione* 25-26, *Sirr II,* 441, Zamaḫšarī, 175, Ibn Yaᶜīš, X, 36, Ibn ᶜUṣfūr, I, 395-396, Howell, IV, fasc. I, 1335-1336), which is the relative noun of *ṣanᶜāʾu* "a city in Yemen".

10.1.4.2. The substitution of the n for the l:

The *n* in *la*ᶜ*anna* is substituted for the *l* of the base form *la*ᶜ*alla* "maybe" (cf. Ibn Ǧinnī, *Sirr II,* 442, Zamaḫšarī, 175, Ibn Yaᶜīš, X, 36, Ibn ᶜUṣfūr, I, 395, Howell, IV, fasc. I, 1336-1337).

10.1.5. The substitution of the ǧ

The ǧ can be substituted for the *y*.

10.1.5.1. The substitution of the ǧ for the y:

The ǧ is substituted for the single *y,* but less often than the double one in pause. Examples referring to the single *y* are *ḥaǧǧatiǧ* underlyingly *ḥaǧǧatiy* "my pilgrimage" (that results in *ḥaǧǧat(i)ī* after the assimilation of the *y* to the *i)* and *biǧ* for *biy* "me" (that results in *b(i)ī* after the assimilation of the *y* to the *i),* which occur in this verse, whose author is, according to the editor of Ibn al-Sarrāǧ, *Uṣūl III,* 274, Abū Zaid: Saᶜīd b. Aus b. Ṯābit al-Anṣārī, the author of *al-Nawādir.* It is also cited by Ibn Ǧinnī, *Sirr I,* 177, *de Flexione* 30, Zamaḫšarī, 176, Ibn Yaᶜīš, X, 50, *Mulūkī* 329, Ibn ᶜUṣfūr, I, 355, Howell, IV, fasc. I, 1376, Lane, I, 47, Vernier, I, 356-357, Åkesson, *Ibn Mas*ᶜ*ūd* 354: (340):

> *"Lāhumma ᵓin kunta qabilta ḥaǧǧatiǧ*
> *fa-lā yazālu šāḥiǧun yaᵓtīka biǧ".*
> "O God, if You have accepted my pilgrimage,
> then a mule shall not cease to bring me to You".

Examples that refer to the doubled *y* are ᶜ*Aliǧǧi* "ᶜAlī" in which the double ǧ is substituted for the double *y* of ᶜ*Aliyyi* in the construct state ᵓ*Abū* ᶜ*Aliǧǧi* "Abū ᶜAlī" of the verse cited below, and *bi-l-*ᶜ*ašiǧǧi* said instead of bi-l-ᶜašiyyi in it. This phenomenon pertains to the dialectal variant of Quḍāᶜa, Banū

Tamīm and Banū Saᶜd, and is known as *al-ᶜağᶜağa*. Both these words occur in this verse said by an inhabitant of the desert, cited by Sībawaihi, II, 315, Ibn Fāris, *Ṣāḥibī* 55, Ibn Ğinnī, *Sirr I,* 175, de Flexione 30, Ibn al-Sarrāğ, *Uṣūl III,* 274, Zamaḫšarī, 176, Ibn Yaᶜīš, X 50, *Mulūkī* 248, 329, 330, Ibn ᶜUṣfūr, I, 353, Howell, IV, fasc. I, 1375-1376, Lane, I, 47, Vernier, I, 356, Åkesson, *Ibn Masᶜūd* 354: (339):

> *"Ḫālī ᶜUwayfun wa-ˀAbū ᶜAliğği*
> *ˀal-muṭᶜimānī l-laḥmi bi-l-ᶜašiğği".*
> "My maternal uncle ᶜUwayf and Abū ᶜAliğği [sc. Abū ᶜAlī],
> they who provide meat for food at evening".

10.1.6. The substitution of the *d*

The *d* can be substituted for the *t*.

10.1.6.1. The substitution of the d for the t:

An example is *fuzdu* in which the *d* is substituted for the *t* of the base form *fuztu* "I succeeded" (cf. Zamaḫšarī, 176, 196, Ibn Yaᶜīš, X, 48, 151, Åkesson, *Ibn Masᶜūd* 332: fol 34b, Howell, IV, fasc. I, 1373). The *-tu* is the suffixed agent pronoun of the 1st person of the singular and the verb is *fawaza* with middle radical *w*.

Another example is *ˀiğdamaᶜū* in which the *d* is substituted for the infixed *t* of the base form VIII *ˀiğtamaᶜū* "they gathered together" (cf. Ibn Fāris, *Ṣāḥibī* 109, Ibn Yaᶜīš, X, 49, Howell, IV, fasc. I, 1372).

10.1.7. The substitution of the *h*

The *h* can be substituted for the following segments: 1- the ˀ, 2- the *ā,* 3- the *y* and 4- the *t*.

10.1.7.1. The substitution of the h for the hamza:

The *h* in Form I *haraqtu* "I spilled" is substituted for the ᵓ of its base form *ᵓaraqtu* (cf. Sībawaihi, II, 341, 364, Åkesson, *Ibn Masᶜūd* 332: fol 34b, de Sacy, I, 247, 224 note 1, Vernier, I, 152).

10.1.7.2. The substitution of the h for the ā:

The last *h* in *ḥayyahalah* "come along!" is substituted for the *ā* of the base form constituted of two words *ḥayya halā* (cf. Zamaḫšarī, 156, 175, Ibn Yaᶜīš, X, 43, Åkesson, *Ibn Masᶜūd* 332: fol 34b) in pause. The other variants are *ḥayya hal* with the sukūn in pause and *ḥayya hala* otherwise (cf. Wright, II, 294). The example *ḥayyahalah* belongs to the category of words that has been determined by Sībawaihi, I, 104 as "nouns in the sing. pertaining to verbs, (whose action they denote)" (for a study see Sībawaihi, I, 105-107, Versteegh, *Zaǧǧāǧī* 63). A verse said by a man of the Banū Bakr b. Waᵓīl, cited by Zamaḫšarī, 62, Ibn Yaᶜīš, IV, 46, Ibn Manẓūr, VI, 4693, Howell, I, fasc. II, 682, Åkesson, *Ibn Masᶜūd* 356: (344) has *ḥayyahaluh* with the ḍamma as a vowel of declension over the *l:*

> *"Wa-hayyaǧa l-ḥayya min dārin fa-ẓalla lahum*
> *yawmun kaṯīrun tanādīhi wa-ḥayyahaluh.*
> "And he [sc. the camel-driver] roused the tribe from an abode;
> and a day, in which the calling of one to another and "make haste" were many, was spent by them".

The *h* in *ᵓanah* is substituted for the *ā* of *ᵓanā* "I" (cf. Ibn Ǧinnī, *Sirr I,* 163, II, 555, de Flexione 22, 28, Zamaḫšarī, 175, Ibn Yaᶜīš, III, 138, IV, 6, IX, 80-81, X, 43, Åkesson, *Ibn Masᶜūd* 332: fol 34b, Howell, I, fasc. II, 577).

10.1.7.3. The substitution of the h for the y:

The h that marks the fem. sing. in the demonstratif pronoun *hāḏihi* "this is" from the phrase *hāḏihi ʾamatu l-lāhi* "this is the servant of God", is substituted for the *y* of the base form *hāḏī* (cf. Rāzī, in Ḫalīl b. Aḥmad ..., *Ḥurūf* 154, Sībawaihi, II, 341, Ibn Ğinnī, *Sirr II,* 556, Zamaḫšarī, 176, Ibn Yaᶜīš, III, 131, X, 44-45, Åkesson, *Ibn Masᶜūd* 332: fol 34b).

10.1.7.4. The substitution of the h for the t:

The *h* in Ṭalḥah "Ṭalḥa" is substituted for the *tāʾ marbūṭa* of its base form Ṭalḥat (cf. Zamaḫšarī, 176, Ibn Yaᶜīš, X, 45, Åkesson, *Ibn Masᶜūd* 332: fols. 34b-35a, Howell, IV, fasc. I, 1364-1365, Fleisch, *Traité I,* 183-184) in pause. This substitution is carried out specifically in nouns ending with the *tāʾ marbūṭa* which marks in them the fem. sing. and not in verbs that occur in the perfect of the fem. sing. ending with the suffixed *tāʾ ṭawīla* that marks the fem. sing., e.g. *ḍarabat* "she hit". It can be noted that the characteristic *tāʾ ṭawīla* suffixed to verbs cannot be substituted by the *h* in pause, i.e. *ḍarabat* cannot become *ḍarabah,* as there is a risk of confounding this *h* with the suffixed pronoun of the accusative of the 3rd person of the masc. sing., the *-hu* "him", because in the written form without vowels both *ḍarabah* and *ḍarabahu* "he hit him" would look alike, i.e. ضربه.

10.1.8. The substitution of the *y*

The *y* or the ī can be substituted for the following segments: 1- the *ā,* 2- the *w,* 3- the ʾ, 4- one of the doubled segments, 5- the *n,* 6- the ᶜ, 7- the *t,* 8- the *b,* 9- the *s* and 10- the *ṯ.*

10.1.8.1. The substitution of the ī for the ā:

The *ī* in *mufaytīḥun* "a little key" is substituted for the *ā*. The example *mufayt(i)īḥun* is the diminutive of *miftāhun,* and is conformable to *fu^{c}ay^c(i)īlun.* It is the last vowelless *ī* in this example that is considered to be substituted for the *ā* (cf. Ibn Ǧinnī, *de Flexione* 23, *Sirr II,* 731-732, Zamaḫšarī, 173, Ibn Ya^{c}īš, X, 21, Åkesson, *Ibn Mas^{c}ūd* 332: fol 35a, Howell, IV, fasc. I, 1256) as it is preceded by a kasra. The pattern *fu^{c}ay^{c}īlun* is appliable to every quinqueliteral noun in which the 4th segment is an *ā, ū* or ī (for examples see Zamaḫšarī, 87, Howell, I, fasc. III, 1167, Wright, II, 166, Vernier, I, 198), e.g. *miṣbāhun: muṣaybīḥun* "little lamp", *qarbūsun: quraybīsun* "a little pommel of a saddle", and *qindīlun: qunaydīlun* "little candelabrum".

10.1.8.2. The substitution of the y for the w:

The *y* in *miyqātun* (which results in *m(i)īqātun* after the assimilation of the *y* to the *i)* is substituted for the vowelless *w* of the base form *miwqātun* "time appointed for performance of an action" (cf. Zamaḫšarī, 173, 185, Ibn Ya^{c}īš, X, 21, Åkesson, *Ibn Mas^{c}ūd* 332: fol. 35a, Howell, IV, fasc. I, 1270-1271), because the *w* is vowelless and influenced by the kasra preceding it.

The *y* in *miyzānun* (which results in *m(i)īzānun* after the assimilation of the *y* to the *i)* is substituted for the vowelless *w* of the base form *miwzānun* "balance" (cf. Ibn Ǧinnī, *Munṣif I,* 220-221, Åkesson, *Ibn Mas^{c}ūd* 282: fol 27a, this study par. 9.1.17.) from the root *w z n.* The reason of this substitution is the vowellessness of the *w* and the influence of the kasra preceding it.

The second *y* of the doubled yā'ˀs in the noun in the sing. *kayyanūnatun* is substituted for the 2nd radical *w* vowelled by a fatḥa of the base form *kaywanūnatun* "being" which is conformable to *fay*ᶜ*alūlatun,* and then the vowelless *y* is assimilated to the *w* (cf. Ibn Ǧinnī, *Munṣif II,* 10, Åkesson, *Ibn Mas*ᶜ*ūd* 282: fol. 27a-27b, this study par. 9.1.12.2.). Likewise, the second of the doubled yāʾs in the noun in the sing. *mayyitun* is substituted for the *w* vowelled by a kasra of the base form *maywitun* "a dead man", and then the vowelless *y* is assimilated to the *w* (cf. Åkesson, *Ibn Mas*ᶜ*ūd* 282: fol. 27b, this study par. 9.1.13.1.).

The *y* in the broken pl. *diy(a)ārun* is substituted for the 2nd radical *w* vowelled by a fatḥa of the base form *diw(a)ārun* "houses" (cf. Åkesson, *Ibn Mas*ᶜ*ūd* 284: fol. 28a, Howell, IV, fasc. I, 1264, this study par. 9.1.9.1.). Other examples are *siy(a)āṭun* in which the *y* is substituted for the 2nd radical *w* vowelled by a fatḥa of the base form *siw(a)āṭun* "whips" and the verbal noun *qiy(a)āmun* in which the *y* is substituted for the 2nd radical *w* vowelled by a fatḥa of the base form *qiw(a)āmun* "standing" (ibid).

10.1.8.3. The substitution of the y for the hamza:

The vowelless *ī* in *ḏ(i)ībun* is possibly substituted for the ʾ of the base form *ḏiʾbun* "a wolf" (cf. Zamaḫšarī, 173, Ibn Yaᶜīš, X, 24, Åkesson, *Ibn Mas*ᶜ*ūd* 332: fol 35a, Howell, IV, fasc. I, 1287).

10.1.8.4. The substitution of the y for one of the doubled segments in the doubled verb:

This substitution is discussed in par. 1.2.1.7. Some examples that are taken up there are Form V *tasarraytu* said instead of *tasarrartu* "I had a concubine" and Form V *taẓannaytu* "I formed an opinion" said instead of *taẓannantu.*

10.1.8.5. The substitution of the y for the n:

The last *y* among the doubled yāʾs in *ʾanāsiyyu* is substituted for the *n* (cf. Ibn Yaᶜīš, X, 27, Ibn Manẓūr, I, 148, Åkesson, *Ibn Masᶜūd* 332: fol. 35a, Howell, I, fasc. III, 100, IV, fasc. I, 1296) of the base form *ʾanās(i)ynu* "men" that results after the assimilation of the *y* to the *i* in *ʾanās(i)īnu.* The example *ʾanāsiyyu* is said to be the pl. of *ʾinsānun,* and not of *ʾinsīyun* "a human being, man".

The y in *d(i)ynārun* is substituted for the *n* of *dinnārun* (cf. Ibn Ǧinnī, *de Flexione* 24, *Sirr II,* 757, Åkesson, *Ibn Masᶜūd* 332: fol. 35a, Howell, IV, fasc. I, 1298, I, fasc. III, 1197, Wright, II, 175).

10.1.8.6. The substitution of the ī for the ᶜ:

The *ī* in *ḍafād(i)ī* is substituted for the ᶜ of the base form *ḍafādiᶜ* "frogs" (cf. Åkesson, *Ibn Masᶜūd* 332: fol. 35a, Nöldeke, *Grammatik* 13). The ᶜ in *ḍafādiᶜ* is counted as heavy on account that it is a guttural segment, and as the kasra preceding it is closer to the *ī,* it became more natural to replace the ᶜ by the *ī.* The example *ḍafādī* occurs in the saying of Ḫalaf al-Aḥmar, whose verse is cited by Sībawaihi, I, 300, Ibn Ǧinnī, *Sirr II,* 762, Zamaḫšarī, 174, Ibn Yaᶜīš, X, 28, Ibn ᶜUṣfūr, I, 376, Ibn Manẓūr, IV, 2594, Howell, IV, fasc. I, 1296, Åkesson, *Ibn Masᶜūd* 361: (355):

> *"Wa-manhalin laysa lahu ḥawāziqu*
> *wa-li-ḍafādī ǧammihi naqāniqu"*
> "And many a watering-place, which has no sides preventing any one from coming down to it, but to which every one is able to come down from all of its sides,
> and the frogs of whose main part have croakings!".

10.1.8.7. The substitution of the y for the t:

The *y* in *ʾiytaṣalat* "it joined" (that results after the assimilation of the *y* to the *i* in *ʾ(i)ītaṣalat)* is substituted for the *w* (cf. Ibn Ǧinnī, *Sirr II,* 764, Ibn Yaᶜīš, X, 26, *Mulūkī* 248, Ibn ᶜUṣfūr, I, 378, Ibn Manẓūr, VI, 4850, Åkesson, *Ibn Masᶜūd* 332: fol. 35a, Howell, IV, fasc. I, 1296) of the base form VIII *ʾiwtaṣalat* "it joined" from *waṣala* "to join". The example *ʾiwtaṣalat* has a vowelless *w,* which is at first assimilated to the infixed *t* of Form VIII resulting in *ʾittaṣalat.* Then the vowelless *t* is anomalously changed into a *y* on account of the influence of the kasra preceding it resulting in *ʾiytaṣalat.* The example *fa-ytaṣalat* occurs in this verse said by an unkown poet, in which he describes a wild cow searching for her calf. It is cited by Ibn Ǧinnī, *Sirr II,* 764, Ibn Yaᶜīš, X, 26, *Mulūkī* 248, Ibn ᶜUṣfūr, I, 378, Ibn Manẓūr, VI, 4850, Howell, IV, fasc. I, 1296, Åkesson, *Ibn Masᶜūd* 362: (356):

> *"Qāmat bi-hā tanšudu kullu l-munšadi*
> *fa-ytaṣalat bi-miṯli ḍawʾi l-farqadi".*
> "She stood in it [sc. the patch of ground], seeking with all inquiry, and joined [a calf] like the light [of the asterism called] al-farqad, [by which one guides oneself]".

10.1.8.8. The substitution of the y for the b:

The *y* in *ṯaᶜāl(i)y* (that results after the assimilation of the *y* to the *i* in *ṯaᶜāl(i)ī)* is substituted for the *b* of *ṯaᶜālib* "foxes" (cf. Åkesson, *Ibn Masᶜūd* 332: fol. 35a). The reason of this substitution seems to be the influence of the kasra preceding the *b.* The example *l-ṯaᶜālī* occurs instead of *l-ṯaᶜālibi* (in the genitive) and *ʾarānīhā* instead of *ʾarānibuhā* (cf. Nöldeke, *Grammatik* 13) in this verse cited by Sībawaihi, I, 300, Ibn Ǧinnī, *Sirr II,* 742, Ibn al-Sarrāǧ, *Uṣūl III,* 467, Zamaḫšarī, 174, Ibn Yaᶜīš, X, 24, 28,

Mulūkī 254, Ibn ᶜUṣfūr, I, 369, Howell, IV, fasc. I, 1297, Åkesson, *Ibn Masᶜūd* 362: (357):

> *"La-hā ʾašārīru min laḥmin tutammiruhu*
> *mina l-ṯaᶜālī wa-waḫzun min ʾarānīhā".*
> "She has bits of flesh that she dries,
> of foxes, and a little of her hares".

10.1.8.9. The substitution of the y for the s:

The *y* in *sād(i)y* (that results after the assimilation of the *y* to the *i* in *sād(i)ī)* is substituted for the *s* of the base form *sādis* "the sixth" (cf. Åkesson, *Ibn Masᶜūd* 332: fol. 35a, Nöldeke, *Grammatik* 13). The reason of this substitution seems to be the influence of the kasra preceding the *s*. The example *sādī* occurs in this verse said by Imruʾu l-Qais, cited by Ibn Ǧinnī, *Sirr II,* 741, Zamaḫšarī, 174, Ibn Yaᶜīš, X, 24, 28, *Mulūkī 255,* Ibn ᶜUṣfūr, I, 368, Ibn Manẓūr, III, 1934, 1979, V, 3414, Howell, IV, fasc. I, 1297, Åkesson, *Ibn Masᶜūd* 362: (358):

> *"ʾIḏā mā ᶜudda ʾarbaᶜatun fisālun*
> *fa-zawǧuki ḫāmisun wa-ʾabūki sādī".*
> "Whenever four mean unmanly fellows are reckoned,
> your husband is fifth, and your father sixth".

10.1.8.10. The substitution of the y for the ṯ:

The *y* in *l-ṯāl(i)y* (that results after the assimilation of the *y* to the *i* in *l-ṯāl(i)ī)* is substituted for the *ṯ* of the base form *l-ṯāliṯ* "the third" (cf. Åkesson, *Ibn Masᶜūd* 332: fol. 35a, Nöldeke, *Grammatik* 13). The reason of this substitution seems to be the influence of the kasra preceding the *ṯ* (cf. Åkesson, *Ibn Masᶜūd* 332: fol. 35a). The example *l-ṯālī* occurs in these verses said by an unknown poet, cited by Rāzī in Ḫalīl b. Aḥmad ..., *Ḥurūf* 155, Ibn Ǧinnī, *Sirr II,* 764, Zamaḫšarī, 174, Ibn Yaᶜīš, X, 28, *Mulūkī* 255, Ibn ᶜUṣfūr, I, 378, Ibn Manẓūr, I, 497, Howell, IV, fasc. I, 1297-1298, Åkesson, *Ibn Masᶜūd* 362: (359):

"Yufdīka yā Zurᶜa ʾabī wa-ḫālī
qad marra yawmāni wa-hāḏa l-ṯālī
wa-ʾanta bi-l-hiğrāni lā tubālī".
"My father and my maternal uncle shall be a ransom for you, O Zurᶜa!
Two days have passed and this is the third; and you do not care for the desertion".

10.1.9. The substitution of the *w*

The *w* or the *ū* can be substituted for the following segments: 1- the *ā*, 2- the *y*, and 3- the *ʾ*.

10.1.9.1. The substitution of the w for the ā:

The *w* in *ḍawāribu* "striking /pl." is necessarily substituted for the *ā* (cf. Ibn Ğinnī, *de Flexione* 24, *Sirr II,* 581-582, Zamaḫšarī, 174, Ibn Yaᶜīš, X, 29, Åkesson, *Ibn Masᶜūd* 334: fol. 35a). The example *ḍawāribu* is the broken pl. of the active participle *ḍāribun* and is conformable to the pattern *fawāᶜilu.* It is assumed that in its base form, the alif that marks the pl. is infixed after the infixed alif of the active participle *ḍāribun* causing a cluster of two vowelless alifs, namely *ḍ(a)āāribun.* The 1st *ā* is substituted by the *w* to prevent this cluster so that it became *ḍawāribu.* The substitution of the *w* for the *ā* is considered as natural as they are both glides (cf. Åkesson, *Ibn Masᶜūd* 334: fol. 35a).

10.1.9.2. The substitution of the w for the y:

The *w* in the active participle Form IV *muwqinun* (that results after the assimilation of the *w* to the *u* in *m(u)ūqinun)* is necessarily substituted for the 1st radical vowelless *y* of the base form *muyqinun* "to be certain" (cf. Sībawaihi, II, 342, Ibn Ğinnī, *de Flexione* 24, *Sirr II,* 584, Zamaḫšarī, 174, Ibn Yaᶜīš, X, 30, Åkesson, *Ibn Masᶜūd* 334: fol. 35a, Howell, IV, fasc. I, 1301) from *ʾayqana* "was certain" with 1st radical *y*. The reason of this substitution is that the vowelless *y* is preceded by a ḍamma (cf. Åkesson, *Ibn Masʿūd* 334: fol. 35a). A similar case is the active participle Form IV *muwsirun* > *m(u)ūsirun* from *ʾaysara* "was prosperous", underlyingly *muysirun* "to be well off", in which the 1st radical vowelless *y* is also substituted by the *w* because it is preceded by a ḍamma (cf. par. 5.4.1.1., par. 9.1.5.).

Another example is the verb in the imperfect Form IV *yuwsiru* "is well off" > *y(u)ūsiru* underlyingly *yuysiru* of which the 1st vowelless radical *y* is changed into a *w* on account of the influence of the ḍamma preceding it (cf. par. 5.4.1.1.).

10.1.9.3. The substitution of the w for the hamza:

The *w* in *luwmun* (that results after the assimilation of the *w* to the *u* in *l(u)ūmun)* is substituted for the ʾ of the base form *luʾmun* "blame" (cf. Åkesson, *Ibn Masʿūd* 334: fol. 35a and this study par. 4.1.2.1.: 2).

10.1.10. The substitution of the *m*

The *m* can be substituted for the following segments: 1- the *w,* 2- the *l,* 3- the *n* and 4- the *b.*

10.1.10.1. The substitution of the m for the w:

The *m* in *famun* is substituted for the *w* (cf. Zağğāğī, *Mağālis* 327, Ibn Ğinnī, *Sirr I,* 413-421, Zamaḫšarī, 174, Ibn Yaʿīš, X, 33-34, Åkesson, *Ibn Masʿūd* 334: fol. 35a, Wright, II, 173, Vernier, I, 16-17) of the base form *fawahun* "mouth" of which the *h* is elided for the purpose of alleviation. According to Sībawaihi, II, 342, the substitution of the *m* for the *w* in *famun* is rare.

10.1.10.2. The substitution of the m for the l:

The *m* in *ᵓam* is substituted for the *l* of the definite article *ᵓal*. *ᵓam* denotes determination in the dialect of Ṭayyī and Ḥimyar which is named *al-ṭumṭumānīyatu* (cf. Rabin, 49). The tradition *laysa mina l-barri l-ṣiyāmu fī l-safari* "fasting in travelling is not an act of piety" has been said with the substitution of the *m* for the *l,* namely *laysa mina m-barri m-ṣiyāmu fī m-safari* by al-Namir b. Tawlab. It is cited by Ibn Ǧinnī, *Sirr I,* 423, Zamaḫšarī, 153, 174, Ibn Yaᶜīš, X, 34, Ibn Hišām, *Muġnī I,* 48, Ibn ᶜUṣfūr, I, 394, Ḥarīrī, *Durra* 183, Åkesson, *Ibn Masᶜūd* 334: fol. 35a-35b, Howell, II-III, 676, IV, fasc. I, 1330, Rabin, 36, Wright, II, 270, Carter, *Linguistics [Širbīnī, Āǧurrūmīya]* 22, 23. According to Ibn Masᶜūd (Åkesson, *Ibn Masᶜūd* 334: fol. 35b), this substitution of the *m* for the *l* is carried out on account of both these segments' common character in being among the voiced segments (for the segments' characters see par. 2.2.2.).

10.1.10.3. The substitution of the m for the n:

The *m* in *ᶜambarun* is substituted for the vowelless *n* of the base form *ᶜanbarun* "a warehouse" (cf. Sībawaihi, II, 342, Ibn Ǧinnī, *de Flexione* 26, Zamaḫšarī, 174-175, Ibn Yaᶜīš, X, 33-36, Åkesson, *Ibn Masᶜūd* 58: fol. 6 b, 334: fol. 35b). The substitution of the *m* for the *n* is necessary when the *n* occurs vowelless before the *b* because of the heaviness implied by the combination of the nasal *n* and the rigid *b.* Another example is *šambāᵓun* said instead of *šanbāᵓun* "having sharp canine teeth".

An example in which this substitution is carried out without that the *n* that precedes the *b* is vowelless is *banām* in which the *m* is substituted anomalously for the vowelled *n* of the base form *banān* "henna" (cf. Nöldeke, *Grammatik* 12). The example *l-*

banāmi occurs in this verse said by al-ᶜAǧǧāǧ in the beginning of a poem in which he is praising Maslama b. ᶜAbd al-Malik. It is cited by Rāzī in Ḫalīl b. Aḥmad ..., *Ḥurūf* 154, Ibn Ǧinnī, *Sirr I,* 422, Zamaḫšarī, 174-175, Ibn Yaᶜīš, X, 33, 35, Ibn ᶜUṣfūr, I, 392, Howell, IV, fasc. I, 1332, Åkesson, *Ibn Masᶜūd* 366: (366):

> *"Yā Hāla ḏāta l-manṭiqi l-tamtāmi*
> *wa-kaffiki l-muḫaḍḍabi l-banāmi".*
> "O Hāla [sc. name of a woman], possessed of the lisping speech, and of your hand dyed in [the tips of] the fingers with henna".

10.1.10.4. The substitution of the m for the b:

The *m* in *rātiman* is substituted for the *b* of the base form *rātiban* (cf. Zamaḫšarī, 175, Ibn Yaᶜīš, X, 35) in the sentence *mā ziltu rātiman* "I have not ceased to be constant" (cf. Åkesson, *Ibn Masᶜūd* 334: fol. 35b). The reason of this substitution is the oneness of both these segments' point of articulation on account that they are both labials (for the segments see par. 2.2.1.).

10.1.11. The substitution of the *ṣ*

The *ṣ* can be substituted for the *s.*

10.1.11.1. The substitution of the ṣ for the s

An example is *ʾaṣbaġa* in which the *ṣ* is allowably substituted for the *s* of its base form *ʾasbaġa* "to make flow in exceeding measure" (cf. Zamaḫšarī, 176, Ibn Yaᶜīš, X, 51-52, Howell, IV, fasc. I, 1378-1380, Fleisch, *Traité I,* 80-81). It occurs in the sur. 31: 20 *(wa-ʾaṣbaġa ᶜalaykum niᶜamahu)* "And has made His bounties flow to you in exceeding measure", underlyingly *wa-ʾasbaġa,* read with both the *s* and the *ṣ* (cf. Ibn Ǧinnī, *Sirr I,*

212). The reason of this substitution is the proximity of the points of articulation of both the *s* and the *ṣ* (cf. Åkesson, *Ibn Masᶜūd* 334: fol. 35b), on account that they both originate from the part which is between the tip of the tongue and the tops of the two upper central incissors and are dentals (for the segments see par. 2.2.1).

10.1.12. The substitution of the *ā*

The *ā* can be substituted for the following segments: 1- the *w*, 2- the *y* and 3- the ᵓ.

10.1.12.1. The substitution of the ā for the w:

An example is *q(a)āla* in which the *ā* is necessarily substituted for the *w* of the base form *qawala* "to say" (cf. Åkesson, *Ibn Masᶜūd* 334: fol. 35b). The reason of this substitution is that the vowelled *w* is found in a measure of a verbal form, namely *faᶜala,* and is preceded by a fatḥa (cf. par. 6.5.1.1.: 1, 9.1.2.1.).

10.1.12.2. The substitution of the ā for the y:

An example is *b(a)āᶜa* in which the *ā* is necessarily substituted for the *y* of the base form *bayaᶜa* "to sell" (cf. ibid). The reason of this substitution is that the vowelled *y* is found in a measure of a verbal form, namely *faᶜala,* and is preceded by a fatḥa (cf. par. 6.5.1.2.: 1, 9.1.2.1.).

10.1.12.3. The substitution of the ā for the hamza:

An example is *r(a)āsun* in which the *ā* is allowably substituted for the ᵓ of the base form *raᵓsun* "head" (cf. Åkesson, *Ibn Masᶜūd* 334: fol. 35b, Nöldeke, *Grammatik* 6). The reason of this change is the vowellessness of the ᵓ and the vowelling of the segment preceding it (see par. 4.1.2.1.: 1).

10.1.13. The substitution of the *l*

The *l* can be substituted for the following segments: 1- the *n* and 2- the *ḍ*.

10.1.13.1. The substitution of the l for the n:

An example is *ʾuṣaylālun* in which the *l* is substituted for the *n* of the base form *ʾuṣaylānun* "evening" (cf. Åkesson, *Ibn Masʿūd* 334: fol. 35b, Wright, II, 175). The example *ʾuṣaylālan* occurs in this verse said by al-Nābiġa al-Ḏubyānī praising al-Nuʿmān b. al-Munḏir, cited by Rāzī in Ḫalīl b. Aḥmad ..., *Ḥurūf* 1538, Ibn Ǧinnī, *Lumaʿ* 28, Muʾaddib, *Taṣrif* 338, Ibn al-Sarrāǧ, *Uṣūl III,* 275, Zamaḫšarī, 176, Ibn Yaʿīš, *Mulūkī* 106, 216, Ibn al-Anbārī, *Inṣāf* Q. 19, 79, Howell, IV, fasc. I, 1367, Åkesson, *Ibn Masʿūd* 368: (370):

> "*Waqaftu fīhā ʾuṣaylālan ʾusāʾiluhā*
> *ʿayyat ǧawāban wa-mā bi-l-rabʿi min ʿaḥad.*
> "I stopped in it a short time at evening, questioning it [about its inmates]:
> it was unable to answer, nor was any one in the abode".

10.1.13.2. The substitution of the l for the ḍ:

An example is *ʾilṭaǧaʿa* in which the *l* is substituted for the *ḍ* of the base form *ʾiḍṭaǧaʿa* "to lay down to sleep" (cf. Åkesson, *Ibn Masʿūd* 334: fol. 35b). The example *fa-lṭaǧaʿ* is found in this verse said by Manẓūr b. Murṯid al-Asadī (cf. Fischer/ Braūnlich, *Šawāhid* 134) describing a wolf that meant to catch a gazelle. It is cited by Ibn Ǧinnī, *Sirr I,* 321, *Ḫaṣāʾiṣ I,* 63, 263, III, 163, Zamaḫšarī, 176, Ibn Yaʿīš, IX, 82, X, 46, *Mulūkī* 216, Ibn ʿAqīl, II, 548, Ibn ʿUṣfūr, I, 403, Suyūṭī, *Ašbāh I,* 601, Ibn Manẓūr, IV, 2554, Howell, IV, fasc. I, 848, 1368, Åkesson, *Ibn Masʿūd* 368: (371):

> "*Lammā raʾā ʾan lā daʿah wa-lā šibaʿ*
> *māla ʾilā ʾarṭāti ḫiqfin fa-lṭaǧaʿ*".

"When he [sc. the wolf] saw that there was no ease, and no glutting of his appetite [in the pursuit of the gazelle],
he turned aside to an Arṭā tree of a curving tract of sand, and lay down to sleep".

10.1.14. The substitution of the *z*

The *z* can be substituted for the following segments: 1- the *s* and 2- the *ṣ*.

10.1.14.1. The substitution of the z for the s:

An example is *yazdulu* in which the *z* is substituted for the *s* of the base form *yasdulu* "he losens (his garment)" (cf. Ibn Ğinnī, *Sirr I,* 196, Zamaḫšarī, 177, Ibn Yaᶜīš, X, 52, Ibn Manẓūr, III, 2036, Åkesson, *Ibn Masᶜūd* 334: fol. 35b, Howell, IV, fasc. I, 1381).

10.1.14.2. The substitution of the z for the ṣ:

An example is *fazdī* in which the *z* is substituted for the *ṣ* of the base form *faṣdī* "my way of bleeding". This substitution is carried out when the *z* is vowelless and occurs before a *d.* The example *fazdī* occurs in this phrase said by Ḥatim when he had slaughtered a she-camel for a guest and he was asked: "Why did you not bleed her?", and he answered: *hākaḏā fazdī ᵓanah* "This is my way of bleeding, mine" (cf. Zağğāğī, *Mağālis* 136, Zamaḫšarī, 177, Ibn Yaᶜīš, X, 52, Åkesson, *Ibn Masᶜūd* 334: fol. 35b, Howell, IV, fasc. I, 856, 1383), with this substitution taking place in *faṣdī* resulting in *fazdī.*

10.1.15. The substitution of the ṭ

The *ṭ* can be substituted for the *t.*

10.1.15.1. The substitution of the ṭ for the t:

This substitution is necessary if the *t* follows one of the segments of covering, namely the *ṣ, ḍ, ṭ* and *ẓ* (for the segments' characters see par. 2.2.2.). This occurs in two cases:

- In Form VIII *ʾiftaᶜala* in which the 1st radical is a segment of covering, e.g. Form VIII *ʾiṣṭabara* in which the *ṭ* is necessarily substituted for the infixed *t* of the base form *ʾiṣtabara* "to have patience" (cf. Åkesson, *Ibn Masᶜūd* 334: fol. 35b and this study par. 2.4.1.1.3.2.: 4), *ʾiḍṭaraba* underlyingly *ʾiḍtaraba* "to be in a state of agitation" (cf. par. 2.4.1.1.3.2.: 5), *ʾiṭṭalaba* originaly *ʾiṭtalaba* "to seek" (cf. par. 2.4.1.1.3.2.: 6), and *ʾiẓṭalama* "to put with wrong" underlyingly *ʾiẓtalama* (cf. par. 2.4.1.1.3.2.: 7).

- In some cases of verbs in the perfect of which the 3rd radical is one of the segments of covering, to which the agent pronoun of the 1st or of the 2nd person of the perfect, namely the *-tu* or the *-ta* respectively, is suffixed to, e.g. *faḥaṣṭu* in which the *ṭ* is substituted for the *t* which is the suffixed agent pronoun of the 1st person of the sing. of *faḥaṣtu* "I scraped a hollow" (cf. Sībawaihi, II, 341, Ibn Ǧinnī, *Sirr I,* 219-220, Zamaḫšarī, 176, Ibn Yaᶜīš, X, 46-48, Ibn ᶜUṣfūr, I, 360-361, Åkesson, *Ibn Masᶜūd* 334: fol. 35b, Howell, IV, fasc. I, 1369-1370, Vernier, I, 356).

Other examples are *ḥafiẓṭu* and *ḥafiẓṭa* said instead of *ḥafiẓtu* "I kept" and *ḥafiẓta* "you kept" respectively and *ḥuṣṭu* and *ḥuṣṭa* said instead of *ḥuṣtu* "I sealed" and *ḥuṣta* "you sealed" respectively.

10.2. Conclusion

As Chapter 10. which treats the substitution of the fifteen segments is distinct from all the other chapters, the work may be said to end with it.

As we have observed, the substitution is carried out mostly between two segments that are close in the point of articulation or that are akin in character. The hamza (cf. 10.1.1.), the glides: the *y* (cf. 10.1.8.), the *w* (cf. 10.1.9.), the *ā* (cf. 10.1.12.), and the infix *t* of Form VIII (cf. 10.1.15.) are more subjected to the substitution than any other segment.

Some of the cases that touch the hamza have been already studied in the chapter treating the phonological changes that are due to the hamza (cf. chapter 4.), those touching the glides have been studied in the chapter referring to the soundness or the unsoundness of the glide (cf. chapter 9.) and those touching the infix -*t* of Form VIII have been studied in the chapter of the assimilation (cf. chapter 2.).

Most of the cases of substitution are due to a specific heaviness in the word, whether it concerns a segment itself, a vowel on a glide, or a combination of two segments.

Some examples of segments that are considered as heavy are, e.g. the guttural segment ^{c} in *ḍafādi*^{c} that is substituted by the lighter *ī* resulting in *ḍafād(i)ī* (cf. 10.1.8.6.), the *t* marker of the fem. in pause that is substituted by the lighter *h*, e.g. Ṭalḥah said instead of Ṭalḥat "Ṭalḥa" (cf. 10.1.7.4.) and the *alif mamdūda* in pause that is substituted by the *h*, e.g. *ḥayyahalah* "come along!" said instead of *ḥayya halā* (cf. 10.1.7.2.).

Some examples of vowels that are found heavy on a glide, which explains why the hamza is substituted for the glide, are the ḍamma vowelling the *w* in *wuǧūhun* that becomes *ʾuǧūhun* "faces" (cf. 10.1.1.2.:2) and the fatḥa vowelling the *y* in *yadayhi* "his hands" that becomes *ʾadayhi* (10.1.1.3.: 1). An example of a heavy combination of two segments is the vowelless nasal *n* followed by the vowelled rigid *b* in *ᶜanbarun* "a warehouse" resulting in the substitution of the *m* for the *n,* i.e. *ᶜambarun* (cf. 10.1.10.3.).

The vowel preceding a glide plays also a role in the segment's substitution by another segment. For instance, the vowelless *w* in *miwqātun* "time appointed for performance of an action" is changed into *y* because of the influence of the kasra preceding it, i.e. *miyqātun* (cf. 10.1.8.2.), the *ᶜ* in *ḍafādiᶜ* is changed into *ī,* i.e. *ḍafād(i)ī* also due to the kasra preceding it (cf. 10.1.8.6.), and the *y* in the verb in the imperfect of Form IV *yuysiru* is changed into *w,* i.e. *yuwsiru* "is well off" due to the influence of the ḍamma preceding it (cf. par. 10.1.9.2.).

Some cases of substitution are due to the usage of a certain dialectal variant, e.g. the substitution of the *t* for the *s,* e.g. *l-nāsi* said instead of *l-nāti* by the Yemenites (cf. 10.1.3.3.), the substitution of the *m* for the *l,* e.g. the definite article *ʾam* said instead of *ʾal* by the Ṭayyī and Ḥimyar (cf. 10.1.10.2.) and the substitution of the *ǧ* for the *y,* e.g. ᶜAliǧǧi "ᶜAlī" said instead of ᶜAliyyi by the Quḍāᶜa, Banū Tamīm and Banū Saᶜd (cf. 10.1.5.1.). Other cases of substitution are due to a metric exigency as the substitution of the *y* for the *ṯ* in *l-ṯāliṯ* "the third" that is said instead of *l-ṯāl(i)ī,* so that the word rimes with *tubālī* in the verses that have been mentioned there (cf. 10.1.8.10.).

BIBLIOGRAPHY

I. Literature

I.1. Primary sources

ᶜAbd al-Raḥīm, *Ṣarf* = ᶜAbd al-Raḥīm, Saᶜd, *Muqaddamat fī ᶜilm al-ṣarf,* Cairo s.a.

ᶜAbd al-Tawwāb, *Taṭawwur* = ᶜAbd al-Tawwāb, R., *al-Taṭawwur al-luġawī, maẓāhiruhu wa-ᶜilaluhu wa-qawānīnuhu,* Cairo 1404/1983.

Åkesson, *Ibn Masᶜūd* = Åkesson, J. , *Arabic Morphology and Phonology based on the Marāḥ al-arwāḥ by Aḥmad b. ᶜAlī b. Masᶜūd, Presented with an Introduction, Arabic Edition, English Translation and Commentary,* Leiden 2001.

Bakkūš, *Taṣrif* = Al-Bakkūš, Ṭ., *al-Taṣrif al-ᶜarabī,* Tunis 1973.

Carter, *Linguistics [Širbīnī, Āǧurrūmīya]* = Carter, M. G., *Arab Linguistics, an introductory classical text with translation and notes,* Amsterdam 1981.

Daqr, *Muᶜǧam* = Daqr, ᶜAbd al-Ġanī, *Muᶜǧam al-naḥw,* Beirut 1407 A.H. /1986.

Ḫalīl b. Aḥmad..., *Ḥurūf* = Ḫalīl b. Aḥmad wa-b. al-Sakīt wa-l-Rāzī, *Ṯalāṯat kutub fī l-ḥurūf,* Ed. R. ᶜAbd al-Tawwāb, Cairo 1982.

Ḥarīrī, *Durra* = Al-Ḥarîrî, Abū Muḥammad al-Qāsim b. ᶜAlī, *Durrat al-ġawwâṣ,* Ed. H. Thorbecke, Leipzig 1871.

Ibn al-Anbārī, *Inṣāf* = Ibn al-Anbārī, Abū l-Barakāt, *Kitāb al-inṣāf fī masāʾil al-ḫilāf bayna l-naḥwīyīn al-baṣrīyīn wa-l-kūfīyīn: Die grammatischen Schulen von Kufa und Basra,* Ed. G. Weil, Leiden 1913.

Ibn ᶜAqīl = Ibn ᶜAqīl, *Bihāʾ al-Dīn ᶜAbdallāh, Šarḥ ᶜalā alfīyat Ibn Mālik,* Ed. ᶜA. al-Ḥamīd, 2 vol., undated.

Ibn Fāris, *Ṣāḥibī* = Ibn Fāris, Aḥmad, *al-Ṣāḥibī fī fiqh al-luġa wa-sanan al-ᶜarab fī kalāmihā,* Ed. M. al-Chouémi, (bibliotheca Philologica; I), Beyrouth 1382/1963.

Ibn Ǧinnī, *de Flexione* = Ibn Ǧinnîi, Abū l-Fatḥ ᶜUṯmān, *de Flexione Libellvs,* Ed. G. Hoberg, Lipsiae, 1885.

Ibn Ǧinnī, *Ḫaṣāʾiṣ* = Ibn Ǧinnī, Abū l-Fatḥ ᶜUṯmān, *al-Ḫaṣāʾiṣ,* Ed. M. A. al-Naǧǧār, 3 vol., Cairo 1371/1952-1376/1956.

Ibn Ǧinnī, *Lumaᶜ* = Ibn Ǧinnī, Abū l-Fatḥ ᶜUṯmān, *Kitāb al-lumaᶜ fi-n-naḥw,* Ed. H. M. Kechrida, Uppsala 1976.

Ibn Ǧinnī, *Munṣif* = Ibn Ǧinnī, Abū l-Fatḥ ᶜUṯmān, *al-Munṣif fī šarḥ taṣrīf al-Māzinī,* Ed. I. Muṣṭafā, ᶜA. Amīn, 3 vol., Cairo 1373/1954-1379/1960.

Ibn Ǧinnī, *Sirr* = Ibn Ǧinnī, Abū l-Fatḥ ᶜUṯmān, *Sirr ṣināᶜat al-iᶜrāb,* Ed. Ḥ. Hindāwī, 2 vol., Damascus 1405/1985.

Ibn Ḫālawaihi, *Qirāʾāt* = Ibn Ḫālawaihi, Abū ᶜAbd Allāh al-Ḥusain b. Aḥmad, *Iᶜrāb al-qirāʾāt al-sabᶜ wa-ᶜilaluhā,* Ed. ᶜAbd al-Raḥmān b. Sulaimān al-ᶜAtīmain, 2 vol., Cairo 1413/1992.

Ibn Hišām, *Muġnī* = Ibn Hišām, Ǧamāl al-Dīn Abū Muḥammad ᶜAbdallāh b. Yūsuf, *Muġnī l-labīb ᶜan kutub al-ʾaᶜārīb,* 2 vol., Ed. M. Mubārak and M. ᶜA. Ḥ. Allāh, Beirut 1972.

Ibn Mālik, *La Alfīya* = Ibn Mālik, Muḥammad b. ᶜAbd Allāh, *La ʾAlfiyyah d'Ibnu-Malik* [pp. 1-227], suivie de (->) *La Lāmiyyah* du meme auteur (pp. 228-353) avec traduction et notes en français et un lexique des termes techniques par A. Goguyer, Beyrouth 1888.

Ibn Manẓūr = Ibn Manẓūr, Ǧamāl al-Dīn, *Lisān al-ᶜArab,* 6 vol., Beirut undated.

Ibn al-Sarrāǧ, *ʾUṣūl* = Ibn al-Sarrāǧ, Abū Bakr, *al-ʾUṣūl fī l-Naḥw,* Ed. ᶜA. Ḥ. al-Fatlī, Beirut 1408/1988.

Ibn ᶜUṣfūr = Ibn ᶜUṣfūr al-Ašbīlī, Abū l-ᶜAbbās ᶜAlī b. Muʾmin, *al-Mumtiᶜ fī l-taṣrīf,* Ed. F. al-Dīn Qabāwih, Aleppo 1390/1970.

Ibn Wallād, *Maqṣūr* = Ibn Wallād, Abū l-ᶜAbbās Aḥmad b. Muḥammad, *Kitāb al-maqṣūr wa-l-mamdūd ᶜalā ḥurūf al-muᶜǧam, Part I, Contributions towards Arabic Philology*, Ed. Paul Brönnle, Leiden 1900.

Ibn Yaᶜīš = Ibn Yaᶜīš, Muwaffaq al-Dīn Abū l-Barāʾ Yaᶜīš, *Šarḥ al-mufaṣṣal, 2* vol., Beirut undated.

Ibn Yaᶜīš, *Mulūkī* = Ibn Yaᶜīš, Muwaffaq al-Dīn Abū l-Barāʾ Yaᶜīš, *Šarḥ al-mulūkī fī l-taṣrīf,* Ed. Faḫr al-Dīn Qabāwa, Aleppo 1393/1973.

Muʾaddib, *Taṣrīf* = Al-Muʾaddib, al-Qāsim b. Muḥammad b. Saᶜīd, *Daqāʾiq al-taṣrīf,* Ed. A. N. al-Qaisī, Ḥ. Ṣ. al-Ḍāmin and Ḥ. Tūrāl, Iraq 1407/1987.

Rāǧiḥī, *Basīṭ* = Rāǧiḥī, ᶜAbdo, *al-Basīṭ fī ᶜilm al-ṣarf,* Alexandria s.a.

Sībawaihi = Sîbawaihi, Abū Bišr ᶜAmr b. ᶜUṯmān, *Le Livre de Sîbawaihi (Kitāb Sībawaihi), Traité de grammaire arabe,* Ed. H. Derenbourg, 2 vol., Paris 1881-1889. Réimpression: 1970.

Širbīnī, Āğurrūmīya = see Carter, *Linguistics.*

Suyūṭī, *Ašbāh* = Al-Suyūṭī, Ğalāl al-Dīn Abū l-Faḍl ᶜAbd al-Raḥmān, *al-ᵓAšbāh wa-l-naẓāᵓir,* Ed. ᶜAbd Allāh Nabhān, 4 vol., Damascus 1406/1985.

Suyūṭī, *Muzhir* = Al-Suyūṭī, Ğalāl al-Dīn Abū l-Faḍl ᶜAbd al-Raḥmān, *al-Muzhir fī ᶜulūm al-luġa wa-anwāᶜihā,* 2 vol., Cairo undated.

ᶜUkbarī, *Masāᵓil* = Al-ᶜUkbarī, Abd Allāh b. al-Ḥusain, *Masāᵓil ḫilāfīya fī l-naḥw,* Ed. M. Ḥ. al-Ḥalawānī, Aleppo, undated.

Versteegh, *Zağğāğī* = Versteegh, K., *The explanation of linguistic causes. Az-Zağğāğī's theory of grammar. Introduction, translation, commentary,* Amsterdam 1995.

Zağğāğī, *Mağālis* = Al-Zağğāğī, Abū Qāsim ᶜAbd al-Raḥmān, *Mağālis al-ᶜulamāᵓ*, Ed. ᶜA. S. M. Harūn, Kuwait 1962.

Zamaḫšarī = Zamaḫsᵓario, Abū l-Qāsim Maḥmūd b. ᶜUmar, *al-Mufaṣṣal,* Ed. J. P. Broch, Christianiae 1840.

II.2. Secondary sources

Åkesson, *Conversion* = Åkesson, J., *Conversion of the yāᵓ into an alif in Classical Arabic* in: ZAL 31, Wiesbaden 1996.

Åkesson, *Ibn Masᶜūd* = Åkesson, J., *Arabic Morphology and Phonology based on the Marāḥ al-arwāḥ by Aḥmad b. ᶜAlī b. Masᶜūd, Presented with an Introduction, Arabic Edition, English Translation and Commentary,* Leiden 2001.

Bohas/Kouloughli, *Linguistic* = Bohas, G., Guillaume, J.-P., Kouloughli, D.E., *The Arabic Linguistic Tradition,* London and New York 1990.

Cantineau, *Études* = Cantineau, J., *Études de linguistique arabe,* Memorial Jean Cantineau, Paris 1960.

Carter, *Linguistics* [Širbīnī, *Āğurrūmīya]* = Carter, M. G., *Arab Linguistics, an introductory classical text with translation and notes,* Amsterdam 1981.

Fischer/Braūnlich, *Šawāhid* = Fischer A. und Bräunlich E., *Schawāhid-Indices, Indices der Reimwörter und der Dichter der in den arabischen Schawāhid-Kommentaren und in verwandten Werken erläuterten Belegverse,* Leipzig und Wien, 1945.

Fleisch, *Traité I* = Fleisch, H., *Traité de Philologie Arabe, vol. I, Préliminaires, Phonétique Morphologie Nominale,* Beyrouth 1961.

Fleisch, *Traité II* = Fleisch, H., *Traité de Philologie Arabe, vol. II, Pronoms, Morphologie verbale, Particules,* Beyrouth 1979.

Howell = Howell, M. S., *Grammar of the Classical Arabic Language,* 4 parts in 7 vol., Allahabad 1880-1911.

Lane = Lane, E.W., *Arabic-English Lexicon,* 8 in 2 vol., London 1863-1893. Reprint. 1984.

Mokhlis, *Taṣrīf* = *Théorie du taṣrīf et traitement du Lexique chez les Grammairiens Arabes,* Frankfurt Am Main 1997.

Nöldeke, *Grammatik* = Nöldeke, T., *Zur Grammatik des Classischen Arabisch im Anhang: Die Handschriftlichen ergänzungen in dem Handexemplar Theodor Nöldekes bearbeitet und mit zuzätzen versehen von Anton Spitaler,* Darmstadt 1963.

Penrice, *Dictionary* = Penrice, J., *A Dictionary and Glossary of the Kor-ân,* London 1873. Reprint: 1971.

Rabin = Rabin, C., *Ancient West-Arabian,* London 1951.

Roman, *Étude* = Roman, A., *Étude de la phonologie et de la morphologie de la koinè arabe,* 2 vol., Publications de l'Université de Provence, Marseille 1983.

De Sacy = De Sacy, S., *Grammaire arabe,* 2 vol., Tunis 1904-1905.

Vernier = Vernier, D., *Grammaire arabe,* 2 vol., Beyrouth 1891.

Versteegh, *Langage* = Versteegh, C. H. M., *The Arabic language,* Edinburgh 1996.

Versteegh, *Zağğāğī* = Versteegh, K., *The explanation of linguistic causes. Az-Zağğāğī's theory of grammar. Introduction, translation, commentary,* Amsterdam 1995.

Wright = Wright, W., *A Grammar of the Arabic Language,* Cambridge, Third Edition 1985.

Wright, *Comparative Grammar* = Wright, W., *Lectures on the Comparative Grammar of the Semitic Languages,* Cambridge 1890.

INDEX OF QUR'ANIC QUOTATIONS

Sur.	v.	par.
1:	7	10.1.1.5.
2:	19	2.3.2.3.
29:	64	9.1.2.2.1.: 3
2:	72	2.4.2.1.1.: 3
2:	237	7.6.
2:	269	2.4.2.1.1.: 4
4:	81	2.4.1.2.
7:	199	3.2.1.1.: 1
9:	12	4.1.2.4.1.
9:	38	2.4.2.1.1: 2.
9:	109	6.5.10.
10:	24	2.4.2.1.1.
10:	35	2.4.2.1.2.
20:	97	1.2.1.4.
20:	132	3.2.1.1.
21:	73	6.5.12.
23:	1	4.1.2.3.1.2.2.
27:	47	2.4.2.1.1.
31:	20	10.1.11.1.

33:	33	1.2.1.6.
36:	49	2.4.2.1.2.
37:	8	2.4.2.1.1.
47:	18	4.1.2.7.2.
48:	29	2.4.2.2.
56:	65	1.2.1.4.
80:	3-4	2.4.2.1.1.
89:	19	10.1.3.1.

INDEX OF VERSES

Fa-taᶜarrafūnī ᵓinnanī ᵓanā ḏākumu	6.5.10.: 2
Fa-yā ẓabyata l-waᶜsāᵓi bayna ğulāğilin	4.1.2.7.1.
Ḫālī ᶜUwayfun wa-ᵓAbū ᶜAliğği	10.1.5.1.
Huwa l-ğawādu l-laḏī yuᶜṭīka nāᶜilahu	2.4.1.1.3.2.: 7
ᵓIḏā l-kirāmu btadarū l-bāᶜa badar	1.2.1.7.
ᵓIḏā mā ᶜudda ᵓarbaᶜatun fisālun	10.1.8.9.
ᵓInna l-ḫalīṭa ᵓağaddū l-bayna fa-nğaradū	5.2.1.2.
ᵓInnamā l-maytu man yaᶜīšu kaᵓīban	9.1.13.1.
La-hā ᵓašārīru min laḥmin tutammiruhu	10.1.8.8.
Lāhumma ᵓin kunta qabilta ḥağğatiğ	10.1.5.1.
Lammā raᵓā ᵓan lā daᶜah wa-lā šibaᶜ	10.1.13.2.
Law šiᵓti qad naqaᶜa l-fuᵓāda bi-šarbatin	5.1.1.
Laysa man māta fa-starāḥa bi-maytin	9.1.13.1.
Qāmat bi-hā tanšudu kullu l-munšadi	10.1.8.7.
Rāḥat bi-Maslamata l-biġālu ᶜašīyata	4.1.2.2.1.: 1
Ṣafqatu ḏī ḏaᶜālitin samūli	10.1.3.5.
ᵓUrī ᶜaynayya mā lam tarᵓayāhu	3.4.1.1.
Wa-baldatin qāliṣatin ᵓamwāᵓuhā	10.1.1.4.
Wa-hayyağa l-ḥayya min dārin fa-ẓalla lahum	10.1.7.2.
Wa-māğa sāᶜātin malā l-wadīqi	10.1.1.6.

Wa-manhalin laysa lahu ḥawāziqu 10.1.8.6.
Waqaftu fīhā ᵓuṣaylālan ᵓusāᵓiluhā 10.1.13.1.
Yā dāra Mayya bi-l-dakādīki l-buraq 10.1.1.5.
Yā Hāla ḏāta l-manṭiqi l-tamtāmi 10.1.10.3.
Yā layta ᵓannā ḍammanā safīnah 9.1.12.2.
Yā qātala l-lāhu banī l-siᶜlāti 10.1.3.3.
Yufdīka yā Zurᶜa ᵓabī wa-ḫālī 10.1.8.10.

INDEX OF NAMES

cAbd al-Raḥīm 5.2.1.4., 6.5.8.1., 6.5.9.1., 6.5.13.1.
cAbd al-Tawwāb 2.4.1.1.3.2., 2.4.2.1.1., 10.1.1.2., 10.1.3.1.
Abū cAmr 2.3.2.3., 2.4.2.1.2.
Abū Bakr 2.4.2.1.2.
Abū l-Fatḥ [Ibn Ǧinnī] 9.1.12.2.
Abū l-Ḥasan 9.1.12.2.
Abū l-Samḥ 4.1.2.4.1.
Abū Umayya al-Faḍl b. al-cAbbās b. cUtba b. Abī Lahab 5.2.1.2.
Abū Zaid 4.1.2.4.1., 10.1.5.1.
cAǧǧāǧ 1.2.1.7., 10.1.10.3.
Åkesson 1., 1.2.1.4., 1.2.1.5., 1.2.1.6., 1.2.1.7., 2.2.2., 2.3.1.1., 2.3.2.1., 2.3.2.2.1., 2.3.2.2.2., 2.4.1.1.3., 2.4.1.1.3.1., 2.4.1.1.3.2., 2.4.2.1.1., 2.4.2.1.2., 3.2.1.1., 3.4.1.1., 3.7., 4.1.1., 4.1.2.1., 4.1.2.2.1., 4.1.2.2.2., 4.1.2.3.1., 4.1.2.3.1.1., 4.1.2.3.1.2.1., 4.1.2.3.1.2.2., 4.1.2.3.2., 4.1.2.3.4., 4.1.2.4., 4.1.2.4.1., 4.1.2.7.1., 4.1.2.7.2., 4.1.3.1., 4.1.3.2., 5.1.1., 5.2.1.1., 5.2.1.2., 5.2.1.6., 5.4.1.1., 6., 6.5.1.1., 6.5.1.2., 6.5.4., 6.5.5., 6.5.6., 6.5.7., 6.5.8.1., 6.5.9.1., 6.5.10., 6.5.13.1., 6.5.15., 7., 7.5.1.1., 7.5.1.2., 7.5.2.1., 7.5.2.2.,

7.5.4., 7.5.5., 7.5.6., 7.5.7., 7.5.8., 7.5.10., 7.5.12., 7.5.13., 7.5.14., 7.5.15., 7.6., 9.1., 9.1.1., 9.1.2.1.1., 9.1.2.2., 9.1.2.2.1., 9.1.3.1., 9.1.4.1., 9.1.5., 9.1.8., 9.1.8., 9.1.9., 9.1.9.1., 9.1.10., 9.1.12.1., 9.1.12.2., 9.1.13.1., 9.1.16.1., 9.1.17., 9.1.18., 10.1.1.1., 10.1.1.2., 10.1.1.3., 10.1.1.4., 10.1.1.5., 10.1.1.6., 10.1.2.1., 10.1.3.1., 10.1.3.2., 10.1.3.3., 10.1.3.4., 10.1.3.5., 10.1.5.1., 10.1.6.1., 10.1.7.1., 10.1.7.2., 10.1.7.3., 10.1.7.4., 10.1.8., 10.1.8.2., 10.1.8.3., 10.1.8.5., 10.1.8.6., 10.1.8.7., 10.1.8.8., 10.1.8.9., 10.1.8.10., 10.1.9.1., 10.1.9.2., 10.1.9.3., 10.1.10.1., 10.1.10.2., 10.1.10.3., 10.1.10.4., 10.1.11.1., 10.1.12.1., 10.1.12.2., 10.1.12.2., 10.1.13.1., 10.1.13.2., 10.1.14.2., 10.1.15.1.

Al-Aḫfaš 6.5.6., 6.5.7.

Arabs 4.1.2.7.2. , 4.1.3.2.1.

Asad 1.2.1.2.

ᶜAṣim 1.2.1.6.

Bakkūš 2.4.1.1.1,. 2.4.1.1.3.2., 5.2.1.4., 6.5.2.1., 6.5.2.2., 6.5.4., 6.5.5., 6.5.13.1.

Bohas 9.1., 9.1.2.2., 9.1.4.1.

Banū ᶜAmir 5.1.1.

Banū Asad 6.5.13.1.

Banū Bakr b. Waᵓīl 10.1.7.2.

Banū ᶜAwf b. Saᶜd 10.1.3.5.

Banū Saᶜd 10.1.5.1., 10.2.

Banū Tamīm 4.1.3.2.1., 10.1.5.1., 10.2.

Braūnlich 2.4.1.1.3.2., 10.1.13.2.

Cantineau 2.4.1.1.3.2., 2.4.2.2.

Carter 9.1.13.1., 10.1.10.2.

Daqr 7.5.5., 7.5.8., 10.1.3.2.

De Sacy 1.2.1.4., 1.2.1.5., 2.3.2.2.1., 2.4.1.1.3.1., 2.4.2.1.1., 2.4.2.1.2., 3.4.1.1., 4.1.2.2.1., 4.1.2.3.2., 5.2.1.3., 5.2.1.5., 6.5.12., 7.5.13., 9.1.18., 10.1.7.1.

Farazdaq 4.1.2.2.1.

Al-Farrāʾ 5.2.1.2.

Fischer 2.4.1.1.3.2., 10.1.13.2.

Fleisch 2.4.1.1.3.1., 2.4.2.1.2., 2.4.2.2., 4.1.1., 10.1.1.2., 10.1.7.4., 10.1.11.1.

Ǧarīr 5.1.1.

Ḫalaf al-Aḥmar 10.1.8.6.

Al-Ḫalīl 4.1.2.7.2, 9.1.12.2., 10.1.1.2., 10.1.3.3., 10.1.7.3., 10.1.8.10., 10.1.10.3., 10.1.13.1.

Harim b. Sinān 2.4.1.1.3.2.

Ḥarīrī 10.1.10.2.

Ḥātim 10.1.14.2.

Ḥiǧāzīs 1.2.1.5., 4.1.2.7.2., 4.1.3.2.1., 10.1.3.2.

Ḥimyar 10.1.10.2., 10.2.

Howell 1.2.1.2., 1.2.1.4., 2.2.2., 2.3.2.1, 2.3.2.1., 2.3.2.2.1., 2.4.1.1.3., 2.4.1.1.3.1., 2.4.1.1.3.2., 2.4.2.1.1., 2.4.2.1.2., 3.2.1.1., 3.4.1.1., 4.1.1., 4.1.2.2.1., 4.1.2.3.1.1., 4.1.2.3.1.2.1., 4.1.2.3.1.2.2., 4.1.2.3.2., 4.1.2.4.1., 4.1.2.7.1., 4.1.2.7.2., 4.1.3.2., 4.1.3.2.1., 5.1.1., 5.2.1.2., 6.5.6., 6.5.10., 6.5.12., 6.5.13.1., 7.5.13., 7.6., 9.1., 9.1.2.1.1., 9.1.2.2.1., 9.1.3.1., 9.1.9.1., 9.1.12.1., 9.1.12.2., 9.1.13.1., 9.1.18., 10.1., 10.1.1.2., 10.1.1.4., 10.1.1.5., 10.1.1.6., 10.1.2.1., 10.1.3.1., 10.1.3.2., 10.1.3.3., 10.1.3.4., 10.1.3.5., 10.1.4.1., 10.1.5.1., 10.1.6.1., 10.1.7.2., 10.1.7.4., 10.1.8.1., 10.1.8.2., 10.1.8.3., 10.1.8.5., 10.1.8.6., 10.1.8.7., 10.1.8.8., 10.1.8.9., 10.1.8.10., 10.1.9.2., 10.1.10.2., 10.1.10.3., 10.1.11.1., 10.1.13.1., 10.1.13.2., 10.1.14.1., 10.1.14.2., 10.1.15.1.

Ibn al-Anbārī 5.2.1.3., 9.1.12.2., 10.1.13.1.
Ibn ᶜAqīl 1.2.1.4., 1.2.1.6., 2.3.2.2.1., 2.4.1.1.3.2., 10.1.1.2., 10.1.13.2.
Ibn Fāris 10.1.3.3., 10.1.6.1.
Ibn Ğinnī 1.1., 1.2.1.7., 2.4.1.1.3.2., 3.2.1.1., 3.4.1.1., 4.1.1., 4.1.2.2.1., 4.1.2.2.2., 4.1.2.3.1.1., 4.1.2.4., 4.1.2.4.1., 4.1.2.7.1., 5.2.1.2., 6.5.1.1., 6.5.1.2., 6.5.2.1., 6.5.4., 6.5.10., 6.5.13.1., 7.5.5., 9.1.8., 9.1.10., 9.1.12.2., 10.1., 10.1.1.1., 10.1.1.2., 10.1.1.4., 10.1.1.5., 10.1.1.6., 10.1.3.3., 10.1.3.5., 10.1.4.1., 10.1.5.1., 10.1.7.2., 10.1.7.3., 10.1.7.4., 10.1.8.1., 10.1.8.2., 10.1.8.5., 10.1.8.6., 10.1.8.7., 10.1.8.8., 10.1.8.9., 10.1.8.10., 10.1.9.1., 10.1.9.2., 10.1.10.1., 10.1.10.2., 10.1.10.3., 10.1.10.3., 10.1.11.1., 10.1.13.1., 10.1.13.2., 10.1.14.1., 10.1.15.1.
Ibn Ḫālawaihi 4.1.2.4.1.
Ibn Hišām 10.1.10.2.
Ibn Mālik 1.2.1.4.
Ibn Manẓūr 1.2.1.6., 2.3.2.2.1., 2.4.1.1.3.1., 2.4.2.1.2., 3.4.1.1., 4.1.1., 4.1.2.3.1.1., 4.1.2.3.1.2.1., 4.1.2.4.1., 5.1.1., 5.2.1.2., 5.2.1.6., 6.5.10., 9.1.1., 9.1.2.2.1., 9.1.12.2., 9.1.13.1., 10.1.1.2., 10.1.1.3., 10.1.1.4., 10.1.1.5., 10.1.1.6., 10.1.3.3., 10.1.3.5., 10.1.7.2., 10.1.8.5., 10.1.8.6., 10.1.8.7., 10.1.8.9., 10.1.8.10., 10.1.13.2., 10.1.14.1.
Ibn Masᶜūd 1., 1.2.1.4., 1.2.1.5., 1.2.1.6., 1.2.1.7., 2.2.2., 2.3.1.1., 2.3.2.1., 2.3.2.2.1., 2.3.2.2.2., 2.4.1.1.3., 2.4.1.1.3.1., 2.4.1.1.3.2., 2.4.2.1.1., 2.4.2.1.2., 3.2.1.1., 3.4.1.1., 3.7., 4.1.1., 4.1.2.1., 4.1.2.2.1., 4.1.2.2.2., 4.1.2.3.1., 4.1.2.3.1.1., 4.1.2.3.1.2.1., 4.1.2.3.1.2.2., 4.1.2.3.2., 4.1.2.3.4., 4.1.2.4., 4.1.2.4.1., 4.1.2.7.1., 4.1.2.7.2., 4.1.3.1., 4.1.3.2., 5.1.1., 5.2.1.1., 5.2.1.2., 5.2.1.6., 5.4.1.1., 6., 6.5.1.1., 6.5.1.2., 6.5.4., 6.5.5., 6.5.6.,

6.5.7., 6.5.8.1., 6.5.9.1., 6.5.10., 6.5.13.1., 6.5.15., 7., 7.5.1.1., 7.5.1.2., 7.5.2.1., 7.5.2.2., 7.5.4., 7.5.5., 7.5.6., 7.5.7., 7.5.8., 7.5.10., 7.5.12., 7.5.13., 7.5.14., 7.5.15., 7.6., 9.1., 9.1.1., 9.1.2.1.1., 9.1.2.2., 9.1.2.2.1., 9.1.3.1., 9.1.4.1., 9.1.5., 9.1.8., 9.1.8., 9.1.9., 9.1.9.1., 9.1.10., 9.1.12.1., 9.1.12.2., 9.1.13.1., 9.1.16.1., 9.1.17., 9.1.18., 10.1.1.1., 10.1.1.2., 10.1.1.3., 10.1.1.4., 10.1.1.5., 10.1.1.6., 10.1.2.1., 10.1.3.1., 10.1.3.2., 10.1.3.3., 10.1.3.4., 10.1.3.5., 10.1.5.1., 10.1.6.1., 10.1.7.1., 10.1.7.2., 10.1.7.3., 10.1.7.4., 10.1.8., 10.1.8.2., 10.1.8.3., 10.1.8.5., 10.1.8.6., 10.1.8.7., 10.1.8.8., 10.1.8.9., 10.1.8.10., 10.1.9.1., 10.1.9.2., 10.1.9.3., 10.1.10.1., 10.1.10.2., 10.1.10.3., 10.1.10.4., 10.1.11.1., 10.1.12.1., 10.1.12.2., 10.1.12.2., 10.1.13.1., 10.1.13.2., 10.1.14.2., 10.1.15.1.

Ibn al-Sarrāǧ 4.1.2.2.1., 10.1.5.1., 10.1.8.8., 10.1.13.1.

Ibn ᶜUṣfūr 3.4.1.1., 5.1.1., 10.1., 10.1.1.2., 10.1.1.4., 10.1.1.6., 10.1.3.2., 10.1.3.3., 10.1.4.1., 10.1.5.1., 10.1.8.6., 10.1.8.7., 10.1.8.8., 10.1.8.9., 10.1.8.10., 10.1.10.2., 10.1.10.3., 10.1.13.2., 10.1.15.1.

Ibn Wallād 9.1.2.2.1.

Ibn Yaᶜīš, 1.2.1.7., 2.3.2.3., 2.4.1.1.3.2., 3.4.1.1., 4.1.2.2.1., 4.1.2.3.1.2.2., 4.1.2.7.1., 5.1.1., 6.5.6., 6.5.7., 7.5.2.2., 9.1.2.1.1., 9.1.8., 9.1.12.2., 9.1.13.1., 10.1., 10.1.1.2., 10.1.1.3., 10.1.1.4., 10.1.1.5., 10.1.1.6., 10.1.3.1., 10.1.3.2., 10.1.3.4., 10.1.4.1., 10.1.5.1., 10.1.6.1., 10.1.7.1., 10.1.7.3., 10.1.7.4., 10.1.8.1., 10.1.8.2., 10.1.8.3., 10.1.8.5., 10.1.8.6., 10.1.8.7., 10.1.8.8., 10.1.8.9., 10.1.8.10., 10.1.9.1., 10.1.9.2., 10.1.10.1., 10.1.10.2., 10.1.10.3., 10.1.10.4., 10.1.11.1., 10.1.13.1., 10.1.13.2., 10.1.14.1., 10.1.14.2., 10.1.15.1.

ᶜIlbāᵓ b. Arqam al-Yaškarī 10.1.3.3.

Ka[c]b 1.2.1.2.
Kouloughli 9.1., 9.1.2.2., 9.1.4.1.
Kūfans 4.1.2.4.1., 5.2.1.3.
Lane 2.3.2.2.2., 2.4.1.1.3.1., 2.4.1.1.3.1., 2.4.1.1.3.2., 2.4.2.1.1., 4.1.2.2.1., 4.1.2.3.1.1., 4.1.2.3.1.2.1., 4.1.2.4.1., 5.2.1.2., 9.1.2.2.1., 10.1.5.1.
Manẓūr b. Murṯid al-Asadī 10.1.13.2.
Maslama b. [c]Abd al-Malik 10.1.10.3.
Mokhlis 10.1.1.2., 10.1.1.3.
Mu[ɔ]addib 1.2.1.7., 2.4.1.1.3.2., 3.4.1.1., 4.1.2.2.1., 4.1.2.7.1., 5.2.1.2., 9.1.13.1., 10.1.13.1.
Al-Nābiġa al-Ḏubyānī 10.1.13.1.
Nāfi[c] 1.2.1.6., 2.4.2.1.2.
Al-Nahšalī 9.1.12.2.
Al-Namir b. Tawlab 10.1.10.2.
Nöldeke 4.1.2.3.1.2.2., 10.1.8.6., 10.1.8.8., 10.1.8.9., 10.1.8.10., 10.1.10.3., 10.1.12.2.
Numair 1.2.1.2.
Al-Nu[c]mān b. al-Munḏir 10.1.13.1.
Penrice 1.2.1.6., 2.4.2.1.1., 2.4.2.1.2.
Quḍā[c]a 10.1.5.1., 10.2.
Quṭrub 1.1.
Rabin 4., 10.1.10.2.
Raddād 4.1.2.4.1.
Rāğiḥī 9.1.
Rāzī 10.1.1.2., 10.1.3.3., 10.1.7.3., 10.1.8.10., 10.1.10.3., 10.1.13.1.
Roman 1.2.1.7., 2.3., 2.4.2.2., 4.1.2.1., 4.1.2.2.1., 4.1.2.3.1.2.2., 4.1.2.3.4.
Sa[c]īd b. Aus b. Ṯābit al-Anṣārī (Abū Zaid) 10.1.5.1.

Sībawaihi 1.2.1.7., 2.2.1., 2.2.2., 2.3., 2.3.1.2., 2.3.2.2.1., 2.3.2.2.2., 2.4.2.2., 3.4.1.1., 4.1.2.2.1., 4.1.2.2.2., 4.1.2.3.1.1., 4.1.2.3.1.2.2., 4.1.2.3.2., 4.1.2.3.4., 4.1.2.4., 4.1.2.7.1., 4.1.2.7.2., 5.2.1.2., 6.5.6., 6.5.7., 6.5.10., 6.5.12., 6.5.13.1., 9.1.2.1.1., 9.1.3.1., 9.1.4.1., 10.1.1.2., 10.1.2.1., 10.1.3.2., 10.1.3.3., 10.1.7.1., 10.1.7.2., 10.1.7.3., 10.1.8.6., 10.1.8.8., 10.1.9.2., 10.1.10.1., 10.1.10.3.

Širbīnī 9.1.13.1.

Surāqa b. Mirdās al-Azdī al-Bāriqī 3.4.1.1.

Suyūṭī 5.2.1.2., 9.1.12.2., 10.1.13.2.

Tamīm 1.2.1.5., 10.1.3.2.

Ṭarīf b. Tamīm al-ᶜAmbarī al-Tamīmi 6.5.10.

Ṭayyī 10.1.10.2., 10.2.

Vernier 2.4.1.1.2., 2.4.1.1.3.2, 3.2.1.1., 4.1.2.3.1.1., 4.1.2.3.1.2.2., 4.1.2.3.2., 4.1.2.4.1., 7.5.13., 7.5.14., 9.1.18., 10.1.1.3., 10.1.5.1., 10.1.7.1., 10.1.8.1., 10.1.10.1., 10.1.15.1.

Versteegh 2.2.1., 10.1.7.2.

Wright 1.2.1.4., 1.2.1.5., 2.3., 2.4.1.1.1., 2.4.1.1.3., 2.4.1.1.3.1., 2.4.2.1.1., 2.4.2.1.2., 2.4.2.2., 3.2.1.1., 3.4.1.1., 4.1.1., 4.1.2.1., 4.1.2.2.1., 4.1.2.3.1.1., 5.2.1.2., 5.2.1.4., 5.2.1.5., 5.4.1.1., 6.5.10., 6.5.12., 7.5.5., 7.5.8., 7.5.10., 7.5.12., 7.5.13., 7.5.14., 9.1.3.1., 9.1.5., 9.1.12.2., 9.1.17., 10.1.7.2., 10.1.8.1., 10.1.8.5., 10.1.10.1., 10.1.10.2., 10.1.12.2.

Yemenites 10.1.3.3., 10.2.

Yūnus 1.1.

Zaǧǧāǧī 10.1.7.2., 10.1.10.1.

Zamaḫšarī 1.2.1.7., 2.2.2., 2.3., 2.3.2.1., 2.3.2.2.1., 2.3.2.3., 2.4.1.1.3.1, 2.4.1.1.3.2, 2.4.2.1.1., 2.4.2.2., 4.1.2.2.1., 4.1.2.2.2., 4.1.2.3.1.1., 4.1.2.3.1.2.2., 4.1.2.4.1., 4.1.2.7.2., 5.2.1.3., 6.5.6., 6.5.7., 6.5.12., 7.5.2.2., 7.5.14., 9.1.2.1.1.,

www.ingramcontent.com/pod-product-compliance
Lightning Source LLC
Chambersburg PA
CBHW071349290426
44108CB00014B/1483
9789197764124